Lecture Notes in Computer Science 14230

Founding Editors

Gerhard Goos
Juris Hartmanis

The series Lecture Notes in Computer Science (LNCS), including its subseries Lecture Notes in Artificial Intelligence (LNAI) and Lecture Notes in Bioinformatics (LNBI), has established itself as a medium for the publication of new developments in computer science and information technology research, teaching, and education.

LNCS enjoys close cooperation with the computer science R & D community, the series counts many renowned academics among its volume editors and paper authors, and collaborates with prestigious societies. Its mission is to serve this international community by providing an invaluable service, mainly focused on the publication of conference and workshop proceedings and postproceedings. LNCS commenced publication in 1973.

Melanie Volkamer · David Duenas-Cid ·
Peter Rønne · Peter Y. A. Ryan ·
Jurlind Budurushi · Oksana Kulyk ·
Adrià Rodriguez Pérez ·
Iuliia Spycher-Krivonosova
Editors

Electronic Voting

8th International Joint Conference, E-Vote-ID 2023
Luxembourg City, Luxembourg, October 3–6, 2023
Proceedings

 Springer

Editors

Melanie Volkamer
Karlsruhe Institute of Technology
Karlsruhe, Germany

David Duenas-Cid
Department of Informatics in Management
Gdańsk University of Technology
Gdańsk, Poland

Peter Rønne
CNRS, LORIA
Université de Lorraine
Nancy, France

Peter Y. A. Ryan
University of Luxembourg
Esch-sur-Alzette, Luxembourg

Jurlind Budurushi
Computer Science and Engineering
Qatar University
Doha, Qatar

Oksana Kulyk
Information Security and Trust
IT University of Copenhagen
Copenhagen, Denmark

Adrià Rodriguez Pérez
Pompeu Fabra University
Barcelona, Spain

Iuliia Spycher-Krivonosova
KPM Center for Public Management
University of Bern
Bern, Switzerland

ISSN 0302-9743   ISSN 1611-3349 (electronic)
Lecture Notes in Computer Science
ISBN 978-3-031-43755-7   ISBN 978-3-031-43756-4 (eBook)
https://doi.org/10.1007/978-3-031-43756-4

This Springer imprint is published by the registered company Springer Nature Switzerland AG
The registered company address is: Gewerbestrasse 11, 6330 Cham, Switzerland

Paper in this product is recyclable.

Preface

This volume contains a selection of papers presented at E-Vote-ID 2023, the Eighth International Joint Conference on Electronic Voting, held during October 3–6, 2023. This was the first time the conference was held in Luxemburg, starting a new era in the conference in which the venue will change at every conference, and we will engage new audiences and organizers in this year's venue, the Abbey Neumunster, keeping the spirit of the traditional Schloss Hofen.

The E-Vote-ID Conference resulted from merging EVOTE and Vote-ID and counting up to 19 years since the first E-Vote conference, in Austria. Since that conference in 2004, over 1600 experts have attended the venue, including scholars, practitioners, representatives of various authorities, electoral managers, vendors, and PhD Students. The conference collected the most relevant debates on the development of Electronic Voting, from aspects relating to security and usability through to practical experiences and applications of voting systems, also including legal, social, or political aspects, amongst others; it has turned out to be an important global referent concerning this issue.

This year, as in previous editions, the conference consisted of:

- Security, Usability, and Technical Issues Track;
- Governance of E-Voting Track;
- Election and Practical Experiences Track;
- PhD Colloquium;
- Poster and Demo Session.

E-VOTE-ID 2023 received 38 submissions for consideration in the first two tracks (Technical and Governance Tracks), each being reviewed by 3 to 5 program committee members using a double-blind review process. As a result, 9 papers were accepted for this volume, representing 24% of the submitted proposals. The selected papers cover a wide range of topics connected with electronic voting, including experiences and revisions of the actual uses of E-voting systems and corresponding processes in elections.

We would like to thank the local organizers, Peter Y. A. Ryan, and event organizer Magali Martin from the University of Luxembourg and the Interdisciplinary Centre for Security, Reliability, and Trust (SnT). The latter we also thank for sponsoring in kind. A special thanks go to the Luxembourg National Research Fund (FNR), which supported this conference generously via the RESCOM scientific event grant. Also, we would like to thank and appreciate the international program members for their hard work in reviewing, discussing, and shepherding papers. They ensured, once again, the high quality of these proceedings with their knowledge and experience.

October 2023

Melanie Volkamer
David Duenas-Cid
Peter Rønne
Peter Y. A. Ryan

Organization

Program Committee

Marta Aranyossy	Corvinus University of Budapest, Hungary
Roberto Araujo	Universidade Federal do Pará, Brazil
Jordi Barrat i Esteve	Election Observation and Democracy Support, Spain
Bernhard Beckert	Karlsruhe Institute of Technology, Germany
Josh Benaloh	Microsoft, USA
Matthew Bernhard	Voting Works, USA
Michelle Blom	University of Melbourne, Australia
Jurlind Budurushi	Qatar University, Qatar
Jeremy Clark	Concordia University, Canada
César Collazos	Universidad del Cauca, Colombia
Veronique Cortier	Centre National de la Recherche Scientifique, Loria, France
Régis Dandoy	Universidad San Francisco de Quito, Ecuador
Staffan Darnolf	International Foundation for Electoral Systems, USA
Alexandre Debant	Inria Nancy – Grand Est, France
Catalin Dragan	University of Surrey, UK
David Duenas-Cid	Gdansk University of Technology, Poland
Helen Eenmaa	University of Tartu, Estonia
Aleksander Essex	University of Western Ontario, Canada
Rosa Mª Fernández	Riveira Universidad Complutense de Madrid, Spain
Bryan Ford	École polytechnique fédérale de Lausanne, Switzerland
David Galindo	Crypto in Motion, UK
Micha Germann	University of Bath, UK
J. Paul Gibson	Institut Mines-Télécom, France
Rosario Giustolisi	IT University of Copenhagen, Denmark
Kristian Gjøsteen	Norwegian University of Science and Technology, Norway
Nicole Goodman	Brock University, Canada
Rajeev Gore	Australian National University, Australia
Ruediger Grimm	University of Koblenz, Germany
Rolf Haenni	Bern University of Applied Sciences, Switzerland

Contents

Investigating Transparency Dimensions for Internet Voting

Samuel Agbesi[1]([⊠]) , Jurlind Budurushi[1,2] , Asmita Dalela[3] ,
and Oksana Kulyk[1]

[1] IT Univserity of Copenhagen, Copenhagen, Denmark
{sagb,jurb,okku}@itu.dk
[2] Qatar University, Doha, Qatar
jurlind@qu.edu.qa
[3] Sammamish, USA

Abstract. While Internet voting is argued to have the potential to improve election processes, concerns about security risks remain one of its main adoption barriers. These concerns are furthermore aggravated by the lack of *transparency* of Internet voting systems that are often perceived as a "black box". Moreover, there is a research gap in conceptualizing the idea of transparency and in studying voters' attitudes towards transparency in Internet voting. In this work, we aim to address this gap by (1) Conducting a systematic literature review, from which we identified five dimensions of transparency; (2) Developing a questionnaire (Transparency Dimensions of Internet Voting, TDIV) to assess voters' attitudes regarding the correlation of these dimensions with transparency; and (3) Conducting an online study (N = 500) to investigate voters' attitudes towards transparency in Internet voting. We conclude that providing information about the security of the Internet voting system; testing it by independent experts for security vulnerabilities prior to the election; monitoring the election process and verifying its integrity; and providing a remedy for security breaches while holding the responsible parties accountable, are perceived by voters as important, and enhance transparency in Internet voting systems.

1 Introduction

Internet voting has been an active topic of public discussions for many years. Its proponents highlight the advantages of voting online, such as increased convenience and accessibility for voters who might have difficulty reaching a physical polling station.

However, critics of Internet voting raise concerns about its security risks, including the potential manipulation of election results and violation of vote secrecy. Addressing these risks and ensuring voters' trust in the security of the system is particularly challenging given the complexity of Internet voting systems and corresponding security measures. One crucial aspect in establishing trust is *transparency*. Transparency allows the public to monitor the voting system's

M. Volkamer et al. (Eds.): E-Vote-ID 2023, LNCS 14230, pp. 1–17, 2023.
https://doi.org/10.1007/978-3-031-43756-4_1

workings and ensure that the election follows proper procedures. Numerous studies [1,9,21] have confirmed the importance of transparency, as also recognized by the German Constitutional Court concerning the use of voting machines [10]. Despite technical proposals to enhance transparency in Internet voting [22,30], little attention has been given to understanding voters' attitudes towards transparency in Internet voting and the proposed measures.

In this work we aim to bridge this gap and to investigate voters' attitudes toward the transparency of Internet voting, our study aims to address the following research question: *What are the measures that can be used to increase transparency in Internet voting systems as proposed in academic research and applied in practice, and what are the voters' attitudes towards these measures and their relation to transparency?*

Our contributions are therefore as follows:

- We conduct a systematic literature review on measures proposed to improve transparency in Internet voting, supplementing the results of our review with a further search on transparency in other domains of technology, such as AI. We propose a taxonomy of these measures by deriving five dimensions, namely, *information availability, understandability, monitoring and verifiability, remedial measures* and *testing*. These differ depending on the involved stakeholders, time period when these measures are applied (e.g. before or during the election) and their effect.
- Based on the taxonomy we develop and empirically validate (N = 50) a questionnaire which we call "Transparency Dimensions of Internet Voting" (TDIV) which is designed to measure voters' assessment of the five dimensions of transparency in Internet voting systems as well as transparency in general (as overall attitudes and as related to specific systems)
- We conduct an online user study (N = 500) by applying the TDIV questionnaire in order to study voters' attitudes towards the measures across the five transparency dimensions and transparency in general. In particular, we conduct a quantitative analysis studying the relationship between the perceived importance of individual dimensions and the perceived importance of transparency in Internet voting in general.

Our findings show that voters' perceptions of four out of five proposed dimensions (namely, *information availability, monitoring and verifiability, remedial measures*, and *testing*) indeed correlate with their perceptions of transparency in Internet voting in general. Thus, our results confirm that providing information about the security and data protection measures used in the election, opportunities both for experts and general public to thoroughly test the voting system prior to the election and to verify the integrity of the election procedures during/after the election, as well as having a remedial plan for the election in case of security breaches indeed has a potential to have a transparency-enhancing effect on Internet voting systems. On the other hand, our study shows mixed effects of *understandability* of the voting system; while some participants mention the importance of being able to understand how the system works, we did not find a significant correlation between the attitudes towards understandability and attitudes towards general transparency, indicating the need for future investigations to better understand the relationship between these two concepts.

The remainder of the paper is as follows: In Sect. 2 we describe the methodology and the results of our literature review, concluding the section with the description of our derived five dimensions of transparency together with hypotheses based on these dimensions that we evaluate in our studies. In Sect. 3 we describe the development and evaluation of the TDIV questionnaire, followed by the description of the methodology for the follow-up study using the questionnaire. Section 4 describes the results of the study. The paper concludes with us discussing our results and their implications for future research in Sect. 5.

2   Literature Review

We describe the systematic literature review conducted to define the concept of transparency and identify its different dimensions as well as the proposed hypothesis.

We used the following search phrases: *("Transparency" OR "TRANS-PARENCY" OR "Openness" OR "Understandability") AND ("Internet Voting" OR "INTERNET VOTING" OR "E-VOTING" OR "E-voting" OR "Online Voting" OR "Remote Voting").* We ran a manual search of databases such as Springer, IEEE, Scopus, Web of Science, ProQuest, and Emerald Insight. We also looked into research publications in the proceedings of the E-Vote-ID conference[1], which is one of the leading conferences dedicated specifically to the subject of electronic voting. Two paper authors evaluated the publications for their relevance to the research inquiry. Our inclusion criteria considered publications published between 2015 and 2022 on transparency and technology in general, as well as empirical and theoretical papers. Technical papers, non-empirical papers, papers that did not discuss transparency and trust, and papers that were not written in English were all excluded. We reviewed the abstracts of the remaining papers and eliminated those that were not relevant to the research topic or aims. Finally, the snowballing approach was used in reviewing the papers. The authors used this method by reviewing the reference list of the initial set of papers extracted and selecting additional relevant papers, which were then added to the list. The review included a total of 21 papers in total.

Based on the reviewed papers, the five main dimensions, *Information Availability, Understandability, Monitoring and verifiability, Remedial Measures*, and *Testing* were identified through an iterative discussion process.

In the following subsections we describe the results of our search, starting with an overview of studies on how transparency of technology influences users' attitudes towards this technology, namely, trust. We then elaborate on our conceptualisation of transparency in Internet voting, describe the five identified dimensions of transparency and provide the hypotheses related to these dimensions that inform our follow-up studies.

---

[1] https://e-vote-id.org, last accessed on 09.02.2023.

2.1   Effects of Transparency on Trust

Transparency in Information Technology. A number of studies have investigated transparency in the context of information technology and how it influences user attitudes. Some of these studies are in the domain of machine learning (ML) and decision support systems [4,17,31], automation systems [19,37], social media algorithms [27] and automatic online comment moderation systems [5]. However, the findings of these studies are inconclusive; for example, Schmidt et al. [31] investigated how users' understanding of the ML-based decision support system affects their willingness to trust the system's predictions. The findings show that transparency, or users having insight to the ML-based decision support tool, negatively impact users' trust in the ML decision support system's predictions [31]. This implies that gaining more insight into the internal logic of the system, it may have a negative impact on users' trust. This finding is also supported by Kizilcec's [17] work, which claims that trust can be influenced by the level of transparency; that is, low and high levels of transparency can decrease users' trust, while medium levels of transparency can increase trust [17]. In contrast, Lyons et al. [19], Yang et al. [37], and Brunk et al. [5] found that transparency increased users' trust in technology.

Transparency in Election Technologies. At the time of writing only few studies have investigated transparency in the context of election technologies, such as electronic voting. For instance, Driza Maurer [7] reviewed how to develop systems that increase transparency to improve voter confidence by identifying design requirements such as verifiability, public intrusion testing, and source code publication. Buckland, Teague and Wen [6] discovered that there is little information available about the Australian electronic voting system, and that the source code and technical documentation are not publicly available. The authors conclude that the lack of transparency negatively influenced voters' attitudes toward the electronically held elections. Note that one of their key recommendations is that source code, technical documentation, user and training manuals, and audit reports should be made public. Volkamer, Spycher and Dubuis [36] concluded that transparency in election technologies is key to voters overall trust and could positively influence voters behaviour towards electronic voting. While these studies have looked at transparency in electronic voting system, they did not fully examine the various dimensions of transparency, that is, there is lack of research for conceptualising transparency. Saldanha et al. [30] attempted to identify the characteristics of transparency in the Brazilian electronic voting system but failed to investigate the significance of these characteristics and how they influence transparency. We complement their work by conceptualising transparency and examining the importance of its various dimensions for voters in the context of Internet voting.

2.2   Conceptualisation of Transparency

Transparency has been defined as the process of ensuring that a system is open and externally accessible to the public [33], as well as the availability of information about the election system and the actors [11]. Jain and Jain [16] also argued that transparency is about information disclosure and openness. Studies have also shown that a transparent election system is the one that supports verifiability of votes, observation and monitoring [22], accountability, as well as public oversight, and comprehension of the election process [15]. Furthermore, Saldanha et al. [30] also identified several characteristics of transparency in election technology, including consciousness, accountability, explanation, and finally testing and auditing. As a result, in the context of our work, transparency is defined as having characteristics such as information availability, understandability, monitoring and verifiability, remedial measures, and testing [11,15,22,30,33], which are further elaborated in the following sections.

Information Availability. The ability to make information about the election system, specifically the Internet voting system, available to relevant stakeholders is referred to as *information availability* [7]. This information could include source code, technical documentation, vendor information and user manuals [7,11]. It is important to emphasise that information availability about Internet voting has been argued to influence transparency [7,15]. Hall [15] argued that even if voters do not understand the source code, the fact that it is available may increase transparency. That is, once the source code is published, experts can review it for any hidden bugs. Note, that level of accessibility of the provided information can vary: as such, some of the information can be made available either publicly or upon request only; similarly, some of the information such as technical documentation might require a relatively high level of expertise to understand it.

Understandability. Is the ability to explain in a way that a lay person can understand how the system works, and in particular, given the concerns about security risks of Internet voting, the extent to which security of the system is guaranteed. Note, while this category is similar to information availability in terms of providing information about the workings of the voting system, the important distinction is that measures aimed at understandability imply that everyone, as opposed to just the experts, can understand the provided information. For example, Saldanha et al. [30] found that explaining the algorithm and security protocols, as well as how the system works, can positively influence voters' attitudes toward transparency. Similarly, "understandability" was identified as a characteristic of transparency in the work of Spycher et al. [34].

Monitoring and Verifiability. Refers to a variety of measures implemented *during* or *after* the election in order to ensure that the election processes run according to a proper procedure. In particular, *end-to-end verifiability* has been widely advocated for by election security experts as a means to detect election manipulations, proposing techniques that enable voters to verify that their own vote has been correctly cast, stored and tallied (individual verifiability) as well as techniques that enable the general public to verify that the stored votes have been tallied correctly [22,26]. Other methods aimed at ensuring the correctness of election processes can include non-technical measures such as ensuring that the important steps of voting and tallying are observed by independent parties. The availability of a vote verification process, according to Solvak's [32], increases voters' confidence that their vote was cast correctly. To improve transparency, many electronic voting system implementations have included verification processes. Puiggali et al. [26], for example, identified countries such as Norway, Switzerland, Estonia, and Australia that have implemented some form of verifiability in their electronic voting system to increase transparency.

Remedial Measures. The various methods for dealing with situations in which something goes wrong, including security breaches as well as other issues that might jeopardise the integrity of the election. This includes both error-correction measures and accountability measures that allow for the identification of individuals or entities responsible for these errors [30]. Voters, for example, may perceive an Internet voting system as transparent if the system can detects errors or breaches, implements corrective measures, and identifies the entities responsible for these breaches [12].

Testing. Refers to the various measures taken *prior* to the election to ensure that the Internet voting system is sufficiently secure. This includes code review measures, public intrusion tests, formal verification, and other auditing-related measures, in particular ones allowing the general public to to participate in the testing and resolution of any discovered vulnerabilities, which can improve transparency [7,25,30].

2.3   Hypotheses

Given the identified dimensions of transparency in Internet voting, we conduct an empirical evaluation in order to understand whether these dimensions are indeed perceived as related to transparency by voters. In doing this, we follow an indirect approach of studying whether the perceived importance of any of the dimensions is correlated with perceived importance of transparency. Such an approach allows us to investigate voters' attitudes independent of a particular voting system, which is of benefits when studying the attitudes of populations that did not yet have experience with voting online. We therefore define the following hypotheses:

H1: There is a positive correlation between perceived importance of information availability and voters' attitude towards transparency.
H2: There is a positive correlation between perceived importance of understandability of Internet voting system and voters' attitude towards transparency.
H3: There is a positive correlation between perceived importance of verifiability of Internet voting system and voters' attitude towards transparency.
H4: There is a positive correlation between perceived importance of remedial measures and voters' attitude towards transparency of Internet voting system.
H5: There is a positive correlation between perceived importance of testing and voters' attitude towards transparency of Internet voting system.

3   Methodology

This section describes the methodology for developing and evaluating the questionnaire, as well as for the study conducted using the questionnaire to investigate the defined hypotheses.

Our goal when developing the questionnaire was two-fold. First, we wanted to propose an instrument that can be used in future studies to evaluate voters' perception of each transparency dimension with respect to any Internet voting system (e.g. whether the voters believe that there is sufficient information provided by the system, that is, the extent to which information availability is ensured). Second, we wanted to understand the relations between individual dimensions of transparency and their related measures, as well as the perceived transparency in general.

As currently very few countries have implemented Internet voting for legally binding elections, we assumed that our questionnaire will target mostly people who do not have a particular system in mind when asked about Internet voting. Nevertheless, our questionnaire can be applied also to people who have used Internet voting, in order to measure and improve the transparency of the corresponding system.

3.1   Questionnaire Development and Testing

Development of TDIV Items. The TDIV instrument consist of the following dimensions (also known as variables or constructs): **Information availability,** **Understandability, Monitoring and verifiability, Remedial measures,** **Testing** and **Transparency**. Based on the literature review and our internal discussion we added at least four (4) closed-ended questions or items to each variable of the TDIV instrument[2]. Each item consisted of a statement about importance of a transparency-enhancing measure related to a corresponding transparency dimension (e.g. "The documentation on how the internet voting system works should be available to the public" for information availability) or transparency in general (e.g. "Transparency is an integral aspect of internet voting system") with the responses measured using a 7-point likert scale (1- Strongly disagree to 7- Strongly agree).

Validation of the TDIV. To ensure the validity of our TDIV instrument, we conducted a face-to-face validation check [2]. Thereby, we asked three experts (cryptography, election technology and security) to examine the various dimensions or variables and items of transparency. The experts were required to determine any ambiguities or inaccuracies, and check if the items address the research questions. The opinions and ideas of the experts were used to update the dimensions and question items. After the first validation, in order to evaluate that the various transparency dimensions and their items are easy to understand we

---

[2] The resulting variables are available at https://github.com/cometitu/constructs/blob/main/Codes_constructs.pdf.

conducted a pilot study with a small number of respondents (sample size of 50, that is 10 percent of the sample size for the main study (500), [2]). The pilot study enabled us to adapt the transparency dimensions and their question items when we detected that the respondents were having difficulties understanding them [2]. Based on the results of the pilot study, we slightly adjusted several of the items and removed some of them. We detected these difficulties through the open-ended questionnaire, where we explicitly asked if the participants encountered any issues in the pilot study[3].

3.2   Study Procedure

Our study applying TDIV has been conducted as an online survey using the SoSci Survey platform[4]. We recruited the participants for our survey from the Prolific[5] platform. The participants were recruited from US, UK, Estonia, Denmark, Sweden and Norway.

To reduce the bias that comes with online surveys like prolific, we conducted a pilot test with a small group of respondents before administering to a larger population. It helped us identify any potential issues with the survey. We furthermore used the option to recruit gender-balanced sample, which according to previous research is reasonably representative of general population with regards to security and privacy related research [28]. Each participant received 1.5 UK pound sterling in compensation for an estimated 10 min of participation, which corresponds to the recommendation of the Prolific platform. Following the recommendation by Aithal and Aithal [2], we aimed to recruit a total of 500 participants. In order to control for quality of the responses, we included attention checks in the survey, namely, two Instruction Manipulation Checks (IMC) [24]. In terms of voting experience, most of the participants (59%) did not have any experience with Internet voting, only 16% had experience ranging from good to excellent. At the beginning of the survey the participants were provided with information about the study and asked to provide their consent for participation. Then they were asked about their previous experience with Internet voting, presented with a hypothetical scenario where they were asked to imagine that their country wants to implement Internet voting for the next elections and asked whether they would be willing vote online in such a scenario. They were then presented with the items from the TDIV questionnaire. For each one of the dimensions, the participants were asked an additional open-ended question for their input on further measures they would like to see in an Internet voting system (e.g. "In your opinion what other information should be available about the internet voting system"). At the end of the TDIV questionnaire the participants were furthermore asked an open-ended question about further measures

---

[3] Items retained for the survey are available at https://github.com/cometitu/constructs/blob/main/Codes_constructs.pdf.

[4] https://www.soscisurvey.de, last accessed 03.02.2023.

[5] https://www.prolific.co/, last accessed 03.02.2023.

that they believe would increase transparency in an Internet voting system. The questionnaire concluded with questions about participants' trust in authorities[6].

Data Analysis. We examined the data after collecting it from the participants for missing values, questionable responses patterns, and data distribution, as common when collecting quantitative data from participants [13]. Furthermore, we tested for outliers and straight line response patterns, and these types of responses were rejected and removed if they also failed the attention checks questions.

For the analysis, the data was analysed using the IBM SPSS statistical program and Partial Least Square Structured Equation Modeling (PLS-SEM) with the SmartPLS software package [29]. We chose this second-generation statistical method (PLS-SEM) over others such as factor or regression analysis because PLS-SEM is suitable for multivariate analysis, it has the capacity to manage and test for complex relationships between independent and dependent variables [13,14]. Note that, even though PLS-SEM is a non-parametric statistical method, it is critical to ensure that the data is not out of normal range, as this can cause mistakes in the results [13]. As a result, we investigated the various measures of distribution, mean and standard deviation (which estimates the amount of data scattered around the mean).

Ethics. Our institution does not require ethical approval for conducting a user study; however, we followed the APA ethical guidelines [3] for conducting both a pilot study and a survey. Before initiating the process, we informed the participants about our study's goals and explained that they could withdraw from the study at any time. According to the privacy and confidentiality section of the APA guideline [3], the participants were informed and assured that their responses would remain confidential and only be used for research purposes. These responses would be used by the researchers involved in the study in an anonymous form during publication. In addition, we also notified our participants before starting the study that attention checks are present and failing them will lead to no compensation from the Prolific platform. We furthermore provided our contact details to participants in case of further questions or concerns.

4 Results

This section presents the findings of the study. We followed a two-step analysis approach, as in PLS-SEM, by evaluating the reflective measurement model followed by the structural model [13,14]. In the evaluation of the reflective measurement model, we assess the model's quality by measuring the relationship between the indicators and the dimensions as well as the relationship between dimensions. Furthermore, we assess the indicator's reliability, internal consistency reliability, convergent validity, and discriminant validity. After assessing

---

[6] For the sake of brevity, we provide our analysis of these responses in the extended version of our paper.

the quality of the measurement model, we evaluate the structural model by examining the collinearity issues in the model, the path coefficient of the structural model, and the model explanatory power. Note that a total of 514 participants have been recruited for the study, of whom 14 were excluded based on low-quality responses and failed attention checks. (see Table 1 and Appendix A in appendix). Out of the remaining 500, 245 identified as women, 252 as men and 3 as non-binary. More than half of the participants (281) were between ages 18 and 40. The full participant's demographics is provided in Table 1 in the appendix.

4.1   Analysis of the Reflective Measurement Model

To test the reflective measurement model, we first examined its reliability by looking at the indicators' outer loading. The rule of thumb is that the outer loading should be 0.708 or higher [13], and almost all indicators' outer loading exceeded the threshold. However, there were a few indicators that were lower than the acceptable 0.708 but greater than 0.4, for example *InfAv_07 = 0.665*, *RemMs_02 = 0.614*, and *Test_04 = 0.657*. These indicators were kept because their removal had no effect on the reliability or validity of our model [13]. Nevertheless, we removed *InfAv_03 = 0.619* and *RemMs_06 = 0.519*, because these indicators were affecting our "Average Variance Expected" (AVE). Furthermore, we examined our model's internal consistency reliability, by using Cronbach's alpha and composite reliability. However, due to the limitations of Cronbach's alpha [13], we used composite reliability (CR) to assess the internal consistency reliability. Our results, refer to Table 2 in Appendix A, revealed that the CR values were within the acceptable range of 0.60 and 0.90 [13], confirming the model's internal consistency reliability. In addition, we assessed the convergent validity of the identified dimensions. Our results, refer to Table 2 in Appendix A, revealed that the AVE of all the latent variables or the dimensions were above 0.50. This demonstrates that on average all latent variables may account for more than half (50 percent) of the variance of their indicators [13]. Further, we evaluated the discriminant validity. Thereby, we adopted Heterotrait-Monotrait ratio (HTMT), which has been suggested to be a more trustworthy measure to determine discriminant validity [13,14]. Our findings showed that the values were below the acceptable threshold level, that is 0.85, indicating that the identified dimensions are conceptually distinct.

4.2   Analysis of the Structural Model

For the structural analysis we followed the method suggested by Hair et al. [13,14]. First, we examined both the outer and inner models for collinearity issues. Our findings showed that collinearity was not an issue for our model. All the values were below the threshold of 5. Hence, there was no collinearity among the dimensions. Further, we examined the significance of the relationships between the structural model. The results, refer to Table 3 in Appendix A, showed that information availability ($\beta = 0.175$, p = 0.003), monitoring and verifiability ($\beta = 0.217$, p = 0.000), remedial measures ($\beta = 0.225$, p = 0.001), and testing ($\beta = 0.217$, p = 0.000) have a positive correlation with transparency. Thus, **supporting the hypotheses *H1*, *H3*, *H4* and *H5***. However, there was no correlation between understandability ($\beta = -0.018$, p = 0.746) and transparency. Hence, the hypothesis *H2* **was not supported**. From the findings, shown in Table 4 in Appendix A), it can be inferred that remedial measures (0.225) have the strongest correlation with transparency, followed by testing, and monitoring and verifiability (0.217), while information availability (0.175) has only a minor correlation. Finally, we investigated our model's explanatory and predictive power. We looked at the coefficient of determination (R^2) of our endogenous dimension (transparency) to test its explanatory power. We found out that our model had 40% explanatory power for transparency, with a R^2 of 0.407. This indicates that our model has moderate explanatory power [14]. To evaluate our model's predictive power, in particular to assess whether our model can be generalisable and make future predictions using different data sets, we used the "PLSpredict" procedure proposed in [13,14]. Thereby, we assessed the dependent variable "transparency" and its root mean square error (RMSE), as well as Q^2 predict. This means that we compared the values generated by PLS-SEM RSME against the values produced by linear regression model (LM) benchmark. The results from our analysis showed that all values for the "transparency" indicators in the PLS-SEM RMSE (Trans_01, Trans_02, Trans_03, Trans_04) were lower than the values for LM_RSME. Consequently, our model has a high predictive power. The Q^2 predict values for the indicators (Trans_01, Trans_02, Trans_03, Trans_04) were all greater than zero, confirming that the our path model performed better than the LM benchmark.

5   Discussion and Conclusion

It has been argued that transparency in Internet voting increases voter's confidence and trust [1,9]. Therefore, our goal in this study was to investigate voters' attitudes towards transparency in Internet voting. Our findings revealed several groups of measures (dimensions) that are important to voters in terms of Internet voting transparency. The findings from our study showed that participants' attitudes towards information availability, monitoring and verifiability, remedial measures, and testing are strongly correlated with their perceived importance of transparency, suggesting that proper implementation of these measures is of significant importance to ensure voters perceiving an Internet voting system as transparent.

The findings demonstrated the significance of making documentation about the Internet voting system publicly available. Such documentation should demonstrate how the Internet voting system functions, as well as the underlying security mechanism(s). Voters also want public information about the vendor(s) who supplied or developed the Internet voting system, allowing them to determine whether the acquisition or implementation of the Internet voting system was not influenced by the government or political parties. As providing such information is inline with common recommendations by election experts [6], our findings confirm its importance.

Our findings also revealed that individual and universal verifiability as well as other measures implemented to monitor the integrity of election processes are linked to voters' positive attitudes toward the transparency of the Internet voting system. The argument that implementing verifiability measures is necessary for voters' trust and perceived transparency has been put forward by previous research [1, 20], as well as supported by other previous studies in the context of Estonian elections [32]. It is worth noting, however, that the attitudes towards verifiability can be paradoxical. Some studies show that voters do not understand the purpose of verifiability and do not see the need to conduct the verification themselves [23]. Furthermore, empirical data from real-world elections show low verification rates among the voters (e.g. around 5% in Estonian elections [8]). It can therefore be argued that while the presence of verifiability options can and does serve as an assurance to the voters, more work needs to be done to ensure that it is understood and utilised to its full extent.

Furthermore, in terms of remedial measures, the findings suggest that stakeholders should not only make an effort to implement measures to detect and prevent any security breaches that may occur during the voting process but also make sure that the existence of such measures and the extent to which independent experts have audited them is properly communicated to the voters. Another aspect of further critical importance is ensuring that the voters have an opportunity to be involved in safeguarding the election process by making sure that explanations regarding the security of the Internet voting system are available to the voters who are interested to know more about them, and by providing easily accessible avenues for voters to report any security issues. Even though studies [30] have found that measures such as accountability do not influence voters' attitudes toward transparency, our findings showed otherwise. Furthermore, our findings showed that voters are much more concerned with the security assurances and safeguards put in place, and they associate this with the transparency of the Internet voting system.

The study also provided sufficient evidence that testing the Internet voting system by experts and the general public prior to its' use has a significant impact on voters' attitudes towards the transparency of the system. Such an approach, in particular, has been used for the Swiss voting system, which provided opportunities for public testing, including election security experts. While the testing revealed a number of serious vulnerabilities, preventing its use in the election, its contribution to the transparency of Internet voting elections was commented positively by experts [7]. Our study showed, that this is likely to be positively perceived by the voters as well.

However, there was insufficient evidence from our study to support that understandability has a correlation to voters' attitudes toward Internet voting transparency. One possible explanation is that while understanding the Internet voting system may be important to voters (e.g. improving their self-efficacy in using the system to vote), it is not necessarily perceived as contributing to transparency. Indeed, previous research shows that voters' understanding of an Internet voting system does not necessarily contribute to voters' trust in the system and might even have a negative impact [38]. Thus, a relationship between understandability, transparency and trust might have a paradoxical nature, in that voters believe that they need to understand how the system works in order to see it as transparent and/or trustworthy, but their actual reactions to being provided with explanations demonstrate a different effect. Therefore, further investigations regarding this *understandability paradox*, which might have similar explanations as the so-called *privacy paradox* [18], are needed.

Finally, while the proposed measures can potentially improve transparency of the voting system and reduce security risks, they have their own limitations that need to be acknowledged, such as verifiability techniques often being difficult for the voters to apply [35] or difficulties in addressing threats such as voter coercion. The decision on whether to provide the option to vote online should therefore be made on case-to-case basis by experts from both technical and social disciplines, and in case such an option is provided, additional channels (e.g. traditional voting in polling places) should be offered to voters who either prefer not to vote online or experience issues with the voting process (as done e.g. in Estonian elections [8]).

Limitations. Despite the fact that the findings highlighted several important aspects of transparency, the survey has some limitations that must be considered. First, as only a few countries implement Internet voting on a large scale, most of our participants did not have personal experience with Internet voting systems. While their experiences still provide valuable insights for introducing Internet voting in countries without such prior experience, the extent to which our findings would differ in countries with extensive history of Internet voting such as Estonia remains to be studied.

Future Work. Our study focused on correlations between voters' perceived importance of various types of measures that are commonly treated as transparency-related by researchers and practitioners when applied to Internet voting, as well as the perceived importance of transparency in general. To further validate our findings more research (e.g. in form of a controlled experiment) is needed to understand whether the presence of these measures in a voting system has a significant effect on perceived transparency of the system, as well as on trust and willingness to use the system for real-world elections. A particular interesting research direction would be to further investigate the effects of understandability. As our study showed mixed results, the extent to which understandability influences perceived transparency and trust, as well as the appropriate ways to provide understandability (e.g. determining the contents as well as the media for provding voters with explanations about the system).

Acknowledgements. This work was supported by a research grant (40948) from VILLUM FONDEN.

A Appendix

Table 1. Participants demographic attribute

Attributes	Dist	Freq	Per
Gender	Female	245	49
	Male	252	50.4
	Non-binary	3	0.6
Age	18 to 30	130	26
	31 to 40	151	30.2
	41 to 50	82	316.4
	51 to 60	68	13.6
	61 to 70	59	11.8
	71 and above	10	2
Education	High School	179	35.8
	Bachelor's degree	84	41.4
	Master's degree	207	16.8
	PhD	13	2.6
	Others	17	3.4

Table 2. Internal Consistency Reliability

	CR	AVE
Info. availability	0.855	0.597
Remedial	0.842	0.574
Testing	0.778	0.540
Transparency	0.922	0.748
Understandability	0.889	0.616
Mon. and Veri	0.848	0.584

Table 3. Path Coefficients

	Path Coefficients	P – values	Confidence intervals		Significance
			Lower	Upper	(p<0.05)
H1:Info availability->transparency	0.175	0.003	0.066	0.294	Yes
H2:Understandability->transparency	–0.018	0.746	–0.121	0.095	No
H3:Mon. and Veri->transparency	0.217	0.000	0.111	0.325	Yes
H4:Remedial->transparency	0.225	0.001	0.088	0.360	Yes
H5:Testing->transparency	0.217	0.000	0.116	0.319	Yes

Table 4. Significant Path Coefficients

	Path Coefficients	P − values
H1:Info availability->transparency	0.175	0.003
H2:Understandability->transparency	−0.018	0.746
H3:Mon. and Veri.->transparency	0.217	0.000
H4:Remedial->transparency	0.225	0.001
H5:Testing->transparency	0.217	0.000

Note: Significant at P = .05

References

1. Agbesi, S., Dalela, A., Budurushi, J., Kulyk, O.: What will make me trust or not trust will depend upon how secure the technology is: factors influencing trust perceptions of the use of election technologies. E-Vote-ID 2022, p. 1 (2022)
2. Aithal, A., Aithal, P.: Development and validation of survey questionnaire & experimental data-a systematical review-based statistical approach. Int. J. Manag. Technol. Soc. Sci. (IJMTS) **5**(2), 233–251 (2020)
3. Association, A.P., et al.: Apa. Ethical principles of psychologists and code of conduct (2017)
4. Branley-Bell, D., Whitworth, R., Coventry, L.: User trust and understanding of explainable ai: exploring algorithm visualisations and user biases. In: Kurosu, M. (ed.) HCII 2020. LNCS, vol. 12183, pp. 382–399. Springer, Cham (2020). https://doi.org/10.1007/978-3-030-49065-2_27
5. Brunk, J., Mattern, J., Riehle, D.M.: Effect of transparency and trust on acceptance of automatic online comment moderation systems. In: 2019 IEEE 21st Conference on Business Informatics (CBI), vol. 1, pp. 429–435. IEEE (2019)
6. Buckland, R., Teague, V., Wen, R.: Towards best practice for E-election systems. In: Kiayias, A., Lipmaa, H. (eds.) Vote-ID 2011. LNCS, vol. 7187, pp. 224–241. Springer, Heidelberg (2012). https://doi.org/10.1007/978-3-642-32747-6_14
7. Driza Maurer, A.: The swiss Post/Scytl transparency exercise and its possible impact on internet voting regulation. In: Krimmer, R., et al. (eds.) E-Vote-ID 2019. LNCS, vol. 11759, pp. 83–99. Springer, Cham (2019). https://doi.org/10.1007/978-3-030-30625-0_6
8. Ehin, P., Solvak, M., Willemson, J., Vinkel, P.: Internet voting in Estonia 2005–2019: evidence from eleven elections. Gov. Inf. Q. **39**(4), 101718 (2022)
9. Faraon, M., Stenberg, G., Budurushi, J., Kaipainen, M.: Positive but skeptical : a study of attitudes towards internet voting in Sweden. In: CeDEM Asia 2014 : Proceedings of the International Conference for E-Democracy and Open Government, pp. 191–205 (2015)
10. Federal Constitutional Court of Germany: Decisions: Order of 03 March 2009–2 BvC 3/07 (2009). http://www.bundesverfassungsgericht.de/SharedDocs/Entscheidungen/EN/2009/03/cs20090303_2bvc000307en.html. Accessed 7 Feb 2016
11. Fragnière, E., Grèzes, S., Ramseyer, R.: How do the swiss perceive electronic voting? Social insights from an exploratory qualitative research. In: Krimmer, R., et al. (eds.) E-Vote-ID 2019. LNCS, vol. 11759, pp. 100–115. Springer, Cham (2019). https://doi.org/10.1007/978-3-030-30625-0_7

12. Garfinkel, S., Matthews, J., Shapiro, S.S., Smith, J.M.: Toward algorithmic transparency and accountability (2017)
13. Hair, J., Hult, G., Ringle, C., Sarstedt, M.: A Primer on Partial Least Squares Structural Equation Modeling (PLS-SEM). SAGE Publications, Thousand Oaks (2021). https://books.google.dk/books?id=6z83EAAAQBAJ
14. Hair Jr, J.F., Hult, G.T.M., Ringle, C.M., Sarstedt, M., Danks, N.P., Ray, S.: Partial least squares structural equation modeling (PLS-SEM) using r: a workbook (2021)
15. Hall, J.L.: Transparency and access to source code in E-voting. In: USENIX/ACCURATE Electronic Voting Technology Workshop (2006)
16. Jain, S.S., Jain, S.P.: Power distance belief and preference for transparency. J. Bus. Res. **89**, 135–142 (2018)
17. Kizilcec, R.F.: How much information? Effects of transparency on trust in an algorithmic interface. In: Proceedings of the 2016 CHI Conference on Human Factors in Computing Systems, pp. 2390–2395 (2016)
18. Kokolakis, S.: Privacy attitudes and privacy behaviour: a review of current research on the privacy paradox phenomenon. Comput. Secur. **64**, 122–134 (2017)
19. Lyons, J.B., et al.: Shaping trust through transparent design: theoretical and experimental guidelines. In: Savage-Knepshield, P., Chen, J. (eds.) Advances in Human Factors in Robots and Unmanned Systems. AISC, vol. 499, pp. 127–136. Springer, Cham (2017). https://doi.org/10.1007/978-3-319-41959-6_11
20. Marky, K., Gerber, P., Günther, S., Khamis, M., Fries, M., Mühlhäuser, M.: Investigating {State-of-the-Art} practices for fostering subjective trust in online voting through interviews. In: 31st USENIX Security Symposium (USENIX Security 22), pp. 4059–4076 (2022)
21. Marky, K., Zollinger, M.L., Roenne, P., Ryan, P.Y., Grube, T., Kunze, K.: Investigating usability and user experience of individually verifiable internet voting schemes. ACM Trans. Comput.-Hum. Interact. (TOCHI) **28**(5), 1–36 (2021)
22. Nurse, J.R.C., et al.: An assessment of the security and transparency procedural components of the Estonian internet voting system. In: Tryfonas, T. (ed.) HAS 2017. LNCS, vol. 10292, pp. 366–383. Springer, Cham (2017). https://doi.org/10.1007/978-3-319-58460-7_26
23. Olembo, M.M., Renaud, K., Bartsch, S., Volkamer, M.: Voter, what message will motivate you to verify your vote? In: Workshop on Usable Security (2014)
24. Oppenheimer, D.M., Meyvis, T., Davidenko, N.: Instructional manipulation checks: detecting satisficing to increase statistical power. J. Exp. Soc. Psychol. **45**(4), 867–872 (2009)
25. Portes, A., N'goala, G., Cases, A.S.: Digital transparency: dimensions, antecedents and consequences on the quality of customer relationships. Recherche et Applications en Marketing (English Edition) **35**(4), 72–98 (2020)
26. Puiggalí, J., Cucurull, J., Guasch, S., Krimmer, R.: Verifiability experiences in government online voting systems. In: Krimmer, R., Volkamer, M., Braun Binder, N., Kersting, N., Pereira, O., Schürmann, C. (eds.) E-Vote-ID 2017. LNCS, vol. 10615, pp. 248–263. Springer, Cham (2017). https://doi.org/10.1007/978-3-319-68687-5_15
27. Rader, E., Cotter, K., Cho, J.: Explanations as mechanisms for supporting algorithmic transparency. In: Proceedings of the 2018 CHI Conference on Human Factors in Computing Systems, pp. 1–13 (2018)
28. Redmiles, E.M., Kross, S., Mazurek, M.L.: How well do my results generalize? Comparing security and privacy survey results from MTurk, web, and telephone

samples. In: 2019 IEEE Symposium on Security and Privacy (SP), pp. 1326–1343. IEEE (2019)

29. Ringle, C.M., Wende, S., Becker, J.M.: Smartpls 4 (2022). http://www.smartpls. com

30. Saldanha, D.M.F., SILVA, M.B.D.: Transparency and accountability of government algorithms: the case of the Brazilian electronic voting system. Cadernos EBAPE. BR **18**, 697–712 (2020)

31. Schmidt, P., Biessmann, F., Teubner, T.: Transparency and trust in artificial intelligence systems. J. Decis. Syst. **29**(4), 260–278 (2020)

32. Solvak, M.: Does vote verification work: usage and impact of confidence building technology in internet voting. In: Krimmer, R., et al. (eds.) E-Vote-ID 2020. LNCS, vol. 12455, pp. 213–228. Springer, Cham (2020). https://doi.org/10.1007/978-3-030-60347-2_14

33. Song, C., Lee, J.: Citizens' use of social media in government, perceived transparency, and trust in government. Public Perform. Manag. Rev. **39**(2), 430–453 (2016)

34. Spycher, O., Volkamer, M., Koenig, R.: Transparency and technical measures to establish trust in Norwegian internet voting. In: Kiayias, A., Lipmaa, H. (eds.) Vote-ID 2011. LNCS, vol. 7187, pp. 19–35. Springer, Heidelberg (2012). https://doi.org/10.1007/978-3-642-32747-6_2

35. Volkamer, M., Kulyk, O., Ludwig, J., Fuhrberg, N.: Increasing security without decreasing usability: a comparison of various verifiable voting systems. In: Eighteenth Symposium on Usable Privacy and Security (SOUPS 2022), pp. 233–252 (2022)

36. Volkamer, M., Spycher, O., Dubuis, E.: Measures to establish trust in internet voting. In: Proceedings of the 5th International Conference on Theory and Practice of Electronic Governance, pp. 1–10 (2011)

37. Yang, X.J., Unhelkar, V.V., Li, K., Shah, J.A.: Evaluating effects of user experience and system transparency on trust in automation. In: 2017 12th ACM/IEEE International Conference on Human-Robot Interaction (HRI), pp. 408–416. IEEE (2017)

38. Zollinger, M.-L., Estaji, E., Ryan, P.Y.A., Marky, K.: Just for the sake of transparency: exploring voter mental models of verifiability. In: Krimmer, R., et al. (eds.) E-Vote-ID 2021. LNCS, vol. 12900, pp. 155–170. Springer, Cham (2021). https://doi.org/10.1007/978-3-030-86942-7_11

OpenVoting: Recoverability from Failures
in Dual Voting

Prashant Agrawal[1], Kabir Tomer[1,3], Abhinav Nakarmi[2], Mahabir Prasad Jhanwar[2],

Subodh Vishnu Sharma[1], and Subhashis Banerjee[1,2(✉)]

[1] Department of Computer Science and Engineering, IIT Delhi, New Delhi, India
{prashant,svs,suban}@cse.iitd.ac.in
[2] Department of Computer Science and Centre for Digitalisation, AI and Society,
Ashoka University, Sonipat, India
abhinav.nakarmi@alumni.ashoka.edu.in,
{mahavir.jhawar,suban}@ashoka.edu.in
[3] Department of Computer Science, UIUC, Champaign, USA
ktomer2@illinois.edu

Abstract. In this paper we address the problem of recovery from failures without re-running entire elections when elections fail to verify. We consider the setting of *dual voting* protocols, where the cryptographic guarantees of end-to-end verifiable voting (E2E-V) are combined with the simplicity of audit using voter-verified paper records (VVPR). We first consider the design requirements of such a system and then suggest a protocol called *OpenVoting*, which identifies a verifiable subset of error-free votes consistent with the VVPRs, and the polling booths corresponding to the votes that fail to verify with possible reasons for the failures.

1 Introduction

Conducting large-scale public elections in a dispute-free manner is not an easy task. On the one hand, there are end-to-end verifiable voting (E2E-V) systems [1,4,8,11,24] that provide cryptographic guarantees of correctness. Although the guarantees are sound, these systems are not yet very popular in large public elections. As the German Constitutional Court observes [18], depending solely on cryptographic guarantees is somewhat untenable as verification of election results requires expert knowledge. Moreover, in case voter checks or universal verifications fail, the E2E-V systems do not provide easy methods of recovery without necessitating complete re-election [6].

On the other hand, there are systems that rely on paper-audit trails to verify electronic tallies [16,21,25]. These systems maintain reliable records of cleartext voter-marked paper ballots or voter-verified paper records (VVPRs) alongside electronic vote records. They use electronic counting for efficiency and conduct easy-to-understand statistical audits, called *risk-limiting audits* (RLAs), to demonstrate that the electronic winners match the winners that would be declared by a full paper count. In case of conflict, the electronic outcome is suggested to be replaced by the paper one. However, these systems require the electorate to trust that the paper records correctly represent voter intent and are not corrupted in the custody chain from the time of voting to that of counting or auditing.

M. Volkamer et al. (Eds.): E-Vote-ID 2023, LNCS 14230, pp. 18–34, 2023.
https://doi.org/10.1007/978-3-031-43756-4_2

Dual voting approaches, where the voting protocols support simultaneous voting for both the cryptographic and the VVPR-based systems [4,5,12,13,17,22], combine the cryptographic guarantees of E2E-V systems with the simplicity and adoptability of paper records. However, in most existing dual voting systems, one typically ends up running two parallel and independent elections, only coupled loosely through simultaneous voting for both in the polling booth. If the electronic and paper record systems are not tightly coupled, and demonstrably in one-to-one correspondence, then it begs the questions: which ought be the legal definition of the vote, and, in case of a tally mismatch, which should be trusted? Why? And how to recover from errors?

It appears that existing approaches either do not provide any recovery mechanism or recover by privileging VVPR counts over electronic counts. In large public elections running simultaneously at multiple polling booths per constituency, failures due to intended or unintended errors by different actors are expected. Polling officers may upload wrong encrypted votes, backend servers may decrypt votes incorrectly, paper records may be tampered with during the custody chain, and voters may put bogus votes in ballot boxes to discredit the election. Discarding the entire election due to failures caused by some bad actors or completely trusting the VVPRs are both unsatisfactory solutions.

In this paper, we study the problem of *recoverability* of a dual voting protocol from audit failures. We consider large, multi-polling booth, first-past-the-post elections like the national elections in India. We observe that except for backend failures, most of the other failures are due to localised corruption of individual polling booths. Therefore, we propose to identify the offending polling booths and perform a local re-election—if at all required—only at those polling booths. Errors—despite the best efforts to minimise them—are inevitable in large elections and such localised recovery may considerably improve the election's overall robustness and transparency.

However, recoverability has a natural tradeoff with vote secrecy. For example, a naive approach that simply publishes and audits votes for each polling booth reveals voting statistics of each booth. In electoral contexts where voters are assigned a specific polling booth according to their residential neighbourhoods, with only a few thousand voters per booth, e.g., in India, revealing booth-level voting statistics poses a significant risk of localised targeting and coercion [3]. Our approach minimises booth-level voting data exposure, disclosing only what is absolutely necessary for recovery.

Main Contributions. 1) We analyse the design requirements for a recoverable and secrecy-preserving dual voting protocol (Sect. 2). **2)** We formalise the notion of recoverability and secrecy in terms of the capability to verifiably identify polling booths contributing to verification failures and extract a verifiable subset of error-free votes in zero-knowledge (Sect. 3). **3)** We propose a novel dual-voting protocol called *OpenVoting* that satisfies our notions of recoverability and secrecy (Sect. 4).

Related Work. Dual voting was introduced by Benaloh [5], following which multiple dual voting protocols emerged [4,12,13,17,22]. Bernhard et al. [6] gives a comprehensive survey of the tradeoffs and open problems in E2E-V and RLA-based voting.

Rivest [23] proposed the notion of *strong software independence* that is similar to our notion of recoverability. It demands that a detected change or error in an election outcome (due to a change or error in the software) can be corrected without re-running the (entire) election. However, "correcting" errors without re-running even parts of an election requires a ground truth, which is usually assumed to be the paper audit trail. Instead, we propose partial recoverability via fault localisation, without completely trusting either paper or electronic votes. The notion of *accountability* [15] is also related, but it is focused on assigning blame for failures and not on recovering from them.

2 Design Requirements

In a typical dual voting protocol, the vote casting process produces a) a VVPR containing the voter's vote in cleartext and b) a voter receipt containing an encryption of the vote. The encrypted votes are published on a bulletin board, typically by a *polling officer*, and are processed by a cryptographic *backend* to produce the electronic tally. The backend typically consists of multiple independent servers which jointly compute the tally from the encrypted inputs, provide a proof of correctness, and preserve vote secrecy unless a threshold number of servers are corrupted. VVPRs counted together produce the paper tally.

Our high-level goal is to publicly verify whether both tallies represent true voter intents and whether all public outputs are consistent with each other. If not, the aim of recovery is to identify booths contributing to the inconsistencies, and segregate the outputs produced by other error-free booths, without leaking any additional information. For this, the protocol design must fundamentally have the following features:

1. The backend must publish individual decrypted votes with matching identifiers with the VVPRs[1], to narrow down tally inconsistencies to individual vote mismatches.
2. The encrypted votes must have voter and booth identifiers. The former enable matching with voter receipts; the latter enable identifying booths in case of errors.
3. The decrypted votes and VVPRs and their identifiers must be unlinkable to encrypted votes, voter receipts or voter identifiers to ensure vote secrecy. They should also be unlinkable to the booth identifiers to hide booth-level voting statistics.
4. For the same reason, VVPRs should be revealed and counted only after aggregating them over all the polling booths.

The encrypted and decrypted votes must be published on two public bulletin boards to enable voters to match their receipts and public verification of the electronic tally. It will also be helpful to upload all VVPRs after scanning, and as many voter receipts as possible, to two other bulletin boards for better transparency and public verifiability. We depict such a design in Fig. 1.

Note that the public outputs in Fig. 1 are effectively *claims* endorsed by various entities as to what should be the correct vote: receipts by voters, encrypted votes by polling officers, decrypted votes by the backend servers, and VVPRs by the VVPR counting authorities. We group disputes between these claims into *input-phase failures*, for mismatches between published voter receipts and encrypted votes, *mixing-phase failures*, for mismatches between encrypted votes and decrypted votes, and *output-phase failures*, for mismatches between decrypted votes and VVPRs (see Fig. 2). Further, we categorise claims of receipts not encrypting voter intents correctly as *cast-as-intended failures*. Given these failures, recoverability requires an audit protocol that verifies whether

---

[1] Homomorphic tallying based backends [1,4] report only the final tally and do not support this.

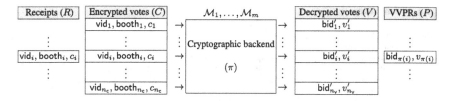

Receipts (R)	Encrypted votes (C)	$\mathcal{M}_1, \ldots, \mathcal{M}_m$	Decrypted votes (V)	VVPRs (P)
	$\text{vid}_1, \text{booth}_1, c_1$ →		→ bid'_1, v'_1	
$\vdots$	$\vdots$	$\vdots$ Cryptographic backend $\vdots$	$\vdots$	$\vdots$
$\boxed{\text{vid}_i, \text{booth}_i, c_i}$	$\text{vid}_i, \text{booth}_i, c_i$ →	(π)	→ bid'_i, v'_i	$\boxed{\text{bid}_{\pi(i)}, v_{\pi(i)}}$
$\vdots$	$\vdots$	$\vdots$	$\vdots$	$\vdots$
	$\text{vid}_{n_c}, \text{booth}_{n_c}, c_{n_c}$ →		→ $\text{bid}'_{n_v}, v'_{n_v}$	

Fig. 1. A recoverable dual voting protocol design. The VVPR for a voter with identifier vid_i voting at booth booth_i contains a ballot identifier bid_i and cleartext vote v_i. Her encrypted vote c_i encrypts a value, e.g., (bid_i, v_i), that when decrypted can be uniquely matched with the corresponding VVPR. Decrypted votes are published by backend servers $\mathcal{M}_1, \ldots, \mathcal{M}_m$ in a permuted order under a secret shared permutation π such that $(\text{bid}'_i, v'_i) = (\text{bid}_{\pi(i)}, v_{\pi(i)})$. Note that n_c and n_v denote the number of encrypted votes and decrypted votes respectively.

the different claims for a given vote are consistent, resolves disputes otherwise, and narrows down the affected votes when the disputes are unresolvable.

To recover from input-phase failures, it is not sufficient if a statistically significant sample of voters from the entire constituency verify their receipts, because in case of any failure, all the uploaded encrypted votes become untrustworthy. Thus, the population for sampling must be each polling booth. This does increase the voter verification overhead, but offers better localisation of errors and recovery.

Recoverability from mixing-phase failures requires that in case the output list of decrypted votes is not correct, individual failing entries—encrypted votes whose decryptions were not available in V and individual decrypted votes that were not decrypted by any encrypted vote on C—should be verifiably identified by the backend servers. And, this must be achieved without leaking any additional information.

Recoverability from output-phase failures requires identifying which of the electronic vote and the VVPR represents the voter's intent. This may be possible in some cases but not always. For example, if the voter's receipt is available on R, then the dispute can be resolved if one can verify in zero-knowledge that the receipt encrypted the electronic vote and not the paper one, or vice versa.

In some cases, the disputes may not be resolvable at all. Consider case FO$_3$ in Fig. 2 and suppose the receipt is not available. FO$_3$ may be due to a) the polling officer uploading an encrypted vote not matching the voter's receipt; b) the voter dropping a bogus VVPR into the ballot box; c) a malicious agent altering the VVPRs post-polling; or d) the backend servers not decrypting the uploaded encrypted vote correctly. Different cases point to failures in either the electronic vote or the VVPR and it is not possible to identify the true voter intent. Thus, a conservative way to recover from this situation is to identify the polling booth where the dispute may have originated and conduct only a local re-election at this booth. This must be done without revealing polling booth statistics of at least the uncorrupted polling booths.

The required action in all the above cases can be reduced to the backend proving in zero-knowledge that an encrypted vote corresponds to one of a set of decrypted votes (a *distributed ZKP of set-membership* [2]), or that a clear-text vote is a decryption of one of a set of encrypted votes (a *distributed ZKP of reverse set-membership* [2]).

Cast-as-intended failures may typically happen in two ways. First, ballots may be malformed. Protection against this threat requires a separate audit of a statistically

Input-phase failures[1,2]	
FI_1	A receipt r against vid exists in R but no encrypted vote against vid exists in C
FI_2	The encrypted vote c in C against vid does not match the receipt r in R against vid
Mixing-phase failures[2,3]	
FM_1	An encrypted vote c in C does not decrypt to any cleartext vote (bid, v) in V
FM_2	A cleartext vote (bid, v) in V is not obtained by decrypting any encrypted vote c in C
FM_3	Two encrypted votes in C decrypt to the same cleartext vote (bid, v) in V
Output-phase failures[2]	
FO_1	An (electronic) decrypted vote (bid, v) exists in V but no VVPR against bid exists in P
FO_2	A VVPR (bid, v) exists in P but no decrypted vote against bid exists in V
FO_3	The decrypted vote v against bid in V does not match the cleartext vote in the VVPR against bid in P
FO_4	Two decrypted votes in V match with a single VVPR (bid, v) in P
FO_5	Two VVPRs in P match with a single decrypted vote (bid, v) in V
Cast-as-intended failures	
FC	A receipt r obtained at a polling booth j does not encrypt the voter's intended vote correctly

[1] A spurious encrypted vote against a vid in C without a receipt in R against that vid is not considered a failure, because some voters may not upload their receipts. Also, we do not consider duplicated receipts and encrypted votes because vids are assumed to be unique identifiers.

[2] We only consider authentic entries in R, C, V and P. Failures where the authenticity of these items cannot be verified are considered equivalent to failures where they are not even uploaded. Receipts and VVPRs are authenticated by official stamps and encrypted and decrypted votes by appropriate digital signatures.

[3] The case of a single encrypted vote in C decrypting to two different entries in V is not considered because this will result in duplicated entries in V, which can be clearly attributed to backend failures and removed without any dispute.

Fig. 2. Potential failures given public outputs (R, C, V, P).

significant sample of ballots before vote casting. Recoverability additionally requires ballot audits to be performed per polling booth. Second, ballots or receipts may be marked incorrectly. In dual voting systems based on hand-marked ballots, the voter may mark the encrypted and the VVPR parts differently, leading to failures. Although this is easily detected and invalidated during VVPR audit, fixing accountability may be difficult and hence voters may do this deliberately to discredit the election. In systems based on ballot marking devices (BMD), such voter errors are avoided but a dispute may be raised that the ballot marking is not according to the voter's choice. Such a dispute between a man and a machine is unresolvable and the only recourse is to allow the voter to revote. This may however cause a deadlock, which can only be resolved through a social process. Still, a BMD should be a preferred option for dual voting since it minimises voter-initiated errors.

3 Formalisation

We now formalise the requirements outlined in the previous section. Given a positive integer x, let $[x]$ denote the set $\{1, \ldots, x\}$. We consider a dual-voting protocol involving α candidates, n voters $(\mathcal{V}_i)_{i \in [n]}$, τ ballot generators $(\mathcal{G}_t)_{t \in [\tau]}$, ℓ polling booths consisting of polling officers $(\mathcal{P}_j)_{j \in [\ell]}$, BMDs $(\mathcal{D}_j)_{j \in [\ell]}$ and physical ballot boxes $(\mathcal{B}_j)_{j \in [\ell]}$, m backend servers $(\mathcal{M}_k)_{k \in [m]}$, and an auditor $\mathcal{A}$. We also assume existence of a public bulletin board where lists R, C, V and P are published. We consider a protocol structure (Setup, BallotGen, Cast, Tally, BallotAudit, ReceiptAudit, TallyAudit) where:

– Setup is a protocol involving $(\mathcal{G}_t)_{t \in [\tau]}$, $(\mathcal{P}_j)_{j \in [\ell]}$ and $(\mathcal{M}_k)_{k \in [m]}$ to generate public/private key pairs and other public election parameters.

- BallotGen is a protocol involving $(\mathcal{G}_t)_{t \in [\tau]}$ to securely print a sealed ballot given a booth identifier $j \in [\ell]$.
- Cast is the vote casting protocol involving $\mathcal{V}_i$ and $\mathcal{P}_j$, $\mathcal{D}_j$, $\mathcal{B}_j$ at booth $j \in [\ell]$ assigned to $\mathcal{V}_i$. $\mathcal{V}_i$'s input is its intended vote v and a ballot b. The protocol outputs a voter receipt r, an encrypted vote c and a VVPR p such that p gets dropped in ballot box $\mathcal{B}_j$, $\mathcal{V}_i$ takes r home and $\mathcal{P}_j$ uploads c on C. The voter may or may not publish r on R. The VVPR is published on P after aggregating VVPRs from all the booths.
- Tally is the vote processing/tallying protocol involving $(\mathcal{M}_k)_{k \in [m]}$ where they take as input the encrypted votes $(c_i)_{i \in [n]}$ published on C, permute and decrypt them and publish a list $(v'_i)_{i \in [n]}$ of decrypted votes on V.
- BallotAudit is a protocol involving $\mathcal{A}$ and $\mathcal{P}_j$ executed at each booth j to verify if ballots at booth j are well-formed.
- ReceiptAudit is a protocol involving $\mathcal{A}$ and the voters to verify that voter receipts at booth j match those uploaded on list C.
- TallyAudit is a protocol involving $\mathcal{A}$, $(\mathcal{M}_k)_{k \in [m]}$ and $(\mathcal{G}_t)_{t \in [\tau]}$ to verify whether the electronic and paper tallies are correct and narrow down errors if not. It takes as input all published lists (R, C, V, P) and lets $\mathcal{A}$ output a tuple (J^*, V^*) where J^* denotes the set of booths that contributed potentially outcome-changing failures and V^* denotes the set of votes from booths not in J^* ($\mathcal{A}$ may also be aborted). The expected usage of the (J^*, V^*) output is that in case of failures/disputes, the election could be rerun at the booths in J^* and the rerun results could be merged with the recovered partial tally from V^* to obtain the complete election tally. Results are announced to the general public only after TallyAudit has finished.

Note that although the above audits are performed by different auditors (even voters) at different times and places, we simplify by representing all the auditors by $\mathcal{A}$.

Let ϵ_b denote the probability that BallotAudit passes at some booth j yet a receipt from the booth does not encrypt the voter's intent correctly, and ϵ_r denote the probability that ReceiptAudit passes for booth j yet a receipt from the booth is not uploaded correctly. Further, let $R^* \subseteq R$, $C^* \subseteq C$ and $P^* \subseteq P$ respectively denote receipts, encrypted votes and VVPRs from booths not in J^*. Finally, let *failures* in a tuple (R, C, V, P) be as defined in Fig. 2 with the added condition that if a receipt or encrypted vote from a booth fails with input-phase or cast-as-intended failures, then all receipts and encrypted votes from that booth are considered as failures.

Definition 1 models our notion of recoverability parametrised by probabilities ϵ_b and ϵ_r denoting the effectiveness of ballot and receipt audits. The case when J^* is empty denotes that no rerun is required at any booth, either because the election ran completely correctly, or because the number of failures are small compared to the reported winning margin. When non-empty, J^* should exactly be the set of booths where re-run is required because of failures that may affect the final outcome and votes V^* must be consistent with receipts, encrypted votes and VVPRs from booths not in J^*.

Note that the auditor is allowed to abort the TallyAudit protocol, since if the mix-servers and the ballot generators holding the election secrets do not cooperate, then recovery cannot happen. This is not an issue because unlike polling booth failures, these failures are centralised and non-cooperation directly puts the blame on these entities.

Definition 1 (Recoverability). *A voting protocol* (Setup, BallotGen, Cast, Tally, BallotAudit, ReceiptAudit, TallyAudit) *is* recoverable *by the audit protocols if for all polynomially bounded adversaries corrupting* $(\mathcal{G}_t)_{t \in [\tau]}$, $(\mathcal{M}_k)_{k \in [m]}$, $(\mathcal{P}_j)_{j \in [\ell]}$, $(\mathcal{D}_j)_{j \in [\ell]}$ *and* $(\mathcal{B}_j)_{j \in [\ell]}$ *such that* $\mathcal{A}$ *outputs a tuple* (J^*, V^*) *and does not abort, the following conditions hold true with probability only negligibly smaller than* $1 - \ell(\epsilon_b + \epsilon_r)$:

- *if* J^* *is empty, then the number of failures in* (R^*, C^*, V^*, P^*) *is less than the reported winning margin computed from* V; *and*
- *if* J^* *is non-empty, then* (R^*, C^*, V^*, P^*) *does not contain any failures and* J^* *is exactly the set of booths that contributed some failing receipt in* R, *some failing encrypted vote in* C, *or some failing VVPR in* P.

Definition 2 models that in the presence of the TallyAudit protocol, the standard vote secrecy guarantee is maintained except that polling booth statistics of the booths contributing some failing items are revealed. This is generally an unavoidable tradeoff.

Definition 2 (Vote Secrecy with Recoverability). *A voting protocol* (Setup, BallotGen, Cast, Tally, BallotAudit, ReceiptAudit, TallyAudit) *protects vote secrecy with recoverability if no polynomially bounded adversary controlling the auditor* $\mathcal{A}$, $(\mathcal{P}_j)_{j \in [\ell]}$, $(\mathcal{D}_j)_{j \in [\ell]}$, $(\mathcal{G}_t)_{t \in [\tau] \setminus \{t^*\}}$ *for some* $t^* \in [\tau]$, $(\mathcal{M}_k)_{k \in [m] \setminus \{k^*\}}$ *for some* $k^* \in [m]$, *and* $(\mathcal{V}_i)_{i \in [n] \setminus \{i_0, i_1\}}$ *for some* $i_0, i_1 \in [n]$ *can distinguish between the following two worlds except with negligible probability:*

- *(World 0)* $\mathcal{V}_{i_0}$ *votes* v_0 *at booth* j_0 *and* $\mathcal{V}_{i_1}$ *votes* v_1 *at booth* j_1, *and*
- *(World 1)* $\mathcal{V}_{i_0}$ *votes* v_1 *at booth* j_0 *and* $\mathcal{V}_{i_1}$ *votes* v_0 *at booth* j_1,

where v_0, v_1 *are any two valid votes and for each failure from booth* j_0, *the adversary must create an identical failure (same failure type and affected vote) from booth* j_1.

4   The *OpenVoting* Protocol

4.1   Preliminaries

Notation. Let $\mathbb{G}_1, \mathbb{G}_2, \mathbb{G}_T$ denote cyclic groups of prime order q ($q \gg \alpha, m, n, \ell$) such that they admit an efficiently computable bilinear map $e : \mathbb{G}_1 \times \mathbb{G}_2 \to \mathbb{G}_T$. We assume that the n-Strong Diffie Hellman (SDH) assumption [7] holds in $(\mathbb{G}_1, \mathbb{G}_2)$, the decisional Diffie-Hellman (DDH) and the discrete logarithm (DL) assumptions hold in $\mathbb{G}_1$, and that generators $g_1, h_1 \in \mathbb{G}_1$ are chosen randomly (say as the output of a hash function) so that nobody knows their mutual discrete logarithm.

Traceable Mixnets [2]. Traceable mixnets extend traditional mixnets [14] to enable the distributed ZKPs of set membership mentioned in Sect. 2. Thus, we use them as our cryptographic backend. In traceable mixnets, the backend servers, often also called *mix-servers*, can collectively prove answers to the following queries in zero-knowledge:

- TraceIn: whether a ciphertext c (from the mixnet's input ciphertext list) encrypts a value in a subset of output plaintexts (denoted as $(v'_i)_{i \in I'}$ for some $I' \subseteq [n]$).
- TraceOut: whether a plaintext v (from the mixnet's output plaintext list) is encrypted in one of a subset of input ciphertexts (denoted as $(c_i)_{i \in I}$ for some $I \subseteq [n]$.).

There are also batched versions of these queries called BTraceIn and BTraceOut, which prove multiple TraceIn and TraceOut queries together.

Formally, a traceable mixnet Π_{TM} is a protocol between a set of senders $S_1, \ldots, S_n$, a set of mix-servers $(\mathcal{M}_k)_{k \in [m]}$ and a querier Q and consists of algorithms/sub-protocols (Keygen, Enc, Mix, BTraceIn, BTraceOut) where:

- Keygen is a distributed key generation protocol involving $(\mathcal{M}_k)_{k \in [m]}$ that outputs a mixnet public key mpk and secret keys $\mathsf{msk}^{(k)}$ for each mix-server $\mathcal{M}_k$.
- Enc is the encryption algorithm that a sender S_i uses to create a ciphertext c_i encrypting its secret input v_i against mpk.
- Mix is the mixing protocol involving $(\mathcal{M}_k)_{k \in [m]}$ that takes as input the list of ciphertexts $(c_i)_{i \in [n]}$ uploaded by $(S_i)_{i \in [n]}$ and outputs a list of permuted plaintexts $(v'_i)_{i \in [n]}$ and a secret witness $\omega^{(k)}$ for each $\mathcal{M}_k$.
- BTraceIn is a protocol involving $(\mathcal{M}_k)_{k \in [m]}$ and Q that takes as input $(c_i)_{i \in [n]}$ and $(v'_i)_{i \in [n]}$ and index sets $I, I' \subseteq [n]$ (each $\mathcal{M}_k$ additionally uses $\omega^{(k)}$). At the end of the protocol, Q either outputs the subset of ciphertexts $\{c_i\}_{i \in I}$ that encrypt some plaintext in $\{v'_i\}_{i \in I'}$ or aborts.
- BTraceOut is a protocol involving $(\mathcal{M}_k)_{k \in [m]}$ and Q that takes exactly the same inputs as BTraceIn. In this case, Q either outputs the subset of plaintexts $\{v'_i\}_{i \in I'}$ that are encrypted by some ciphertext in $\{c_i\}_{i \in I}$ or aborts.

The *soundness property of traceable mixnets* states that an adversary controlling all $(\mathcal{M}_k)_{k \in [m]}$ cannot make Q output an incorrect set. Their *secrecy property* states that an adversary controlling $(\mathcal{M}_k)_{k \in [m] \setminus \{k^*\}}$ for some $k^* \in [m]$, Q and $(S_i)_{i \in [n] \setminus \{i_0, i_1\}}$ for some $i_0, i_1 \in [n]$ cannot distinguish between a world where (S_{i_0}, S_{i_1}) respectively encrypt (v_0, v_1) and the world where they encrypt (v_1, v_0), if the BTraceIn and BTraceOut query outputs do not leak this information, i.e., if in all BTraceIn queries, $v_0 \in \{v'_i\}_{i \in I'}$ iff $v_1 \in \{v'_i\}_{i \in I'}$ and in all BTraceOut queries, $i_0 \in I$ iff $i_1 \in I$.

An Instantiation of Traceable Mixnets. [2] also provides a concrete instantiation of a traceable mixnet, which we use. In this instantiation, mpk is of the form $((\mathsf{pk}_{\mathcal{M}_k})_{k \in [m]}, \mathsf{pk}_{\mathsf{EG}}, \mathsf{pk}_{\mathsf{Pa}})$, where $\mathsf{pk}_{\mathcal{M}_k}$ is the public key of any IND-CPA secure encryption scheme E, and $\mathsf{pk}_{\mathsf{EG}}$ and $\mathsf{pk}_{\mathsf{Pa}}$ are respectively public keys of $\mathsf{E}_{\mathsf{EG}}^{\mathsf{th}}$, the threshold ElGamal encryption scheme [10] with message space $\mathbb{G}_1$, and $\mathsf{E}_{\mathsf{Pa}}^{\mathsf{th}}$, the threshold Paillier encryption scheme proposed in [9] with message space $\mathbb{Z}_N$ for an RSA modulus N. The secret key $\mathsf{msk}^{(k)}$ for each $\mathcal{M}_k$ consists of the secret key $\mathsf{sk}_{\mathcal{M}_k}$ corresponding to $\mathsf{pk}_{\mathcal{M}_k}$ and the kth shares of the secret keys corresponding to $\mathsf{pk}_{\mathsf{EG}}$ and $\mathsf{pk}_{\mathsf{Pa}}$. Further, Enc on input a value $v \in \mathbb{Z}_q$ outputs a ciphertext of the form $(\epsilon, \gamma, (\mathsf{ev}^{(k)}, \mathsf{er}^{(k)})_{k \in [m]}, \rho_\gamma, \epsilon_r)$, where

- $\epsilon \leftarrow \mathsf{E}_{\mathsf{Pa}}^{\mathsf{th}}.\mathsf{Enc}(\mathsf{pk}_{\mathsf{Pa}}, v)$ is an encryption of v (interpreted as $v \in \mathbb{Z}_N$) under $\mathsf{E}_{\mathsf{Pa}}^{\mathsf{th}}$,
- $\gamma = g_1^v h_1^r$ is a Pedersen commitment [20] to v in $\mathbb{G}_1$ under randomness $r \in \mathbb{Z}_q$,
- $\mathsf{ev}^{(k)} \leftarrow \mathsf{E}.\mathsf{Enc}(\mathsf{pk}_{\mathcal{M}_k}, v^{(k)})$ is an encryption of a secret share $v^{(k)}$ of v,
- $\mathsf{er}^{(k)} \leftarrow \mathsf{E}.\mathsf{Enc}(\mathsf{pk}_{\mathcal{M}_k}, r^{(k)})$ is an encryption of a secret share $r^{(k)}$ of r,
- $\rho_\gamma \leftarrow \mathsf{NIZKPK}\{(v, r) : \gamma = g_1^v h_1^r\}$ is a noninteractive ZKP of knowledge of the opening of γ, and
- $\epsilon_r \leftarrow \mathsf{E}_{\mathsf{Pa}}^{\mathsf{th}}.\mathsf{Enc}(\mathsf{pk}_{\mathsf{Pa}}, r)$ is an encryption of r (interpreted as $r \in \mathbb{Z}_N$) under $\mathsf{E}_{\mathsf{Pa}}^{\mathsf{th}}$.

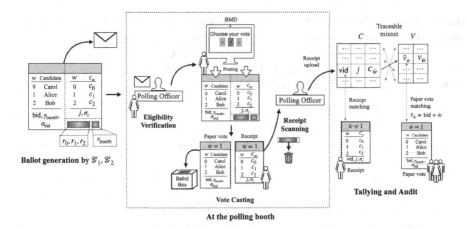

Fig. 3. Overview of the *OpenVoting* protocol: w represents the candidate index in the ballot and $\dot{w}$ represents the voter's choice.

In our protocol, the encrypted votes are encryptions under Enc, where we instantiate scheme E with the (non-threshold) Paillier encryption scheme [19]. We need it for its following homomorphic property: given two Paillier ciphertexts c_1, c_2 encrypting messages $m_1, m_2 \in \mathbb{Z}_q$ respectively (m_1, m_2 interpreted as messages in $\mathbb{Z}_N$), the ciphertext $c_1 c_2$ encrypts the message $m_1 + m_2 \mod N = m_1 + m_2$ if $N > 2q$. We also require a public-key digital signature scheme $\Pi_S := (\mathsf{Keygen}, \mathsf{Sign}, \mathsf{Ver})$ with the usual existential unforgeability property under chosen message attacks (EUF-CMA).

4.2 The Proposed Protocol

Figure 3 depicts the high-level *OpenVoting* protocol. Two ballot generators ($\mathcal{G}_1$ and $\mathcal{G}_2$) jointly generate sealed ballots to protect voter-vote association from both. Voters use the sealed ballots and a BMD to cast their votes. Each ballot contains two halves. The BMD prints the voter's choice on both halves without learning the vote. The left half becomes the VVPR and is deposited by the voter in a physical ballot box, while the right half becomes the voter receipt. Polling officers scan the voter receipts and upload the encrypted votes to C. The encrypted votes are processed by a traceable mixnet backend to produce decrypted votes V. Voters can verify their receipts against the encrypted votes, and VVPRs can be matched with the decrypted votes. The tally audit process uses the traceable mixnet's querying mechanism to identify polling booths contributing to failures without leaking additional information. Results are announced only after this audit step. Now we describe the sub-protocols of *OpenVoting* in detail.

Setup. During the Setup protocol, $\mathcal{G}_1$ and $\mathcal{G}_2$ generate public/private keys $\mathsf{pk}_{\mathcal{G}_1}, \mathsf{sk}_{\mathcal{G}_1}$ and $\mathsf{pk}_{\mathcal{G}_2}, \mathsf{sk}_{\mathcal{G}_2}$ under Π_S. Polling officers $(\mathcal{P}_j)_{j \in [\ell]}$ also generate public/private keys $(\mathsf{pk}_{\mathcal{P}_j}, \mathsf{sk}_{\mathcal{P}_j})_{j \in [\ell]}$ under Π_S. Mix-servers $(\mathcal{M}_k)_{k \in [m]}$ jointly run the Π_{TM}.Keygen protocol of the traceable mixnet to generate the mixnet public key mpk and individual secret keys $(\mathsf{msk}^{(k)})_{k \in [m]}$ for each $(\mathcal{M}_k)_{k \in [m]}$. An official candidate list $(\mathsf{cand}_0, \ldots, \mathsf{cand}_{\alpha-1})$ is created such that cand_a denotes the ath candidate.

Ballot Design. Our ballot (Fig. 3 - left) customises the Scratch & Vote ballot [1] for dual voting and BMD support. It consists of two halves connected by a perforated line. The left half serves as the VVPR, while the right half serves as the voter receipt. These halves are unlinkable after the vote is cast.

The left half includes a randomly drawn ballot identifier bid from $\mathbb{Z}_q$. It displays a circular rotation of the official candidate list. For each $w \in \{0, \ldots, \alpha - 1\}$, row w corresponds to the candidate $\mathsf{cand}_{\mathsf{bid}+w \bmod \alpha}$. For example, if the official candidate list is ("Alice", "Bob", "Carol"), and bid $= 302$, the candidate printed on row $w = 1$ would be $\mathsf{cand}_{302+1 \bmod 3} = \mathsf{cand}_0$ (i.e., "Alice"). The right half contains corresponding encryptions c_w obtained by running the $\Pi_{\mathsf{TM}}.\mathsf{Enc}$ algorithm on input $\bar{v}_w = \mathsf{bid} + w$, except that they do not include the ρ_{γ_w} component; this is added during the Tally protocol. We call values $\bar{v}_w \in \mathbb{Z}_q$ the *extended votes* and values $v_w := \bar{v}_w \bmod \alpha \in [\alpha]$ the *raw votes*. The randomnesses r_w used in creating encryption c_w are kept secret and placed under a detachable scratch surface on the ballot.

Both halves feature a designated gray area at the top. During the Cast protocol, the BMD prints the voter-selected w in this gray area on both halves. Additionally, the right half includes a polling booth identifier j for the designated polling booth of the ballot, while the left half contains its commitment $\gamma_{\mathsf{booth}} = g^j h^{r_{\mathsf{booth}}}$. Randomness $r_{\mathsf{booth}} \xleftarrow{\$} \mathbb{Z}_q$ is also put under a separate scratch surface. The commitment γ_{booth} is revealed when the polling booth of a disputed VVPR needs to be identified in the TallyAudit protocol.

Due to the size of encryptions c_w (around 20 KB each [2]), they may not fit within standard QR codes on the paper ballot. However, conceptually, the actual encryptions could be stored in a backend server, with only a binding hash printed on the ballot. For simplicity, we ignore this complication.

Ballot Generation. During the BallotGen protocol, a ballot is jointly generated by $\mathcal{G}_1$ and $\mathcal{G}_2$ to hide the voter-vote association from any one of them (see Fig. 4). $\mathcal{G}_1$, who selects the ballot secrets, does not learn the encryptions printed on the receipt half and cannot match voters to their ballot secrets, while $\mathcal{G}_2$, who creates the receipt half, does not know the ballot secrets.

$\mathcal{G}_2$ knows the destination booth j but keeps it hidden from $\mathcal{G}_1$ to hide booth-level voting statistics. It generates a commitment γ_{booth} for j and shares it with $\mathcal{G}_1$ (lines 1–2), who prints it on the left half of the ballot. $\mathcal{G}_1$ generates a secret ballot identifier bid and signs it (lines 2–3), computes $\bar{v}_w = \mathsf{bid} + w$ for each w and accordingly prints candidate names on the left half and randomnesses r_w under a scratch surface on the right half (lines 6,10). It then sends the partially printed ballot to $\mathcal{G}_2$, keeping the left half hidden. This can be done, e.g., by folding the ballot along the perforation line, sealing it and letting $\mathcal{G}_2$ print its contents on the *back side* of the right half. It also sends encryptions of each $\bar{v}_w$ under $\Pi_{\mathsf{TM}}.\mathsf{Enc}$, except the ρ_{γ_w} components, to $\mathcal{G}_2$ (lines 7–9,12).

$\mathcal{G}_2$ re-randomises the obtained commitments/encryptions and homomorphically computes fresh shares of $\bar{v}_w$ and the commitment randomnesses using the additive homomorphism of E in $\mathbb{Z}_q$ (lines 13–19). It then prints these re-randomised encryptions on the right half of the received ballot and signs them. The re-randomisation ensures that $\mathcal{G}_1$ cannot identify the ballot corresponding to a voter from their receipt. The commitment randomness r_{booth} of γ_{booth} is printed on another scratch surface on the right half.

---

1 $\mathcal{G}_2$: $r_{\text{booth}} \xleftarrow{\$} \mathbb{Z}_q$; $\gamma_{\text{booth}} \leftarrow g_1^j h_1^{r_{\text{booth}}}$
2 $\mathcal{G}_2$: send γ_{booth} to $\mathcal{G}_1$
3 $\mathcal{G}_1$: bid $\xleftarrow{\$} \mathbb{Z}_q$
4      $\sigma_{\text{bid}} \leftarrow \Pi_{\text{S}}.\text{Sign}(\text{sk}_{\mathcal{G}_1}, \text{bid})$
5 **for** $w \in \{0, \ldots, \alpha-1\}$:
6      $\bar{v}_w \leftarrow \text{bid} + w$; $r_w \xleftarrow{\$} \mathbb{Z}_q$; $\gamma_w \leftarrow g_1^{\bar{v}_w} h_1^{r_w}$
7      $\epsilon_{\bar{v}_w} \leftarrow \text{E}_{\text{P}_a}^{\text{th}}.\text{Enc}(\text{pk}_{\text{P}_a}, \bar{v}_w)$; $\epsilon_{r_w} \leftarrow \text{E}_{\text{P}_a}^{\text{th}}.\text{Enc}(\text{pk}_{\text{P}_a}, r_w)$ // interpret v_w, r_w as elements of $\mathbb{Z}_N$
8      $(\bar{v}_w^{(k)})_{k \in [m]} \leftarrow \text{Share}_{(m,m)}(\bar{v}_w)$; $(r_w^{(k)})_{k \in [m]} \leftarrow \text{Share}_{(m,m)}(r_w)$
9      $(\text{ev}_w^{(k)})_{k \in [m]} \leftarrow (\text{E.Enc}(\text{pk}_{\mathcal{M}_k}, \bar{v}_w^{(k)}))_{k \in [m]}$; $(\text{er}_{w_i}^{(k)})_{k \in [m]} \leftarrow (\text{E.Enc}(\text{pk}_{\mathcal{M}_k}, r_{w_i}^{(k)}))_{k \in [m]}$
10 print ballot's left half ($\text{cand}_{\bar{v}_w \bmod \alpha}$ on row w) and $(r_w)_{w \in \{0, \ldots, \alpha-1\}}$ under a scratch surface as per Fig. 3 - left
11 send the ballot to $\mathcal{G}_2$ with its left half sealed
12 send $(\epsilon_{\bar{v}_w}, \gamma_w, (\text{ev}_w^{(k)}, \text{er}_w^{(k)})_{k \in [m]}, \epsilon_{r_w})_{w \in \{0, \ldots, \alpha-1\}}$ to $\mathcal{G}_2$ electronically
13 $\mathcal{G}_2$: **for** $w \in \{0, \ldots, \alpha-1\}$:
14      $r'_w \xleftarrow{\$} \mathbb{Z}_q$; $\gamma'_w \leftarrow \gamma_w h_1^{r'_w}$
15      $\epsilon_{\bar{v}_w}' \leftarrow \text{E}_{\text{P}_a}^{\text{th}}.\text{REnc}(\text{pk}_{\text{P}_a}, \epsilon_{\bar{v}_w})$; $\epsilon_{r_w}' \leftarrow \text{E}_{\text{P}_a}^{\text{th}}.\text{REnc}(\text{pk}_{\text{P}_a}, \epsilon_{r_w})$ // $\text{E}_{\text{P}_a}^{\text{th}}.\text{REnc}(\text{pk}_{\text{P}_a}, \epsilon) = \epsilon \text{E}_{\text{P}_a}^{\text{th}}.\text{Enc}(\text{pk}_{\text{P}_a}, 0)$
16      $(v'^{(k)}_w)_{k \in [m]} \leftarrow \text{Share}_{(m,m)}(0)$; $(r'^{(k)}_w)_{k \in [m]} \leftarrow \text{Share}_{(m,m)}(r'_w)$
17      $(\text{ev}'^{(k)}_w)_{k \in [m]} \leftarrow (\text{ev}_w^{(k)} \cdot \text{E.Enc}(\text{pk}_{\mathcal{M}_k}, v'^{(k)}_w))_{k \in [m]}$
18      $(\text{er}'^{(k)}_w)_{k \in [m]} \leftarrow (\text{er}_w^{(k)} \cdot \text{E.Enc}(\text{pk}_{\mathcal{M}_k}, r'^{(k)}_w))_{k \in [m]}$
19      $c_w := (\epsilon_{\bar{v}_w}', \gamma'_w, (\text{ev}'^{(k)}_w, \text{er}'^{(k)}_w)_{k \in [m]}, \epsilon_{r_w}')$
20      $\sigma_c \leftarrow \Pi_{\text{S}}.\text{Sign}(\text{sk}_{\mathcal{G}_2}, H((c_w)_{w \in \{0, \ldots, \alpha-1\}}))$, where H is a hash function
21 print ballot's right half and r_{booth} under another scratch surface as per Fig. 3 - left
22 store (j, r_{booth}) indexed by γ_{booth}

Fig. 4. The BallotGen protocol for generating a ballot for booth j known only to $\mathcal{G}_2$.

Vote Casting. The Cast protocol for voter $\mathcal{V}_i$ at booth j is as follows (Fig. 3 - center):

– *Ballot pick-up and eligibility verification:* $\mathcal{V}_i$ picks up a random sealed ballot from a set of ballots kept at the polling booth. The polling officer $\mathcal{P}_j$ verifies $\mathcal{V}_i$'s eligibility in the presence of polling agents and allows $\mathcal{V}_i$ to proceed to a private room containing a BMD $\mathcal{D}_j$.
– *Vote casting:* $\mathcal{V}_i$ feeds the top gray region of the ballot to $\mathcal{D}_j$ and presses a button on the onscreen display to select w corresponding to her preferred candidate. We denote the voter's chosen w as $\dot{w}$. $\mathcal{D}_j$ can only access the top gray region for printing and cannot read any part of the ballot (it should not have any attached scanner or camera). $\mathcal{D}_j$ prints $\dot{w}$ on both the left and the right halves of this gray region.
  $\mathcal{V}_i$ needs to verify that indeed her intended choice is printed on both the halves. If satisfied, $\mathcal{V}_i$ separates the left half of the marked ballot (the VVPR), folds it and drops it into a physical ballot box $\mathcal{B}_j$ kept near $\mathcal{P}_j$ such that $\mathcal{P}_j$ can verify that the voter dropped an official VVPR. The right half (the receipt) is given to $\mathcal{P}_j$ for scanning. If not satisfied, $\mathcal{V}_i$ shreds the marked ballot and raises a dispute. In this case, $\mathcal{V}_i$ is allowed to re-vote. Note that the vote casting phase can also completely avoid the BMD and require the voter to hand-mark the two ballot halves, but this design is prone to more voter errors (see Sect. 2).

– *Receipt scanning:* $\mathcal{P}_j$ checks that the scratch surface on $\mathcal{V}_i$'s receipt is intact, i.e., the ballot secrets are not compromised, and shreds the scratch region in front of $\mathcal{V}_i$. From the scanned receipt, $\mathcal{P}_j$ extracts $c_{\dot{w}}$ and uploads $(\mathsf{vid}_i, j, c_{\dot{w}})$ to C, along with $\sigma_{\mathsf{vid}_i} \leftarrow \Pi_{\mathsf{S}}.\mathsf{Sign}(\mathsf{sk}_{\mathcal{P}_j}, (\mathsf{vid}_i, j, c_{\dot{w}}))$. $\mathcal{P}_j$ also affixes vid_i to $\mathcal{V}_i$'s receipt, stamps it for authenticity, and returns it to $\mathcal{V}_i$.

Chain Voting and Randomisation Attacks. With minor modifications, these sophisticated coercion attacks can also be handled. For chain voting, $\mathcal{P}_j$ can stamp a serial number on the receipt half of the sealed ballot after identity verification to prevent the use of rogue ballots. This number is matched before accepting the voter's receipt. Under a *randomisation attack*, voters may be asked to choose a fixed $\dot{w}$, thereby randomising their votes. To counter this, voters should be allowed to choose their ballots in a private room. The ballot cover should contain a detachable slip showing the candidate order, allowing coerced voters to choose a ballot so that they can vote for their preferred candidate while producing the $\dot{w}$ satisfying the coercer. Before proceeding to $\mathcal{P}_j$, the voter should detach the slip.

Vote Tallying. Post polling, $(\mathcal{M}_k)_{k \in [m]}$ process the tuples $\{(\mathsf{vid}_i, j_i, c_i)\}_{i=0}^{n-1}$ uploaded on C by $(\mathcal{P}_j)_{j \in [\ell]}$, where c_i denotes $c_{\dot{w}}$ for the ith voter (Fig. 3 - right). $(\mathcal{M}_k)_{k \in [m]}$ proceed as per Fig. 5 where they first add the ρ_{γ_i} components to the encryptions c_i by engaging in a distributed NIZK proof of knowledge (lines 2–9) and then processing $(c_i)_{i \in [n]}$ through the traceable mixnet's Mix protocol (line 13). At the end, the permuted extended votes $(\bar{v}_i')_{i \in [n]}$ are obtained from which the raw votes are computed (line 14). Both extended and raw votes are published on V.

The VVPRs from each polling booth's ballot box are collected and mixed in a central facility. VVPRs are revealed to the public only after this mixing phase and post audit, to avoid leaking polling booth-level voting statistics. A VVPR containing ballot identifier bid and voter choice $\dot{w}$ can be matched with the corresponding decrypted vote by computing bid $+ \dot{w}$, finding it on V and checking if the corresponding raw vote matches the candidate name printed on the $\dot{w}^{\mathrm{th}}$ row on the VVPR.

Ballot and Receipt Audits. In the BallotAudit protocol, a statistically significant number of ballots at each polling booth must be audited to keep the probability ϵ_b of a cast-as-intended failure (see Sect. 3) small. Ballot audits can happen before, during or after polling, and even be initiated by voters. When auditing a ballot, its sealed cover is opened and secrets under its scratch surfaces are revealed. For each $w = 0 \ldots \alpha - 1$, it is checked that encryption c_w is created correctly on message bid $+ w$ using r_w and the candidate name printed at row w is $\mathsf{cand}_{\mathsf{bid}+w \bmod \alpha}$, where bid is looked up from the left half and r_w from the scratch surface. Further, it is checked that $\gamma_{\mathsf{booth}} \overset{?}{=} g_1^j h_1^{r_{\mathsf{booth}}}$, where j is the audited booth's identifier and r_{booth} is obtained from the scratch surface, and that signatures by $\mathcal{G}_1, \mathcal{G}_2$ verify. Since the secrets of audited ballots are revealed, audited ballots cannot be used for vote casting and must be spoiled.

Similarly, in the ReceiptAudit protocol, a statistically significant number of voter receipts from each polling booth must be checked for their existence on list C to keep ϵ_r small. All audited receipts should be uploaded to R to aid audit and recovery.

$$
\begin{array}{ll}
1 & (\mathcal{M}_k)_{k\in[m]}: \textbf{for } i \in [n]: \\
2 & \quad \bar{v}_i^{(k)} \leftarrow \mathsf{E.Dec}(\mathsf{sk}_{\mathcal{M}_k}, \mathsf{ev}_i^{(k)}) \quad \text{// decryption under } \mathsf{E} \\
3 & \quad r_i^{(k)} \leftarrow \mathsf{E.Dec}(\mathsf{sk}_{\mathcal{M}_k}, \mathsf{ev}_i^{(k)}) \\
4 & \quad \text{// Generate a distributed NIZK PoK } \rho_{\gamma_i} \text{ of the opening of } \gamma_i \text{ using shares } (\bar{v}_i^{(k)}, r_i^{(k)})_{k\in[m]} \\
5 & \quad r_{v_i}^{(k)}, r_{r_i}^{(k)} \overset{\$}{\leftarrow} \mathbb{Z}_q; a_i^{(k)} \leftarrow g_1^{r_{v_i}^{(k)}} h_1^{r_{r_i}^{(k)}}; \text{ publish } a_i^{(k)}. \\
6 & \quad c_i \leftarrow H(\gamma_i \| \prod_{k\in[m]} a_i^{(k)}); z_{\bar{v}_i}^{(k)} \leftarrow r_{v_i}^{(k)} - \bar{v}_i^{(k)} c_i; z_{r_i}^{(k)} \leftarrow r_{r_i}^{(k)} - r_i^{(k)} c_i; \text{ publish } z_{\bar{v}_i}^{(k)}, z_{r_i}^{(k)}. \\
7 & \quad \rho_{\gamma_i} := (a_i, c_i, (z_{\bar{v}_i}, z_{r_i})) \leftarrow (\prod_{k\in[m]} a_i^{(k)}, H(\gamma_i \| \prod_{k\in[m]} a_i^{(k)}), (\sum_{k\in[m]} z_{\bar{v}_i}^{(k)}, \sum_{k\in[m]} z_{r_i}^{(k)})). \\
8 & \quad \text{// } \rho_{\gamma_i} \text{ can be verified by checking if } c_i \overset{?}{=} H(\gamma_i \| a_i) \text{ and } \gamma_i^{c_i} g_1^{z_{\bar{v}_i}} h_1^{z_{r_i}} \overset{?}{=} a_i \\
9 & \quad \text{update } c_i \text{ by inserting } \rho_{\gamma_i} \text{ into it} \\
10 & \textbf{endfor} \\
11 & \text{// Mixing protocol to generate permuted } extended \text{ votes} \\
12 & \text{// Each } \mathcal{M}_k \text{ gets secret input } \mathsf{msk}^{(k)} \text{ and secret output } \omega^{(k)} \text{ (see Section 4.1)} \\
13 & (\mathcal{M}_k)_{k\in[m]}: (\bar{v}_i')_{i\in[n]}, (\mathcal{M}_k[\![\omega^{(k)}]\!])_{k\in[m]} \leftarrow \Pi_{\mathsf{TM}}.\mathsf{Mix}(\mathsf{mpk}, (c_i)_{i\in[n]}, (\mathcal{M}_k[\![\mathsf{msk}^{(k)}]\!])_{k\in[m]}) \\
14 & \quad (v_i')_{i\in[n]} \leftarrow (\bar{v}_i' \bmod \alpha)_{j\in[n]} \\
15 & \quad \text{publish } (\bar{v}_i')_{i\in[n]}, (v_i')_{i\in[n]} \text{ to } V; \mathcal{M}_k \text{ stores } \omega^{(k)}
\end{array}
$$

Fig. 5. The Tally protocol involving $(\mathcal{M}_k)_{k\in[m]}$ on input mpk, $(c_i)_{i\in[n]}$ and $\mathcal{M}_k$'s input $\mathsf{msk}^{(k)}$ containing $\mathsf{sk}_{\mathcal{M}_k}$.

Tally Audit. Our tally audit protocol (see Fig. 6) depends on BTraceIn and BTrace-Out queries of a traceable mixnet (see Sect. 4.1). Given (R, C, V, P), first, all input-phase failures are marked (lines 1–3). Here, as per the discussion in Sect. 2, we mark all receipts/encrypted votes from a booth as failed if any one of them fails and the encrypted votes as failed if the ballot audit at that booth failed. For marking mixing phase failures on C and V, we run the BTraceIn/BTraceOut queries against the complete set of entries on V and C respectively (lines 4–5). Output-phase failures are marked by comparing the VVPRs with the decrypted extended votes (lines 6–7).

If the total number of failures is less than the winning margin, then $J^* = \emptyset$ and $V^* = V$ are reported, signalling that no rerun is required (lines 9–10). Otherwise, polling booths contributing all the failing items are identified: for receipts and encrypted votes, the booth identifiers directly exist on R and C (line 12); for VVPRs without an electronic entry, they are identified by asking $\mathcal{G}_2$ to open the opening of γ_{booth} printed on the VVPR (line 13); for decrypted votes, a BTraceOut query against the set of cipher-texts cast at a booth j is run for all booths $j \in [\ell]$ (lines 14–18). The set of all such booths is reported in J^* (line 19). The decrypted votes V^* contributed by the good booths are obtained by running another BTraceOut query against the entries on C contributed by booths outside of J^* (line 21).

Recovery. The suggested recovery is to rerun the election only on booths in J^* and later merge this tally with the tally reported in V^*. However, if J^* is small, one can also consider rerunning on a few randomly selected good booths too, to avoid specialised targeting of the booths in J^*. Further, the general approach of TraceIn/TraceOut queries can also support other recovery options for dual voting systems. For example, one can immediately recover from case FO_3 if a TraceOut query is run for the decrypted vote against the set of encrypted votes that successfully matched with voter receipts. If the answer is yes, then it provides solid evidence that the VVPR is wrong, without leaking any additional information. A similar query run for the VVPR provides solid evidence

1   $J_{\text{PC}} \leftarrow \{j \in [\ell] \mid \text{BallotAudit fails at booth } j\}$
2   $R_{\text{FI}} \leftarrow \{r \in R \mid r \text{ fails against } C \text{ under } \text{Fl}_1, \text{Fl}_2\}; R_{\text{FI}} \leftarrow \{(\text{vid}, j, c) \in R \mid (\text{vid}', j, c') \in R_{\text{FI}}\}$
3   $C_{\text{FI}} \leftarrow \{c \in C \mid c \text{ fails against } R \text{ under } \text{Fl}_2\}; C_{\text{FI}} \leftarrow \{(\text{vid}, j, c) \in C \mid (\text{vid}', j, c') \in C_{\text{FI}} \vee j \in J_{\text{PC}}\}$
4   $C_{\text{FM}} \leftarrow \{c_i\}_{i \in [n_c]} \setminus \text{BTraceIn}(\text{mpk}, (c_i)_{i \in [n_c]}, (\bar{v}_i)_{i \in [n_v]}, [n_c], [n_v], (\mathcal{M}_k[\text{msk}^{(k)}, \omega^{(k)}])_{k \in [m]}, \mathcal{A}[\,])$
5   $V_{\text{FM}} \leftarrow \{v'_i\}_{i \in [n_v]} \setminus \text{BTraceOut}(\text{mpk}, (c_i)_{i \in [n_c]}, (\bar{v}_i)_{i \in [n_v]}, [n_c], [n_v], (\mathcal{M}_k[\text{msk}^{(k)}, \omega^{(k)}])_{k \in [m]}, \mathcal{A}[\,])$
6   $V_{\text{FO}} \leftarrow \{\bar{v} \in V \mid \bar{v} \text{ fails against } P \text{ under } \text{FO}_1, \text{FO}_3, \text{FO}_4\}$
7   $P_{\text{FO}} \leftarrow \{p \in P \mid p \text{ fails against } V \text{ under } \text{FO}_2, \text{FO}_3, \text{FO}_5\}$
8   $R_{\text{F}} \leftarrow R_{\text{FI}}; C_{\text{F}} \leftarrow C_{\text{FI}} \cup C_{\text{FM}}; V_{\text{F}} \leftarrow V_{\text{FM}} \cup V_{\text{FO}}; P_{\text{F}} \leftarrow P_{\text{FO}}$
9   **if** $|R_{\text{F}}| + |C_{\text{F}}| + |V_{\text{F}}| + |P_{\text{F}}| <$ winning margin calculated from V:
10     $J^* \leftarrow \emptyset; V^* \leftarrow V$
11   **else**:
12     $\text{badbooths}_r \leftarrow \{j \mid (\text{vid}, j, c) \in R_{\text{F}}\}; \text{badbooths}_c \leftarrow \{j \mid (\text{vid}, j, c) \in C_{\text{F}}\}$
13     $\text{badbooths}_p \leftarrow \{j \mid \mathcal{G}_2 \text{ supplies } (j, r_{\text{booth}}) \text{ to } \mathcal{A} \text{ for } \gamma_{\text{booth}} \text{ printed on some } p \in P_{\text{F}} \text{ s.t. } \gamma_{\text{booth}} = g_1^j h_1^{r_{\text{booth}}}\}$
14     $\text{badbooths}_v \leftarrow \emptyset$
15   **for** j **in** $[\ell]$:
16   // I_j denotes indices of booth j's entries in C; $I'_{V_{\text{F}}}$ denotes indices of V_{F} entries on V
17       $V_{\text{F}_j} \leftarrow \text{BTraceOut}(\text{mpk}, (c_i)_{i \in [n_c]}, (v'_i)_{i \in [n_v]}, I_j, I'_{V_{\text{F}}}, (\mathcal{M}_k[\text{msk}^{(k)}, \omega^{(k)}])_{k \in [m]}, \mathcal{A}[\,])$
18   **if** $V_{\text{F}_j} \neq \emptyset$: $\text{badbooths}_v \leftarrow \text{badbooths}_v \cup \{j\}$
19     $J^* \leftarrow \text{badbooths}_r \cup \text{badbooths}_c \cup \text{badbooths}_p \cup \text{badbooths}_v$
20   // $I_{\text{goodbooths}}$ denotes indices of booths outside J^* in C; $I'_{V \setminus V_{\text{F}}}$ denotes indices of entries outside V_{F} on V
21     $V^* \leftarrow \text{BTraceOut}(\text{mpk}, (c_i)_{i \in [n_c]}, (v'_i)_{i \in [n_v]}, I_{\text{goodbooths}}, I'_{V \setminus V_{\text{F}}}, (\mathcal{M}_k[\text{msk}^{(k)}, \omega^{(k)}])_{k \in [m]}, \mathcal{A}[\,])$
22   **return** J^*, V^*

Fig. 6. The TallyAudit protocol involving $\mathcal{A}$, $(\mathcal{M}_k)_{k \in [m]}$ and $\mathcal{G}_2$ with public input (R, C, V, P), each $\mathcal{M}_k$'s input its mixnet secret key $\text{msk}^{(k)}$ and witness $\omega^{(k)}$ output by the traceable mixnet during the Tally protocol, and $\mathcal{G}_2$'s input being (j, r_{booth}) stored indexed by γ_{booth} at the end of the BallotGen protocol.

that the electronic vote was wrong. Of course, what queries to allow must be carefully decided depending on the situation to best optimise the recoverability-secrecy tradeoff.

5   Security Analysis

Theorem 1. *Under the DL assumption in $\mathbb{G}_1$, the n-SDH assumption in $(\mathbb{G}_1, \mathbb{G}_2)$ [7] and the EUF-CMA security of Π_S, the OpenVoting protocol is recoverable as per Definition 1.*

Proof (Sketch). We focus on the event that for each booth, BallotAudit passing implies that all receipts correctly captured voter intents and ReceiptAudit passing implies that all receipts were correctly uploaded. This event happens with probability $1 - \ell(\epsilon_b + \epsilon_r)$.

Let J^*, V^* be $\mathcal{A}$'s output in the TallyAudit protocol. From Fig. 6, we consider the two cases: first when the branch on line 8 is taken and the second when it is not taken. In the first case, $J^* = \emptyset$ and thus we must show that the number of failures in (R^*, C^*, V^*, P^*) is less than the winning margin, where $R^* = R$, $C^* = C$ and $P^* = P$ for $J^* = \emptyset$ and $V^* = V$ by line 10. By the condition on line 9, the number of *reported* failures is less than the winning margin. By the soundness of Π_{TM} under the stated assumptions [2], sets C_{FM} and V_{FM} correctly represent the set of true failures. This, combined with the definitions of R_{FI}, C_{FI}, V_{FO} and P_{FO}, implies that the number of real failures in (R^*, C^*, V^*, P^*) is less than the winning margin.

In the second case, J^* is, as required, exactly the non-empty set of booths that contributed some failing item in R_{F}, C_{F} (by the definitions on line 12), P_{F} (by line 13 and the computational binding of Pedersen commitments under the DL assumption in $\mathbb{G}_1$) or V_{FO} (by lines 14–18 and the soundness property of Π_{TM}; note that V_{FM} entries in V_F are mix-server errors and, as required, are not reported here). Finally, by line 21 and the soundness of Π_{TM}, V^* is exactly the set of votes decrypted from encrypted votes sent by booths outside J^*. Thus, by the definitions of R^*, C^* and P^*, (R^*, C^*, V^*, P^*) does not contain any failures.

Theorem 2. *Under the DDH assumption in $\mathbb{G}_1$ and the DCR assumption [19], the OpenVoting protocol satisfies vote secrecy with recoverability as per Definition 2 in the random oracle model.*

Proof (Sketch). If the adversary corrupts $\mathcal{G}_2$ but not $\mathcal{G}_1$, then it does not learn the ballot secrets of ballots used by $\mathcal{V}_{i_0}$ and $\mathcal{V}_{i_1}$ by the perfect hiding of Pedersen commitments under the DDH assumption and the IND-CPA security of Paillier schemes E and $\mathsf{E}_{\text{Pa}}^{\text{th}}$ under the DCR assumption (see Fig. 4). Post-printing, ballots get sealed and are opened only by the voter during vote casting, where the adversary-controlled BMD does not see any information about the ballot used. The receipts and the tallying protocol does not reveal any information to the corrupted mix-servers by the secrecy property of Π_{TM} under the stated assumptions [2]. VVPRs are collected after mixing and the ballot identifiers used therein cannot be linked to the identifiers of $\mathcal{V}_{i_0}$ and $\mathcal{V}_{i_1}$. Finally, during the TallyAudit protocol, it is required that if the adversary causes a failure in either the receipt, encrypted vote or VVPR contributed by $\mathcal{V}_{i_0}$'s booth j_0 then it should also cause a failure in $\mathcal{V}_{i_1}$'s booth j_1. Thus, sets R_{FI} to P_{FO} in Fig. 6 do not help it distinguish between the two worlds. Outputs V_{F_j} do not help because for each failure in booth j_0, the adversary is required to create an identical failure in booth j_1. Further, the partial tally V^* includes either both v_0, v_1 or none of them. The secrecy property of Π_{TM} ensures that no additional information beyond the query outputs is revealed.

If the adversary corrupts $\mathcal{G}_1$ but not $\mathcal{G}_2$, then it obtains ballot secrets but it cannot identify which of $\mathcal{V}_{i_0}$ or $\mathcal{V}_{i_1}$ used which ballot. The rest of the proof is similar.

6 Conclusion and Future Work

We have introduced and formalised the notion of recoverability and secrecy for dual voting protocols and suggested a protocol that achieves this notion. Based on existing reports for the underlying traceable mixnet construction, the total time taken by the recovery process remains within a few hours for $n = 10000$ ciphertexts, which can be optimised further using the construction's high degree of task parallelism [2].

Although we have shown our protocol's recoverability properties, the potential non-termination of the revoting process during vote casting seems like an inherent limitation of BMD protocols and designing voting frontends that overcome this limitation yet remain usable and minimise voter errors appears to be a challenging open problem. Further, although we have focused on recoverability for first-past-the-post voting where exact winning margins are computable, extending to other more complex voting rules also appears to be an interesting avenue for future work.

Acknowledgments. Prashant Agrawal is supported by the Pankaj Jalote Doctoral Grant. Abhinav Nakarmi was supported by a research grant from MPhasis F1 Foundation.

References

1. Adida, B., Rivest, R.L.: Scratch & vote: self-contained paper-based cryptographic voting. In: WPES, pp. 29–40 (2006)
2. Agrawal, P., Nakarmi, A., Jhawar, M.P., Sharma, S., Banerjee, S.: Traceable mixnets (2023). [arXiv; cs.CR:2305.08138]
3. Banerjee, M.: Blocking the introduction of the Totaliser is not good for the secret ballot in India. LSE South Asia Center Blog (2017). Accessed 19 May 2023
4. Bell, S., et al.: STAR-vote: a secure, transparent, auditable, and reliable voting system. In: EVT/WOTE (2013)
5. Benaloh, J.: Administrative and public verifiability: can we have both? In: EVT, pp. 5:1–5:10 (2008)
6. Bernhard, M., et al.: Public evidence from secret ballots. In: EVOTE-ID, pp. 84–109 (2017)
7. Boneh, D., Boyen, X.: Short signatures without random oracles. In: Cachin, C., Camenisch, J.L. (eds.) EUROCRYPT 2004. LNCS, vol. 3027, pp. 56–73. Springer, Heidelberg (2004). https://doi.org/10.1007/978-3-540-24676-3_4
8. Chaum, D., et al.: Scantegrity: end-to-end voter-verifiable optical-scan voting. IEEE S&P **6**(3), 40–46 (2008)
9. Damgård, I., Jurik, M., Nielsen, J.B.: A generalization of Paillier's public-key system with applications to electronic voting. Intl. J. Inf. Secur. **9**, 371–385 (2010)
10. Desmedt, Y.: Threshold cryptography. Eur. Trans. Telecommun. **5**(4), 449–458 (1994)
11. Essex, A., Clark, J.: Punchscan in practice: an E2E election case study. In: WOTE (2007)
12. Essex, A., Henrich, C., Hengartner, U.: Single layer optical-scan voting with fully distributed trust. In: EVOTE-ID, pp. 122–139 (2012)
13. Farhi, N.: An implementation of dual (paper and cryptograhic) voting system. Master's thesis, The Blatavnik School of Computer Sciences, Tel Aviv University (2013)
14. Haines, T., Müller, J.: SoK: techniques for verifiable mix nets. In: CSF, pp. 49–64 (2020)
15. Küsters, R., Truderung, T., Vogt, A.: Accountability: definition and relationship to verifiability. In: CCS, pp. 526–535 (2010)
16. Lindeman, M., Stark, P.B., Yates, V.S.: BRAVO: ballot-polling risk-limiting audits to verify outcomes. In: EVT/WOTE (2012)
17. Lundin, D., Ryan, P.Y.A.: Human readable paper verification of Prêt à voter. In: ESORICS, pp. 379–395 (2008)
18. NDI: The constitutionality of electronic voting in Germany (2019). Accessed 8 June 2019
19. Paillier, P.: Public-key cryptosystems based on composite degree residuosity classes. In: International Conference on Theory and Applications of Cryptographic Techniques, pp. 223–238 (1999)
20. Pedersen, T.P.: Non-interactive and information-theoretic secure verifiable secret sharing. In: Feigenbaum, J. (ed.) CRYPTO 1991. LNCS, vol. 576, pp. 129–140. Springer, Heidelberg (1992). https://doi.org/10.1007/3-540-46766-1_9
21. Stark, P.B.: Super-simple simultaneous single-ballot risk-limiting audits. In: EVT/WOTE (2010)
22. Popoveniuc, S., Regenscheid, A.: Sigma ballots. In: EVOTE-ID, vol. P-167, pp. 179–190 (2010)
23. Rivest, R.L.: On the notion of software independence in voting systems. Philos. Trans. Roy. Soc. A: Math. Phys. Eng. Sci. **366**(1881), 3759–3767 (2008)
24. Ryan, P.Y.A., Bismark, D., Heather, J., Schneider, S., Xia, Z.: Prêt à Voter: a voter-verifiable voting system. Trans. Inf. Forensics Secur. **4**(4), 662–673 (2009)
25. Stark, P.B.: Conservative statistical post-election audits. Ann. Appl. Stat. **2**, 550–581 (2008)

Adaptively Weighted Audits
of Instant-Runoff Voting Elections:
AWAIRE

Alexander Ek[1] , Philip B. Stark[2] , Peter J. Stuckey[3] ,
and Damjan Vukcevic[1]([✉])

[1] Department of Econometrics and Business Statistics, Monash University,
Clayton, Australia
`damjan.vukcevic@monash.edu`
[2] Department of Statistics, University of California, Berkeley, CA, USA
[3] Department of Data Science and AI, Monash University, Clayton, Australia

Abstract. An election audit is *risk-limiting* if the audit limits (to a pre-specified threshold) the chance that an erroneous electoral outcome will be certified. Extant methods for auditing instant-runoff voting (IRV) elections are either not risk-limiting or require cast vote records (CVRs), the voting system's electronic record of the votes on each ballot. CVRs are not always available, for instance, in jurisdictions that tabulate IRV contests manually.

We develop an RLA method (AWAIRE) that uses adaptively weighted averages of test supermartingales to efficiently audit IRV elections when CVRs are not available. The adaptive weighting 'learns' an efficient set of hypotheses to test to confirm the election outcome. When accurate CVRs are available, AWAIRE can use them to increase the efficiency to match the performance of existing methods that require CVRs.

We provide an open-source prototype implementation that can handle elections with up to six candidates. Simulations using data from real elections show that AWAIRE is likely to be efficient in practice. We discuss how to extend the computational approach to handle elections with more candidates.

Adaptively weighted averages of test supermartingales are a general tool, useful beyond election audits to test collections of hypotheses sequentially while rigorously controlling the familywise error rate.

1 Introduction

Ranked-choice or *preferential* elections allow voters to express their relative preferences for some or all of the candidates, rather than simply voting for one or more candidates. Instant-runoff voting (IRV) is a common form of ranked-choice

---

Authors listed alphabetically.

© The Author(s) 2023
M. Volkamer et al. (Eds.): E-Vote-ID 2023, LNCS 14230, pp. 35–51, 2023.
https://doi.org/10.1007/978-3-031-43756-4_3

voting. IRV is used in political elections in several countries, including all lower house elections in Australia.[1]

A risk-limiting audit (RLA) is any procedure with a guaranteed minimum probability of correcting the reported outcome if the reported outcome is wrong. RLAs never alter correct outcomes. (*Outcome* means the political outcome—who won—not the particular vote tallies.) The *risk limit* α is the maximum chance that a wrong outcome will not be corrected. Risk-limiting audits are legally mandated or authorised in approximately 15 U.S. states[2] and have been used internationally. RAIRE [2] is the first method for conducting RLAs for IRV contests. RAIRE generates 'assertions' which, if true, imply that the reported winner really won. Such assertions are the basis of the SHANGRLA framework for RLAs [5].

A *cast vote record* (CVR) is the voting system's interpretation of the votes on a ballot. RAIRE uses CVRs to select the assertions to test.[3] Voting systems that tabulate votes electronically (e.g., using optical scanners) typically generate CVRs, but in some jurisdictions (e.g., most lower house elections in Australia) votes are tabulated manually, with no electronic vote records.[4] Because RAIRE requires CVRs, it cannot be used to check manually tabulated elections. Moreover, while RAIRE generates a set of assertions that are expected to be easy to check statistically if the CVRs are correct, if the CVRs have a high error rate, then the assertions it generates may not hold *even if the reported winner actually won*, leading to an unnecessary full hand count.

In this paper we develop an approach to auditing IRV elections that does not require CVRs. Instead, it adapts to the observed voter preferences as the audit sample evolves, identifying a set of hypotheses that are efficient to test statistically. The approach has some statistical novelty and logical complexity. To help the reader track the gist of the approach, here is an overview:

- Tabulating an IRV election results in a *candidate elimination order*. A candidate elimination order that yields a winner other than the reported winner is an *alt-order*. If there is sufficiently strong evidence that no alt-order is correct, we may safely conclude that the reported winner really won.
- Each alt-order can be characterised by a set of *requirements*, necessary conditions for that elimination order to be correct. If the data refute at least one requirement for each alt-order, the reported outcome is confirmed.

---

[1] Instant-runoff voting has been used in more than 500 political elections in the U.S. https://fairvote.org/resources/data-on-rcv/ (accessed 18 July 2023). It is also used by organisations; for instance, the 'Best Picture' Oscar is selected by instant runoff voting: https://www.pbs.org/newshour/arts/how-are-oscars-winners-decided-heres-how-the-voting-process-works (accessed 15 May 2023).

[2] See https://www.ncsl.org/elections-and-campaigns/risk-limiting-audits (accessed 15 May 2023).

[3] If the CVRs are linked to the corresponding ballot papers, then RAIRE can use *ballot-level comparison*, which increases efficiency. See, e.g., Blom et al. [1].

[4] IRV can be tabulated by hand, making piles of ballots with different first-choices and redistributing the piles as candidates are eliminated, with scrutineers checking that each step is followed correctly.

- We construct a *test supermartingale* for each requirement; a (predictable) convex combination of the test supermartingales for the requirements in an alt-order is a test supermartingale for that alt-order.
- As the audit progresses, we update the convex combination for each alt-order to give more weight to the test supermartingales that are giving the strongest evidence that their corresponding requirements are false.
- The audit has attained the risk limit α when the intersection test supermartingale for every alt-order exceeds $1/\alpha$ (or when every ballot has been inspected and the correct outcome is known).

The general strategy of adaptively re-weighting convex combinations of test supermartingales gives powerful tests that rigorously control the sequential familywise error rate. It is applicable to a broad range of nonparametric and parametric hypothesis testing problems. We believe this is the first time these ideas have been used in a real application.

To our knowledge, the SHANGRLA framework has until now been used to audit only social choice functions for which correctness of the outcome is implied by *conjunctions* of assertions: if all the assertions are true, the contest result is correct. The approach presented here—controlling the familywise error rate within groups of hypotheses and the per-comparison error rate across such groups—allows SHANGRLA to be used to audit social choice functions for which correctness is implied by *disjunctions* of assertions as well as conjunctions. This fundamentally extends SHANGRLA.

2 Auditing IRV Contests

We focus on IRV contests. The set of candidates is $\mathcal{C}$, with total number of candidates $C := |\mathcal{C}|$. A *ballot* b is an ordering of a subset of candidates. The number of ballots cast in the election is B.

Each ballot initially counts as a vote for the first-choice candidate on that ballot. The candidate with the fewest first-choice votes is eliminated (the others remain 'standing'). The ballots that ranked that candidate first are now counted as if the eliminated candidate did not appear on the ballot: the second choice becomes the first, etc. This 'eliminate the candidate with the fewest votes and redistribute' continues until only one candidate remains standing, the winner. (If at any point there are no further choices of candidate specified on a ballot, then the ballot is *exhausted* and no longer contributes any votes.) Tabulating the votes results in an *elimination order*: the order in which candidates are eliminated, with the last candidate in the order being the winner.

2.1 Alternative Elimination Orders

In order to audit an IRV election we need to show that if any candidate other than the reported winner actually won, the audit data would be 'surprising,' in the sense that we can reject (at significance level α) the null hypothesis that any other candidate won.

Example 1. Consider a four-candidate election, with candidates 1, 2, 3, 4, where 1 is the reported winner. We must be able to reject every elimination order in which any candidate other than 1 is eliminated last (every *alt-order*): $[1, 2, 3, 4]$, $[1, 2, 4, 3]$, $[1, 3, 2, 4]$, $[1, 3, 4, 2]$, $[1, 4, 2, 3]$, $[1, 4, 2, 3]$, $[2, 1, 3, 4]$, $[2, 1, 4, 3]$, $[2, 3, 1, 4]$, $[2, 4, 1, 3]$, $[3, 1, 2, 4]$, $[3, 1, 4, 2]$, $[3, 2, 1, 4]$, $[3, 4, 1, 2]$, $[4, 1, 2, 3]$, $[4, 1, 3, 2]$, $[4, 2, 1, 3]$, $[4, 3, 1, 2]$. The other 6 elimination orders lead to 1 winning: they are not alt-orders.   □

To assess an alt-order, we construct *requirements* that necessarily hold if that alt-order is correct—then test whether those requirements hold. If one or more requirements for a given alt-order can be rejected statistically, then that is evidence that the alt-order is not the correct elimination order. Blom et al. [2] show that elimination orders can be analysed using two kinds of statements, of which we use but one:[5]

> 'Directly Beats': $\mathbf{DB}(i, j, \mathcal{S})$ holds if candidate i has more votes than candidate j, assuming that only the candidates $\mathcal{S} \supseteq \{i, j\}$ remain standing. It implies that i cannot be the next eliminated candidate (since j would be eliminated before i) if only the candidates $\mathcal{S}$ remain standing.

2.2   Sequential Testing Using Test Supermartingales

Each requirement can be expressed as the hypothesis that the mean of a finite list of bounded numbers is less than $1/2$. Each such list results from applying an *assorter* (see Stark [5]) to the preferences on each ballot. The assorters we use below all take values in $[0, 1]$. For example, consider the requirement $\mathbf{DB}(1, 2, \mathcal{C})$ that candidate 1 beats candidate 2 on first preferences. That corresponds to assigning a ballot the value 1 if it shows a first preference for candidate 2, the value 0 if it shows a first preference for 1, and the value $1/2$ otherwise. If the mean of the resulting list of B numbers is less than $1/2$, then the requirement $\mathbf{DB}(1, 2, \mathcal{C})$ holds.

A stochastic process $(M_t)_{t \in \mathbb{N}}$ is a *supermartingale* with respect to another stochastic process $(X_t)_{t \in \mathbb{N}}$ if $\mathbb{E}(M_t \mid X_1, \ldots, X_{t-1}) \leqslant M_{t-1}$. A *test supermartingale* for a hypothesis is a stochastic process that, if the null hypothesis is true, is a nonnegative supermartingale with $M_0 := 1$. By Ville's inequality [7], which generalises Markov's inequality to nonnegative supermartingales, the chance that a test supermartingale ever exceeds $1/\alpha$ is at most α if the null hypothesis is true. Hence, we reject the null hypothesis if at some point t we observe $M_t \geqslant 1/\alpha$. The maximum chance of the rejection being in error is α.

Let $X_1, X_2, \ldots$ be the result of applying the assorter for a particular requirement to the votes on ballots drawn sequentially at random without replacement from all of the B cast ballots. We test the requirement using the ALPHA test supermartingale for the hypothesis that the mean of the B values of the assorter is at most μ_0 is

---

[5] Blom et al. [2] called these statements 'IRV' rather than 'DB'.

$$M_j = \prod_{i=1}^{j} \left(\frac{X_i}{\mu_i} \cdot \frac{\eta_i - \mu_i}{1 - \mu_i} + \frac{1 - \eta_i}{1 - \mu_i} \right), \quad j = 1, 2, \ldots, B,$$

where

$$\mu_j = \frac{B\mu_0 - \sum_{i=1}^{j-1} X_i}{B - j + 1}$$

is the mean of the population just before the jth ballot is drawn (and is thus the value of $\mathbb{E}X_j$) if the null hypothesis is true. The value of M_j decreases monotonically in μ_0, so it suffices to consider the largest value of μ_0 in the null hypothesis, i.e., $\mu_0 = 1/2$ [6]. The value η_j can be thought of as a (possibly biased) estimate of the true assorter mean for the ballots remaining in the population just before the jth ballot is drawn. We use the 'truncated shrinkage' estimator suggested by Stark [6]:

$$\eta_j = \min \left[\max \left(\frac{d\eta_0 + \sum_{i=1}^{j-1} X_i}{d + j - 1}, \mu_j + \epsilon_j \right), 1 \right].$$

The parameters $\epsilon_j = (\eta_0 - \mu)/(2\sqrt{d + j - 1})$ form a nonnegative decreasing sequence with $\mu_j < \eta_j \leqslant 1$. The parameters η_0 and d are tuning parameters. The ALPHA supermartingales span the family of *betting* supermartingales, discussed by [9]: setting η_j in ALPHA is equivalent to setting λ_j in betting supermartingales [6].

3 Auditing via Adaptive Weighting (AWAIRE)

3.1 Eliminating Elimination Orders Using 'requirements'

We can formulate auditing an IRV contest as a collection of hypothesis tests. To show that the reported winner really won, we consider every elimination order that would produce a different winner (every alt-order). The audit stops without a full hand count if it provides sufficiently strong evidence that no alt-order occurred. Suppose there are m alt-orders. Let H_0^i denote the hypothesis that alt-order i is the true elimination order, $i = 1, \ldots, m$. These partition the global null hypothesis,

$$H_0 = H_0^1 \cup \cdots \cup H_0^m.$$

If we reject all the null hypotheses $H_0^1, \ldots, H_0^m$, then we have also rejected H_0 and can certify the outcome of the election.

For each alt-order i, we have a set of *requirements* $R_i = \{R_i^1, R_i^2, \ldots, R_i^{r_i}\}$ that necessarily hold if i is the true elimination order, i.e.,

$$H_0^i \subseteq R_i^1 \cap R_i^2 \cap \cdots \cap R_i^{r_i}.$$

If any of these requirements is false, then alt-order i is not the true elimination order. If

$$H_0^i = R_i^1 \cap R_i^2 \cap \cdots \cap R_i^{r_i}$$

then R_i is a *complete* set of requirements: they are necessary and sufficient for elimination order i to be correct. One way to create a complete set is to take all **DB** requirements that completely determine each elimination in the given elimination order.

Example 2. A complete set of requirements for the elimination order $[1, 2, 3, 4]$ is: $\mathbf{DB}(4, 3, \{3, 4\})$, $\mathbf{DB}(4, 2, \{2, 3, 4\})$, $\mathbf{DB}(3, 2, \{2, 3, 4\})$, $\mathbf{DB}(4, 1, \{1, 2, 3, 4\})$, $\mathbf{DB}(3, 1, \{1, 2, 3, 4\})$, and $\mathbf{DB}(2, 1, \{1, 2, 3, 4\})$. If we reject any of these, then we can reject the elimination order $[1, 2, 3, 4]$.   □

We can rule out alt-order i by rejecting the intersection hypothesis $R_i^1 \cap \cdots \cap R_i^{r_i}$. The test supermartingales for the individual requirements are dependent because all are based on the same random sample of ballots. Section 3.2 shows how to test the intersection hypothesis, taking into account the dependence.

'Requirements' vs 'Assertions'. SHANGRLA [5] uses the term 'assertions.' Requirements and assertions are statistical hypotheses about means of assorters applied to the votes on all the ballots cast in the election. 'Assertions' are hypotheses whose conjunction is *sufficient* to show that the reported winner really won: if all the assertions are true, the reported winner really won. 'Requirements' are hypotheses that are *necessary* if the reported winner really lost—in a particular way, e.g., because a particular alt-order occurred. Loosely speaking, assertions are statements that, if true, allow the audit to stop; while requirements are statements that, if false, allow the audit to stop. To stop without a full hand count, an assertion-based audit needs to show that every assertion is true. In contrast, a requirement-based audit needs to show that at least one requirement is false in each element H_0^i of a partition of the null hypothesis $H_0 = \cup_i H_0^i$. (In AWAIRE, the partition corresponds to the alt-orders.)

3.2   Adaptively Weighted Test Supermartingales

Given the sequentially observed ballots, we can construct a test supermartingale (such as ALPHA) for any particular requirement. To test a given hypothesis H_0^i, we need to test the intersection of the requirements in the set R_i. We now describe how we test that intersection hypothesis, despite the dependence among the test supermartingales for the separate requirements. The test involves forming weighted combinations of the terms in the test supermartingales for individual requirements in such a way that the resulting process is itself a test supermartingale for the intersection hypothesis. This is somewhat similar to the methods of combining test supermartingales described by Vovk & Wang [8].

The quantities defined in this section, such as $E_{r,t}$, are for a given set of requirements R_i and thus implicitly depend on i. For brevity, we omit i in the notation.

At each time t, a ballot is drawn without replacement, and the assorter corresponding to each R_i^r, $r = 1, \ldots, r_i$ is computed, producing the values X_t^r,

$r = 1, \ldots, r_i$. Let $(E_{r,t})$ be the test supermartingale for requirement r. The test supermartingale can be written as a telescoping product:[6]

$$E_{r,t} := \prod_{k=0}^{t} e_{r,k},$$

with $E_{r,0} := 1$ for all r and

$$\mathbb{E}(e_{r,k} \mid (X_\ell^r)_{\ell=0}^{k-1}) \leqslant 1, \tag{1}$$

where the conditional expectation is computed under the hypothesis that requirement r is true. (This last condition amounts to the supermartingale property.) We refer to these as *base* test supermartingales.

For each k, let $\{w_{r,k}\}_{r=1}^{r_i}$ be nonnegative *predictable* numbers: $w_{r,t}$ can depend on the values $\{X_k^r\}$, $r = 1, \ldots, r_i$, $k = 0, \ldots, t-1$ but not on data collected on or after time t. Define the stochastic process formed by multiplying convex combinations of terms from the base test supermartingales using those weights:

$$E_t := \prod_{k=1}^{t} \frac{\sum_{r=1}^{r_i} w_{r,k} e_{r,k}}{\sum_{r=1}^{r_i} w_{r,k}}, \quad t = 0, 1, \ldots,$$

with $E_0 := 1$. This process, which we call an *intersection* test supermartingale, is a test supermartingale for the intersection of the r_i hypotheses: Clearly $E_t \geqslant 0$ and $E_0 := 1$, and if all the hypotheses are true,

$$\mathbb{E}\left(E_t \mid (X_k^r)_{k=1}^{t-1}, r = 1, \ldots, r_i\right) = \mathbb{E}\left(E_{t-1} \frac{\sum_{r=1}^{r_i} w_{r,k} e_{r,k}}{\sum_{r=1}^{r_i} w_{r,k}} \mid (X_k^r)_{k=1}^{t-1}, r = 1, \ldots, r_i\right)$$

$$= E_{t-1} \mathbb{E}\left(\frac{\sum_{r=1}^{r_i} w_{r,k} e_{r,k}}{\sum_{r=1}^{r_i} w_{r,k}} \mid (X_k^r)_{k=1}^{t-1}, r = 1, \ldots, r_i\right)$$

$$= E_{t-1} \frac{\sum_{r=1}^{r_i} w_{r,k} \mathbb{E}\left(e_{r,k} \mid (X_k^r)_{k=1}^{t-1}\right)}{\sum_{r=1}^{r_i} w_{r,k}}$$

$$\leqslant E_{t-1} \frac{\sum_{r=1}^{r_i} w_{r,k}}{\sum_{r=1}^{r_i} w_{r,k}} = E_{t-1},$$

where the penultimate step follows from Eq. 1. Thus (E_t) is a test supermartingale for the intersection of the requirements. The base test supermartingale for any requirement that is false is expected to grow in the long run (the growth rate depends on the true assorter values and the choice of base test supermartingales). We aim to make E_t grow as quickly as the fastest-growing base supermartingale by giving more weight to the terms from the base supermartingales that are growing fastest.

For example, we could take the weights to be proportional to the base values in the previous timestep, $w_{r,t} = E_{r,t-1}$. More generally, we can explore other functions of those previous values, see below for some options. Unless stated otherwise, we set the initial weights for the requirement to be equal.

---

[6] This is always possible, by taking $e_{r,t} := E_{r,t}/E_{r,t-1}$.

This describes how we test an individual alt-order. The same procedure is used in parallel for every alt-order. Because the audit stops without a full hand-count only if *every* alt-order is ruled out, there is no multiplicity issue.

Setting the Weights. We explored three ways of picking the weights:

Linear. Proportional to previous value, $w_{r,t} := E_{r,t-1}$.
Quadratic. Proportional to the square of the previous value, $w_{r,t} := E_{r,t-1}^2$.
Largest. Take only the largest base supermartingale(s) and ignore the rest, $w_{r,t} := 1$ if $r \in \arg\max_{r'} E_{r',t-1}$; otherwise, $w_{r,t} := 0$.

Using ALPHA with AWAIRE. The adaptive weighting scheme described above can work with any test supermartingales. In our implementation, we use ALPHA with the truncated shrinkage estimator to select η_t (see Sect. 2.2); it would be interesting to study the performance of other test supermartingales, for instance, some that use the betting strategies in Waudby-Smith & Ramdas [9].

In our experiments (see Sect. 4), the intersection test supermartingales were evaluated after observing each ballot. However, for practical reasons, we updated the weights only after observing every 25 ballots rather than every ballot; this does not affect the validity (the risk limit is maintained), only the adaptivity. Initial experiments seem to indicate that updating the weights more frequently often slightly favours lower sample sizes, but not always.

Using CVRs. If accurate CVRs are available, then we can use them to 'tune' AWAIRE and ALPHA to be more efficient for auditing the given contest. We explore several options in Sect. 4.3. If CVRs are available and are 'linked' to the paper ballots in such a way that the CVR for each ballot card can be identified, AWAIRE can also be used with a ballot-level comparison audit, which could substantially reduce sample sizes compared to ballot-polling. See, e.g., Stark [5]. We have not yet studied the performance of AWAIRE for ballot-level comparison audits, only ballot-polling audits.

4 Analyses and Results

To explore the performance of AWAIRE, we simulated ballot-polling audits using a combination of real and synthetic data (see below). Each sampling experiment was repeated for 1,000 random permutations of the ballots, each corresponding to a sampling order (without replacement). For each contest, the same 1,000 permutations were used for every combination of tests and tuneable parameters.

In each experiment, sampling continued until either the method confirmed the outcome or every ballot had been inspected. We report the mean sample size (across the 1,000 permutations) for each method.

The ballots were selected one at a time without replacement, and the base test supermartingales were updated accordingly. However, to allow the experiments to complete in a reasonable time, we only updated the weights after every 25 ballots were sampled. This is likely to slightly inflate the required sample sizes due to the reduced adaptation.

We repeated all of our analyses with a risk limit of 0.01, 0.05, 0.1, and 0.25. The results were qualitatively similar across all choices, therefore we only show the results for $\alpha = 0.01$.

4.1 Data and Software

We used data from the New South Wales (NSW) 2015 Legislative Assembly election in Australia.[7] We took only the 71 contests with 6 or fewer candidates (due to computational constraints: future software will support elections with more candidates). The contests each included about 40k–50k ballots. Our software implementation of AWAIRE is publicly available.[8]

We supplemented these data with 3 synthetic 'pathological' contests that were designed to be difficult to audit, using the same scheme as Everest et al. [4]. Each contest had 6 candidates and 56k ballots, constructed as follows. Candidates: a the (true) winner, b an alternate winner, and candidates c_1, c_2, c_3, c_4. Ballots:

- $16000 + 2m$ ballots of the form $[a]$,
- $8000 - 2m$ ballots of the form $[b]$,
- 8000 ballots of the form $[c_i, b, a]$ for each $i \in \{1, 2, 3, 4\}$.

We used $m \in \{2.5, 25, 250\}$ to define the 3 pathological contests.

In each of these contests, b is eliminated first, then each of the c_i is eliminated, making a the winner. If any c_i is eliminated first by mistake (e.g., due to small errors in the count), then b does not get eliminated and instead will collect all of the votes after each elimination and become the winner. A random sample of ballots, such as is used in an audit, will likely often imply the wrong winner.

We calculated the *margin* of each contest using `margin-irv` [3] to allow for easier interpretation of the results. The margin is the minimum number of ballots that need to be changed so that the reported winner is no longer the winner, given they were the true winner originally. For easier comparison across contests, we report the margin as proportion of the total ballots rather than as a count.

4.2 Comparison of Weighting Schemes

We tested AWAIRE with the three weighting schemes described earlier (Linear, Quadratic, and Largest). For the test supermartingales, we used ALPHA with $\eta_0 = 0.52$ and $d = 50$. For each simulation, we first set the true winner to be the reported winner, and then repeated it with the closest runner-up candidate

---

[7] Source: https://github.com/michelleblom/margin-irv (accessed 17 April 2023).
[8] https://github.com/aekh/AWAIRE.

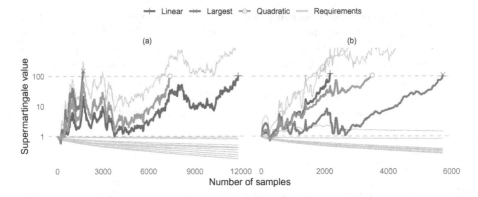

Fig. 1. Examples of test supermartingales for a set of requirements. The plots show how our test supermartingales evolved as we sampled increasingly more ballots in a particular audit with risk limit $\alpha = 0.01$. Each panel refers to a particular null hypothesis (i.e., a single alt-order) for a particular contest. The lines in light blue show the test supermartingales for each requirement used to test that hypothesis; the bold lines show our adaptively weighted combination across all requirements (using the weighting schemes as indicated by colour). Panel (a): NSW 2015 Upper Hunter contest (true elimination order $[1, 2, 3, 0, 4, 5]$) with a hypothesised order $[1, 2, 3, 0, 5, 4]$. Panel (b): NSW 2015 Prospect contest (true elimination order $[3, 0, 4, 1, 2]$) with a hypothesised order $[0, 3, 4, 2, 1]$. The horizontal lines indicate the start (1) and target ($1/\alpha = 100$) values; we stop sampling and reject the null hypothesis when the intersection test supermartingale exceeds the target value.

(based on the margin) as the reported winner. This allowed us to explore scenarios where the reported winner was false, in order to verify the risk limit (in all cases, the proportion of such simulations the led to certifying the wrong winner was lower than the risk limit).

Figure 1 illustrates an example of how the test supermartingales evolved in two simulations. Panel (a) is a more typical scenario, while panel (b) is an illustration of the rare scenarios where Largest is worst (due to competing and 'wiggly' base supermartingales).

Figure 2 summarises the performance of the different weighting schemes across a large set of contests. Some more details for a selected subset of contests are shown in top part of Table 1.

The three weighting schemes differ in how 'aggressively' they favour the best-looking requirements at each time point. In our experiments, the more aggressive schemes consistently performed better, with the Largest scheme achieving the best (lowest) mean sample sizes. On this basis, and the simplicity of the Largest scheme, we only used this scheme for the later analyses.

Fig. 2. Comparison of weighting schemes. The mean sample size (across 1,000 simulations; shown on a log scale) versus the margin, both shown as a proportion out of the total ballots in a contest. Each point depicts a single contest and weighting scheme, the latter distinguished by colour and point type as indicated. The 'Fixed' scheme is only shown for reference: adaptive weighting was disabled and only the best requirements were used.

A key feature of AWAIRE is that it uses the observed ballots to 'learn' which requirements are the easiest to reject for each elimination order and adapts the weights throughout the audit to take advantage. To assess the statistical 'cost' of the learning, we also ran simulations that used a fixed weight of 1 for the test supermartingales for the requirements that proved easiest to reject, and gave zero weight to the other requirements (we call this the 'Fixed' scheme).[9] The performance in this mode is shown in Fig. 2 as green crosses. The Fixed version gave smaller mean sample sizes, getting as small as 55% of the Largest. This shows that adaptation less than doubles the sample size.

4.3   Using CVRs (Without Errors)

We compare AWAIRE to RAIRE [2], the only other extant RLA method for IRV contests. Since RAIRE requires CVRs, we considered several ways in which we could use AWAIRE when CVRs are available. We explored choices for the following:

Starting weights. Using the CVRs we can calculate the (reported) margin for each requirement, allowing us to determine the easiest requirement to reject for each null hypothesis (assuming the CVRs are accurate). We gave each such requirement a starting weight of 1, and the other requirements a starting weight of 0. Other choices are possible (e.g., weights set according to some function of the margins) but we did not explore them.

---

[9] This is equivalent to a scenario where we have fully accurate CVRs available and decide to keep weights fixed. We explore such options in the next section.

Table 1. Selected results. The mean sample size from experiments using a risk limit of $\alpha = 0.01$, across a subset of contests, in 1,000 replications. The contest margins range from very close (Lismore) to a very wide margin (Castle Hill). The top part of the table shows results from analyses that did not use CVRs; the bottom part shows results from analyses using CVRs without errors. The column labeled d is the value of the ALPHA d parameter.

Contest:			Lismore	Monaro	Auburn	Maroubra	Cessnock	Castle Hill
No. candidates:			6	5	6	5	5	5
Margin:			0.44%	2.43%	5.15%	10.1%	20.0%	27.3%
Total ballots:			47,208	46,236	44,011	46,533	45,942	48,138
Method	**Weights**	d	**Mean sample size**					
No CVRs								
AWAIRE	Linear	50	34,246	5,822	1,354	378	117	73
	Quadratic	50	32,988	5,405	1,195	343	107	69
	Largest	50	32,534	5,217	1,130	320	98	65
With error-free CVRs								
AWAIRE	Largest	50	32,312	5,172	1,074	283	60	33
	Largest	500	31,790	4,458	942	265	59	33
	Fixed	50	29,969	4,317	876	230	55	31
	Fixed	500	29,756	3,912	781	212	54	31
RAIRE	—	50	31,371	4,260	876	230	56	34
	—	500	31,034	3,862	781	212	54	33

Weighting scheme. If the CVRs are accurate, then it would be optimal to keep the starting weights fixed across time (similar to RAIRE). Alternatively, we can allow the weights to adapt as usual to the observed ballots, in case the CVRs are inaccurate. We explored both choices, using only the Largest weighting scheme (which performed best in our comparison, above).

Test supermartingales. Having CVRs available allows us to tune ALPHA for each requirement by setting η_0 to the reported assorter mean (based on the CVRs). We allowed ALPHA to adapt by setting $d = 500$ (adapt slowly) or $d = 50$ (adapt quickly). For any requirements that the CVRs claim are true (i.e., consistent with the null hypothesis, with the assorter mean at most 0.5), we used a default value of $\eta_0 = 0.52$.

For comparison, we ran RAIRE with the same set of choices for the test supermartingales. For this analysis, we used accurate CVRs (no errors), the best-case scenario for RAIRE and for any choices where adaptation is slow or 'switched off' (such as keeping the weights fixed).

Figure 3 summarises the results, with a selected subset shown in the bottom part of Table 1. RAIRE and AWAIRE Fixed are on par when the CVRs are perfectly accurate, with both methods being equal most of the time. For margins up to 10%, RAIRE is ahead (albeit slightly) more often than AWAIRE Fixed is; for margins above 10%, AWAIRE Fixed is instead more often slightly ahead.

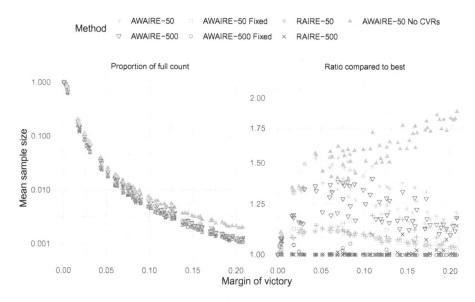

Fig. 3. Comparison of methods when using accurate CVRs. Left panel: similar to Fig. 2 but now showing different variants of AWAIRE all using the Largest scheme, and RAIRE. Right panel: showing mean sample size as a ratio compared to the best method for each contest. 'Fixed' means the weights were kept fixed throughout the audit. 'No CVRs' means AWAIRE was not provided the CVRs to set the starting weights. The numbers 50/500 specify the value d used for ALPHA.

For both AWAIRE and RAIRE, the 'less adaptive' versions performed better than their 'more adaptive' versions (there is no need to adapt if there are no errors). The largest ratio between the best setup and 'AWAIRE-50 No CVRs' is 2.14, which occurs around a margin of 27.3%. However, at that margin, it translates to a difference of less than 35 ballots.

Interestingly, the difference between the various versions of AWAIRE is small. Across the different margins, they maintain the relative order from the least informed (No CVRs) to the most informed and least adaptive (Fixed weights, $d = 500$). The cost of non-information in terms of mean sample size is surprising low, particularly when the margin of victory is small: there is little difference between 'AWAIRE-50 No CVRs' and 'AWAIRE-50'. As the margin grows, the relative difference becomes more substantial but the ratio never exceeds 1.97, and at this stage the absolute difference is small (within 50 ballots).

Table 1 gives more detail on a set of elections. For the smallest margin election, AWAIRE Fixed using CVRs outperforms RAIRE, which outperforms AWAIRE Largest using CVRs, which outperforms AWAIRE without CVRs; but the relative difference in the number of ballots required to verify the result is small (about 14%). In this case, the variants of AWAIRE have similar workloads, with or without CVRs. For larger margins ($> 5\%$), the auditing effort falls, and the relative differences between AWAIRE and RAIRE become negligible.

Overall, while AWAIRE with no CVRs can require much more auditing effort than when perfect CVRs are available, for small margins the relative cost difference is small, and for larger margins the absolute cost difference is small. This shows that AWAIRE is certainly a practical approach to auditing IRV elections without the need for CVRs (if doing a ballot-polling audit).

4.4   Using CVRs with Permuted Candidate Labels

We sought to repeat the previous comparison but with errors introduced into the CVRs. There are many possible types of errors and, as far as we are aware, no existing large dataset from which we could construct a realistic error model. A thorough analysis of possible error models is beyond the scope of this paper. For illustrative purposes, we explored scenarios where the candidate labels are permuted in the CVRs, the same strategy adopted by Everest et al. [4].

While this type of error can plausibly occur in practice, we use it here for convenience: it allows us to easily generate scenarios where the reported winner is correct but the elimination order implied by the CVRs is incorrect. This is likely to lead RAIRE to escalate to a full count if it selects a suboptimal choice of assertions. We wanted to see whether in such scenarios AWAIRE could 'recover' from a poor starting choice by taking advantage of adaptive weighting.

We simulated audits for a particular 5-candidate contest, exploring all $5! = 120$ possible permutations of the candidate labels in the CVRs. The results are summarised in Table 2. Without label permutation, the results were consistent with Sect. 4.3. Swapping the first two eliminated candidates made little difference. Permuting the first three eliminated candidates exposed the weakness of the Fixed strategies, which nearly always escalated to full counts. When the runner-up candidate was moved to be reportedly eliminated earlier in the count, RAIRE nearly always escalated to a full count, but AWAIRE performed substantially better (at least for $d = 50$), demonstrating AWAIRE's ability to 'recover' from CVR errors. For permutations where the reported winner was incorrect, AWAIRE always led to full count, while RAIRE incorrectly certified 0.3% of the time.

5   Discussion

AWAIRE is the first RLA method for IRV elections that does not require CVRs. AWAIRE may be useful even when CVRs are available, because it may avoid a full handcount when the elimination order implied by the CVRs is wrong but the reported winner really won—a situation in which RAIRE is likely to lead to an unnecessary full handcount.

Comparisons of AWAIRE workloads with and without the adaptive weighting shows that the 'cost' of this feature is relatively small (i.e., how many extra samples are required when 'learning', compared to not having to do any learning). However, we also saw a sizable difference in performance between AWAIRE

Table 2. Comparison of methods when using CVRs with errors. Mean sample sizes for experiments using the NSW 2015 Strathfield contest (46,644 ballots, 1.65% margin) and CVRs with different permutations of the candidate labels (leading to different reported elimination orders). The columns refer to groups of one or more permutations for which we observed largely similar results for each of the auditing methods; the corresponding mean sample sizes reported in the table were the average across the permutations in the group ('all' = 46,644). The true elimination order is $[1, 2, 3, 4, 5]$. Notation for reported elimination orders: an integer means the given candidate is in that place in the order, a crossed-out integer means the given candidate is *not* in that place, a dot (·) means any unmentioned candidate can be in that place, and the final column includes all orders with incorrect winners.

Method	Reported elimination order						Other
	$\begin{bmatrix}1\\2\\3\\4\\5\end{bmatrix}$	$\begin{bmatrix}2\\1\\3\\4\\5\end{bmatrix}$	$\begin{bmatrix}\cdot\\\cdot\\\not3\\4\\5\end{bmatrix}$	$\begin{bmatrix}\cdot\\\cdot\\4\\\cdot\\5\end{bmatrix}$	$\begin{bmatrix}\cdot\\4\\\cdot\\\cdot\\5\end{bmatrix}$	$\begin{bmatrix}4\\\cdot\\\cdot\\\cdot\\5\end{bmatrix}$	
AWAIRE-50 No CVRs	9,821	9,821	9,821	9,821	9,821	9,821	all
AWAIRE-50	9,694	9,717	9,810	14,229	15,714	15,929	all
AWAIRE-500	8,656	8,863	9,052	25,410	29,274	29,786	all
AWAIRE-50 Fixed	7,912	7,914	all	46,462	all	all	all
AWAIRE-500 Fixed	7,315	7,315	all	46,460	all	all	all
RAIRE-50	7,875	7,875	7,875	46,504	46,504	46,504	46,621
RAIRE-500	7,301	7,301	7,301	46,318	46,272	46,225	46,621

with adaptive weighting and methods that had both access to and complete faith in (correct) CVRs (i.e., RAIRE and AWAIRE Fixed).

In some scenarios, RAIRE was slightly more efficient than AWAIRE (similarly configured). The two main differences between these methods are (i) RAIRE uses an optimisation heuristic to select its assertions and (ii) RAIRE has a richer 'vocabulary' of assertions to work with than the current form of AWAIRE, which only considers **DB** for alternate candidate elimination orders. AWAIRE can be extended to use additional requirements, similar to the **WO** assertions of Blom et al. [1] (which asserts that one candidate always gets more votes initially than another candidate ever gets). Rejecting one such assertion can rule out many alt-orders. Adding requirements to AWAIRE that are similar to these assertions may reduce the auditing effort, since they are often easy to reject.

Our current software implementation becomes inefficient when there are many candidates, because the number of null hypotheses we need to reject is factorial in the number of candidates C, and the number of **DB** requirements we need to track is $O(C!\,C^2)$. Future work will investigate a *lazy* version of AWAIRE, where rather than consider all requirements for all alt-orders, we only consider a limited set of requirements (e.g., only those concerning the last 2 remaining candidates). Once we have rejected many alt-orders with these few requirements, which we are likely to do early on, we can then consider further requirements for the remaining alt-orders (e.g., concerning the last 3 candidates). Again, once even more alt-orders have been rejected, with the help of these newly introduced requirements, we can then consider the last 4 remaining candidates, and so on. This lazy expansion process should result in considering far fewer than the $O(C!\, C^2)$ **DB** requirements in all.

This work extends SHANGRLA in a fundamental way, allowing it to test disjunctions of assertions, not just conjunctions. The adaptive weighting scheme we develop using convex combinations of test supermartingales is quite general; it solves a broad range of statistical problems that involve sequentially testing intersections and unions of hypotheses using dependent or independent observations.

Acknowledgements. We thank Michelle Blom, Ronald Rivest and Vanessa Teague for helpful discussions and suggestions. This work was supported by the Australian Research Council (Discovery Project DP220101012, OPTIMA ITTC IC200100009) and the U.S. National Science Foundation (SaTC 2228884).

References

1. Blom, M., Conway, A., King, D., Sandrolini, L., Stark, P., Stuckey, P., Teague, V.: You can do RLAs for IRV. In: E-Vote-ID 2020, pp. 296–310. TALTECH Press, Tallinn (2020), Preprint: arXiv:2004.00235
2. Blom, M., Stuckey, P.J., Teague, V.: RAIRE: Risk-limiting audits for IRV elections. arXiv:1903.08804 (2019), Preliminary version appeared in E-Vote-ID 2018, LNCS, vol. 11143. Springer
3. Blom, M., Stuckey, P.J., Teague, V.J.: Computing the margin of victory in preferential parliamentary elections. In: E-Vote-ID 2018. LNCS, vol. 11143, pp. 1–16. Springer (2018). https://doi.org/10.1007/978-3-030-00419-4_1, Preprint: arXiv:1708.00121
4. Everest, F., Blom, M., Stark, P.B., Stuckey, P.J., Teague, V., Vukcevic, D.: Ballot-polling audits of instant-runoff voting elections with a Dirichlet-tree model. In: Computer Security. ESORICS 2022 International Workshops. LNCS, vol. 13785, pp. 525–540. Springer (2023). https://doi.org/10.1007/978-3-031-25460-4_30, Preprint: arXiv:2209.03881
5. Stark, P.B.: Sets of half-average nulls generate risk-limiting audits: SHANGRLA. In: Financial Cryptography and Data Security, FC 2020. LNCS, vol. 12063, pp. 319–336. Springer (2020). https://doi.org/10.1007/978-3-030-54455-3_23, Preprint: arXiv:1911.10035
6. Stark, P.B.: ALPHA: audit that learns from previously hand-audited ballots. Ann. Appl. Stat. **17**(1), 641–679 (2023). https://doi.org/10.1214/22-AOAS1646, Preprint: arXiv:2201.02707
7. Ville, J.: Etude critique de la notion de collectif. No. 3 in Monographies des Probabilites, Gauthier-Villars, Paris (1939)
8. Vovk, V., Wang, R.: E-values: calibration, combination and applications. Ann. Stat. **49**(3), 1736–1754 (2021). https://doi.org/10.1214/20-AOS2020, Preprint: arXiv:1912.06116

9. Waudby-Smith, I., Ramdas, A.: Estimating means of bounded random variables by betting. J. Roy. Stat. Soc. Series B: Stat. Methodol. (2023). https://doi.org/10.1093/jrsssb/qkad009, Preprint: arXiv:2010.09686

Online Voting in Ontario Municipalities: A Standards-Based Review

James Brunet and Aleksander Essex(✉)

Western University, London, Canada
{jbrunet8,aessex}@uwo.ca

Abstract. Over two hundred municipalities now offer online voting in Ontario, Canada, representing one of the largest deployments of digital elections worldwide. Many have eliminated the paper ballot altogether. Despite this, no provincial or federal-level standards exist. This gap leaves local election officials to create and apply their own cybersecurity requirements with varying degrees of success.

Until a standard can be developed and adopted, we turn to perhaps the most natural and immediate stand-in: The Council of Europe's (CoE) standards for e-voting. We use this baseline to present the first standards-based analysis of online voting practices in Ontario.

Our results find the province is broadly *non-compliant*, with only 14% of the CoE's 49 standards and 93 implementation guidelines categorized as fully met. We summarize these differences and identify areas for improvement in the hope of underscoring the need for domestic e-voting standards.

Keywords: Online voting · Standards · Cybersecurity

1 Introduction

Ontario's municipal elections represent some of the highest concentrations of online voting globally. Although turnout by voting-method is not published, a recent study estimated as many as one million voters cast a ballot online in the 2018 Ontario Municipal election [10]. Online voting adoption has grown steadily across the province since 2003. In 2022, the province reached a critical milestone: More than half of Ontario's cities now offer online voting, and many have moved to eliminate the paper ballot altogether.

Given the critical nature of elections, the stakes are high. A natural and necessary question has emerged: How well does this technology align with the principles of free and fair elections? How well do these deployments measure up to an objective democratic benchmark? What should that benchmark even be?

The answer in Ontario is short but not nearly so sweet: There is no accepted benchmark. There are currently *no* federal or provincial standards or guidelines for the implementation of online voting, including no requirements surrounding

© The Author(s) 2023
M. Volkamer et al. (Eds.): E-Vote-ID 2023, LNCS 14230, pp. 52–68, 2023.
https://doi.org/10.1007/978-3-031-43756-4_4

certification, testing, or, crucially, auditing. Instead, Ontario cities are given broad leeway to adopt, procure, and deploy this technology based on their own internal (and largely non-public) deliberations.

Therefore, the impetus of this work is to provide *some* objective measure for the province to identify critical areas of cyber and democratic risk toward prioritizing areas for improvement. In the absence of a domestic standard, we turn to perhaps the most natural and immediate alternatives: The Council of Europe's Standards for E-Voting (SeV). The SeV offers a set of broad-ranging and well-suited requirements and guidelines for online voting.

In this paper, we conduct a review of online voting in Ontario and analyze compliance against each of the 141 requirements and guidelines of the CoE's SeV. We summarize divergences and identify areas for improvement in hopes of underscoring the urgent need for *domestic* e-voting standards and oversight.

2   Background and Preliminaries

The province of *Ontario, Canada* consists of 444 municipalities distinguished across upper-, lower- and single-tier categories. However, only the lower- and single-tier municipalities conduct elections. Of these 417 municipalities, 217 (52%) offered an online interface to receive and cast a ballot in the 2022 Ontario Municipal Election, an increase of 42 cities over the prior 2018 election.[1]

The *Council of Europe* is an international organization focusing on human rights, democratic governance, and the rule of law. Founded in 1949, it predates the European Union. The CoE articulates its core values by developing standards and monitoring how well those standards are applied among member states.[2] The CoE consists of 46 member states, including all 27 members of the European Union, amounting to a combined population of over 700 million citizens. On the topic of online voting, the Council of Europe takes the view that such systems must be "secure, reliable, efficient, technically robust, open to independent verification and easily accessible" to build public confidence, which is a "prerequisite for holding e-elections" [1].

2.1   Terminology

The Council of Europe's Standards of E-Voting (SeV) fall across three main documents [2–4]. Although distinct from the CoE SeV, the US Voluntary Voting System Guidelines (VVSG) [6] provides a model for conceptualizing standards as a hierarchy of four successive components: principles, requirements, guidelines and test assertions. Requirements are derived from principles. Guidelines flow from requirements and so on. We use the following terminology in this analysis:

---

[1] 2022 Municipal Election - Context. Association of Municipalities of Ontario. Available: https://www.amo.on.ca/municipal-election-statistics.

[2] https://www.coe.int/en/web/portal/european-union.

Principles. Principles articulate the highest-level priorities. The CoE articulates principles in Section 14 of the explanatory memorandum [2]. These principles are democratic in focus (universal suffrage, equal suffrage, free suffrage, etc.), as opposed to the VVSG's principles, which are more engineering-focused (quality design, quality implementation, interoperability, etc.).

Requirements. Requirements are properties of the election that must be upheld. The CoE articulates its requirements in its main standards document [4]. For example, Requirement 10 (under the principle of free suffrage) requires a voter's intention to be free of undue influence.

Guidelines. Guidelines provide some specificity around what is minimally necessary to meet a requirement. The CoE articulates guidelines for some (but not all) of its requirements [3]. For example, toward the requirement of freedom from undue influence, Guideline 10(d) advises that the voting system "offer mechanisms ... to protect voters from coercion to cast a vote in a specific way."

Directives. For the sake of our analysis, we combine the concepts of requirements and guidelines into a single category: *directives*. In total, we examined 141 directives consisting of 49 requirements and 92 guidelines.

2.2 Information Collection About Ontario Municipal Online Voting Practices

We consulted various information sources to determine whether practices in Ontario complied with directives. We sampled public-facing election documents on municipal websites, read minutes from municipal council meetings, viewed advertised security claims by the five private online election vendors active in Ontario, used search engines to find news reports and press releases about technical incidents, and searched Twitter with incident-related keywords to identify incident response communications from municipalities and vendors. We collected tutorial videos created by municipalities for each vendor, and evaluated a public interactive demonstration system from one vendor as well as a private interactive demonstration system from another. On election day, we performed a passive security analysis of the voting portals of five municipalities, each using a different one of the five online voting vendors active in Ontario.

We indicated that **information was broadly unavailable** if, after a thorough search, no information about compliance with a directive was publicly available. For example, we are not aware of a single penetration test report being made public by any of Ontario's 217 municipalities despite five years of research in this area: We are confident that the publication of these documents is, at the very least, extraordinarily rare.

Legal Standing. Canada and the United States have observer status in the CoE. Although Canada is deeply aligned with the legal and ethical values of the CoE, as a non-member state, the SeV has no legal standing in Canada. Consequently, our findings of compliance (or, more importantly, *non-compliance*) are entirely moot from a legal perspective. As such, there is no explicit expectation that any of the directives be met—except where they overlap with the governing legislation (i.e., Ontario Municipal Elections Act [15]).

2.3   Related Work

Del Blanco et al. [8] and Luis Panizo et al. [7] performed a cryptographic analysis of the nvotes and Helios Voting e-voting systems, respectively, on the CoE's requirements for e-voting. This research identified technical limitations with respect to these systems' coercion resistance and end-to-end verifiability, among other aspects. Our study diverges from previous work because it not only analyzes the technology of e-voting systems but also the *real-world implementation* of these systems by municipal governments. Our analysis is broader in that it examines additional categories of CoE directives: namely those related to procurement, transparency, certification, regulation, reliability, and accountability.

2.4   Compliance Categories

We began the analysis by attempting to assign each directive to one of three broad compliance categories (*met, partially met, unmet*). As the analysis proceeded, we identified several additional cases and sub-cases. Each directive was eventually assigned one to one the following categories defined as follows:

1. **Directive broadly *met* (●)**
   (a) Most (or all) cities meaningfully meet directive.
2. **Directive *partially met* (◐)**
   (a) Some cities fully meet directive.
   (b) A substantial number of cities meaningfully attempt to meet directive.
3. **Directive broadly *unmet* (○)**
   (a) Few cities meaningfully attempt to meet directive.
   (b) Almost all (or all) cities fail to meaningfully attempt to meet directive.
   (c) No cities (to our knowledge) meaningfully attempt to meet directive.
   (d) General failure of provincial jurisdiction.
4. **Information broadly unavailable (⊗)**
   (a) The required information to assess is generally not publicly available.
5. **Not applicable (⊙)**
   (a) Assessing the directive is outside authors' recognized area of expertise.
   (b) Directive does not apply to the Ontario legal/electoral case.
   (c) Directive does not apply to the online voting setting.

3 Summary of Findings

Our analysis shows that Ontario municipalities are broadly non-compliant with the CoE's directives. A summary of our analysis is shown in Table 1. A substantial effort has only been made to satisfy 28% of applicable directives, and half of those (14%) are only partially met. One in four directives could not be evaluated because of a lack of transparency by vendors and municipalities.

When viewing directives by category, we identify three key trends. First, the majority of directives relating to Regulatory & Organizational Requirements are unmet because Ontario has no standards for e-voting. Second, a disproportionate number of directives within the Reliability and Security category could not be evaluated, because both municipalities and vendors do not disclose information about voting system internals and procedures. Finally, two-thirds of the applicable directives in Transparency and Observation were unmet, which is indicative of the lack of transparency in municipal e-voting in Ontario.

Table 1. Summary of compliance

Principle	Met	Partial	Unmet	No Info	N/A
Accountability	1	9	3	–	–
Equal Suffrage	3	4	–	1	2
Free Suffrage	3	2	7	2	2
Regulatory & Organisational	3	2	16	5	1
Reliability and Security	1	6	8	17	1
Secret Suffrage	4	2	8	2	1
Transparency and Observation	3	1	10	1	1
Universal Suffrage	1	–	–	1	7
Total	18	18	58	32	15
Proportion (Applicable)	14%	14%	46%	25%	–

4 Analysis of Selected Directives

The Council of Europe's standards for e-voting consist of 141 directives for electoral authorities, legislators, and vendors. Our categorization for each directive is available in Appendix A, but a detailed analysis of each directive is not possible due to space constraints. In this section, we provide a selection of our more interesting findings, with the titles of directives paraphrased and shortened.

4.1 Directive Broadly Met

4. Election must be obviously real. Voters receive official notification by mail of an election, indicating that the election is real. Demonstration/test systems are generally unavailable [9], so voters are unlikely to be confused.

5. Voting information (e.g. list of candidates) should not be presented differently on different channels. A legal principle of the Municipal Elections Act is that "voters and candidates shall be treated fairly and consistently" [21]. Specifically, Section 41(2) of the Municipal Elections Act (MEA) specifically outlines how candidates appear on the ballot [15]. Our observations show that cities present information about candidates neutrally and consistently, with no additional information about candidates on the online or in-person ballots, which satisfies implementation guidelines 5(a) and 5(b).

12. Voters should not be rushed and should have confirmation. To the best of our knowledge, all online voting systems in Ontario offer confirmation pages and do not rush voters. A recent study tested the confirmation pages of Scytl, Simply Voting and Neuvote [9] and found the confirmation pages allow voters to alter their choice, which satisfies implementation guideline 12(a).

22. Voter list should only be accessible to authorised parties. We interpret this to mean voter lists. Unlike American states like Ohio,[3] voter lists are not made publicly available and are only accessible to authorized parties (candidates, municipalities, and other election-related authorities).

32. Voters should be provided information about online election. Almost all, if not all, cities provide detailed information about e-voting, including technical support and documentation (satisfying 32(a)). Common methods of outreach include direct mail, city websites (although we observed many cities had outages of their websites on election night), videos posted to YouTube, and Tweets (satisfying 32(b)).

45. No release of information about votes and voters before counting commences. We did not see election results released prematurely in any municipality, other than turnout data [16].

4.2 Directive Fully Met by Some Cities

9. Count one vote per voter. There were several examples of voters receiving multiple voting credentials,[4] which could allow them to vote twice. This is due to duplicate entries on the municipal voters list, or entries for deceased voters not being removed. The severity of this issue varies by municipality, as some have more robust processes in place to identify and remove duplicates.

10(b). Only official information on e-ballot. Two online voting vendors did not have HTTP Strict Transport Security (HSTS) preloading configured, which could allow for a Machine-in-the-Middle (MITM) [11]. Additionally, these vendors did not set X-Frame-Options header. Combined, this allows for a MITM to add unofficial information to an embedded version of the e-ballot. This vulnerability will be reported in detail in future work.

15. Individual verifiability. Individual verifiability exists for some cities using Scytl or Neuvote, including Markham [13] and Ignace [17], respectively.

---

[3] https://www6.ohiosos.gov/ords/f?p=VOTERFTP:STWD:::#stwdVtrFiles.

[4] https://www.thorold.ca/en/news/thorold-residents-encouraged-to-hold-on-to-all-voter-letters-they-receive.aspx.

While there are limitations to these approaches (closed-source verifier app), the directive is met. Scytl's individual verifiability comes at the expense of SeV Requirement 23, because it shows who you voted for and could be used to prove to others how you voted [13]. However, most cities in Ontario use unverifiable voting systems offered by Dominion, Simply Voting, and Intelivote.

23(b). No residual information about voter's choice after voting. Simply Voting's unverifiable voting service purges information about the voter's choice from the browser cache. However, the proofs offered by municipalities using Scytl's individually verifiable voting violate this directive [13].

25. Previous choices (deleted) by the voter in the voting process should also be secret. Ontario does not allow for multiple votes to be cast as a feature against coercion resistance, so this directive was interpreted to refer to the secrecy of a voter's potential choice (before they confirm their choice). For most online voting vendors we had demo access to, confirmation pages were generated on a client-side basis, so deleted choices are kept secret. However, in the case of Simply Voting municipalities, a voter's potential choice is sent to the server, and the server generates a confirmation page. The vote is only protected in transit and can be read by the server [9]. This practice could jeopardize the secrecy of both a voter's unconfirmed choices and their final vote.

29(a). Transparent procurement. Procurement rules vary by municipality, but generally, in Ontario, the purchase of online voting technology is not distinct from any other purchase of goods. Smaller contracts of under $25,000 are generally partially exempt from procurement transparency/competitiveness requirements. In some municipalities, contracts below $10,000 do not require a competitive process at all. For example, in 2022 Township of Central Huron had 6863 electors.[5] In 2018, they entered a contract with Simply Voting at the cost of $1.30 per elector [22], which is well below their threshold of $25,000 for a competitive public procurement process [12].

32(c). Public demo of e-voting system. Most vendors do not offer public demos of their e-voting systems [9].

40(a). No downtime. Municipalities using Dominion as a vendor experienced service disruptions in 2018 [10] and in 2022.[6,7,8]

40(i). Disaster recovery plans should exist. Before 2018, cities generally did not have disaster recovery plans [10] Because of outages in 2018 that led to emergency extensions of voting periods, disaster recovery plans were created by some affected municipalities. These plans are generally not available to the public.

---

[5] https://www.centralhuron.ca/en/your-municipal-government/2022-official-municipal-school-board-election-results.aspx.

[6] https://twitter.com/NewTecumseth/status/1584694858471690240.

[7] https://twitter.com/TwpofScugog/status/1584689666259030016.

[8] https://www.thecounty.ca/county_news_notices/online-voting-extended-until-830-pm-on-october-24/.

4.3   Directive Partially Met by Most or All Cities

9(c). Generally, voters should be prevented from casting multiple votes. Cities often use electronic poll books to prevent cross-channel multiple voting. However, the recurring issue of duplicate entries on the voters' list could allow voters to vote twice online.

39. Open and comprehensive auditing, with active reporting on issues/threats. Most voting vendors offer some form of logging, intrusion detection systems, and/or auditing features, but these audit systems are not comprehensive to the extent described in the explanatory memorandum [2]. For example, most municipalities do not offer individual or universal verifiability, so audit systems generally cannot provide proof of the authenticity of votes.

4.4   Directive Unmet: Meaningful Attempts from Some Cities

10. Voting system must be protected from MITM, client-side malware, etc. Our analysis of the security posture of online voting services showed that Simply Voting is the only vendor with effective protection (HSTS pre-loading) against Machine-in-the-Middle attacks. Individual verifiability can protect against client-side malware but is only offered by cities using Neuvote/Scytl/Voatz. Cities using Intelivote/Dominion have neither of these features.

24. Disclosure of premature results should be prevented by system. For Simply Voting and Dominion's online voting services, the encryption of ballots occurs only in transit between the voter's device and the server (TLS) [9,14], which means that the online voting provider has real-time access to and could prematurely disclose the count of votes for a candidate. By comparison, with cryptographically verifiable voting systems like the SwissPost e-voting system, the results stay encrypted until after the voting period. From observing their demonstration system, Scytl may offer some form of cryptographic protection against the release of premature results. Information is not available about the protections in place for other vendors.

42(a). Equipment should be checked and approved by a municipality -defined protocol before each election. Some municipalities conduct penetration tests against online voting systems on an informal and irregular basis. However, to the extent of our knowledge, no municipalities check/approve equipment used by the vendor before each election.

4.5   Directive Unmet by Almost All Cities

10(a). Voter should be told how to verify connection to server. This directive is challenging to satisfy because there is no single voting portal in Ontario. The URL for online voting varies by vendor, and sometimes the URL varies between different elections. Few Ontario municipalities offer meaningful instructions to verify connections and protect against phishing. An example of ineffective instructions is the municipality of Clarington, which has a document titled "How can I verify I am accessing the actual voting site and not a fake site?"

with the instructions "When accessing the voting website, HTTPS and an image of a padlock will appear in the search bar, confirming a secure connection".[9] These instructions are potentially dangerous, because phishing sites often use HTTPS, and no instructions are provided to check that the URL in the address bar exactly matches the official URL of the voting website.

`10(d)`. `Coercion resistance`. The Municipal Elections Act does not specifically address the possibility of coercion in unsupervised remote voting. While it is an offence under the Act to coerce a voter, there are no legislated means to enforce or protect against this. Some cities offer supervised remote voting, where coercion could be difficult. This is offered for accessibility purposes; there are few in-person locations in a municipality, and a coercer could direct you to vote remotely instead.

`11`. `Procedural steps ensure e-voting ballot is authentic`. We are aware of informal logic and accuracy testing conducted by scrutineers and clerks, which may detect errors. However, these procedural steps are not required by law, and details of informal procedures are not made public. An example of non-binding, unclear procedures is "...the Clerk can test the system by running a mock election, and may investigate the feasibility of including candidates and scrutineers in this process..." [19]. Two cities had serious errors which could have been prevented by sufficient procedural steps. Thunder Bay had some voters receive the wrong ballot [23], while Cambridge presented an e-ballot to voters that was missing candidates [18].

`19`. `Ballot secrecy`. For most cities, the e-voting system can see a voter's date of birth and the city a voter is voting in. If combined with that city's voter list, many voters can be re-identified merely with their birthday [10].

`27`. `Gradual introduction to e-voting`. Adoption of online voting in Ontario has been rapid—doubling each election cycle between 2003 to 2018. Cities do not generally run pilot projects (fails Directives 27(b), 27(d)), and while some cities conduct feasibility studies, they are often not available to the public. Three examples of sudden adoption with no hybrid voting include Adjala-Tosorontio, which transitioned from exclusive in-person paper ballots in 2018 to exclusive remote e-voting in 2022, Algonquin Highlands, which transitioned from exclusive mail-in voting in 2018 to exclusive remote e-voting in 2022, and Arran Elderslie, which transitioned from exclusive mail-in voting in 2018 to exclusive remote e-voting in 2022.[10,11]

4.6   Directive Unmet by All Cities

`17`, `19`, `10(c)`. `Directives that require universal verifiability`. No cities in Ontario offered universal verifiability where any interested person could verify that votes are counted correctly.

---

[9] https://votes.clarington.net/en/voters/voter-faqs/.

[10] Vote methods in 2018: https://whisperlab.org/ontario-online.csv.

[11] Vote methods in 2022: https://elections2022.amo.on.ca/web/en/home.

21. **Authentication data should be protected.** Voter dates of birth are used for authentication, which cannot be meaningfully protected. As well, credentials delivered by mail are sometimes visible through envelopes when held up to light [10].

23. **Proofs of who a voter voted for can't be used by third parties.** The verification method employed by Scytl shows the voter which choice they selected [13]. Any third party, given a QR code and a voter's credentials, could verify this proof themself. Most other vendors offer no proof.

23(c). **Voters should be informed of risks to ballot secrecy and mitigations.** We did not find evidence of cities informing voters of risks to ballot secrecy. Instead, several municipalities in 2022 repeated vendor claims of perfect secrecy on social and traditional media.[12,13] This claim appears to originate from a 2018 document provided by Simply Voting to municipalities:

> Whether you use the internet or telephone to vote, your vote is instantly encrypted and stored with no possibility of your vote being traced back to your identity, just like a traditional paper ballot. It is impossible for municipal staff, Simply Voting employees or any other person to see how you have voted [5].

However, a recent analysis of Simply Voting's demonstration system shows that no application-layer cryptographic mechanism separates a voter's choice from authentication data like their birthday before a vote is cast. Another study found over 50% of Ontario voters are uniquely re-identifiable from their city and date of birth [10].

29. **Legislation to regulate e-voting systems should ensure an electoral management body has control over them.** E-voting systems are broadly unregulated: Vendors have control over e-voting systems and are entirely responsible for deploying and managing remote e-voting infrastructure (fails to satisfy 29(d)).

30. **Observability and responsibility of count.** The vendor is responsible for the counting process, not an electoral management body. In addition, the widespread absence of satisfactory universal verifiability means the evidence of correct counting is not sound (fails to satisfy 30(b) and 30(c)).

31, 31(a-b), 33, 33(a-f), 34. **Transparency, disclosure, and observation.** Private vendors are not subject to access-to-information law, have little transparency, and use proprietary systems. Testing of e-voting systems is conducted privately. Observers are not able to access meaningful documentation on e-voting systems, inspect physical/electronic safety mechanisms, or inspect or test devices.

36, 36(a), 37, 37(a-f), 38, 40, 43. **Directives relating to certification requirements or standards.** No certification requirements or standards exist in Ontario.

---

[12] https://twitter.com/ClaringtonON/status/1555184785089347596.

[13] https://www.baytoday.ca/2022-municipal-election-news/election-officials-easing-concerns-about-online-voting-system-5944887.

41. Only people authorized by municipality can have access to infrastructure. Private vendors are wholly responsible for managing remote e-voting infrastructure. They, not municipalities, are responsible for authorizing their staff members according to their policies.

4.7 Directive Unmet Due to Failure Within Provincial Jurisdiction

28, 28(a-f). Legislative directives for remote e-voting. The Municipal Elections Act is limited, delegating responsibility for authorization of "alternative voting methods" to cities, which can pass bylaws to authorize online voting. These bylaws are extremely limited in scope; Below is Markham's entire bylaw to authorize online voting:

> That the use of internet voting is hereby authorized for the purposes of voting in municipal elections in the City of Markham [20].

Neither provincial law nor municipal bylaws have procedures for e-voting implementation, set-up, operation, or counting. They do not specify how to determine e-vote validity, have rules for problems/failures/discrepancies for verification tools, or specify timelines for e-voting. Although some data destruction is required by law, it is described in the context of paper elections, and procedures for digital data destruction are not legislated [15]. Provisions exist for candidates or municipalities to appoint observers, but these provisions appear to be written in the context of paper elections: no provisions define roles or access provided to observers in online elections. Municipal clerks (executive, not legislative) are responsible for determining procedures for e-elections.

4.8 N/A—Outside of Expertise

Directives 1, 1(a), 1(c), 2, 2(a), 2(b), 3, 40(f) require a usability background to properly evaluate. These are outside of our expertise.

4.9 N/A—Not Applicable to Ontario

We are not aware of municipalities that have coercion-resistant multiple voting and voters are not allowed to cast votes over multiple channels, so 9(a) and 9(b) do not apply in the Ontario context. 28(i) is also not applicable because Ontario municipalities have a grace period for in-person and online voting. This allows voters to submit their ballot after voting has ended, provided that they have begun the voting process before the end of the voting period.

4.10 N/A—Not Applicable to E-Voting

15(a), 15(b), and 23(a) refer specifically to the use of e-voting machines in supervised environments. These are not applicable to our study of remote e-voting systems in Ontario.

4.11   Information Not Available

We were unable to evaluate many directives because of a lack of transparency from vendors and municipalities. We encountered issues in four areas:

Directives Requiring Access to 'Live' Election Systems. Our access was limited to the login page of each vendor as well as demonstration systems offered by two vendors using mock elections. For that reason, we were not able to evaluate whether voters could cast an abstain vote (13) or whether they are advised of invalid votes (14), among other directives.

Directives Requiring Knowledge of Vendor Procedures. Vendors are not subject to access-to-information law and do not disclose details of their procedures to the public. For that reason, we were not able to evaluate which auditing directives vendors satisfied (39(a,b)) or whether e-voting infrastructure is properly secured (40(d)), among other directives.

Directives Requiring Knowledge of Online Voting System Internals. Online voting products made by private vendors are proprietary and not subject to access-to-information law. Source code, configuration, and technical documentation are not available to the public. For that reason, we were unable to evaluate how voter information is separated from their decision (26(a)) or whether irregular votes can be identified by the system (49), among other directives.

Directives Requiring Knowledge of Municipal Procedures. Municipalities generally do not disclose their internal procedures for conducting elections besides the few documents they must make publicly available (e.g. mandatory accessibility reports). For that reason, we were unable to evaluate whether the two-person rule is followed when sensitive data is accessed 41(b,c), whether the authenticity and integrity of voter lists are confirmed (48), or whether online and non-online votes are aggregated securely (6), among other directives.

5   Recommendations and Conclusion

With only 18 of 126 (14%) of applicable directives in the Council of Europe's Standard for E-Voting fully met, Ontario and its 217 municipalities engaging in online voting have much to do. We conclude with five key recommendations:

Recommendation 1. Cities Should Be Familiar with International Democratic Principles, Expectations and Norms. There is a valid role for criticism of online voting in the province, especially if the technology diverges from internationally accepted democratic norms. Toward understanding which forms of criticisms of online voting are (and are not) justified or warranted, cities ought to, at a minimum, become acquainted with the CoE's Standards for E-Voting.

Recommendation 2. Cities Should Conduct Their Own Internal Review. Cities should conduct their own internal review of their compliance relative to the SeV. This could help cities identify areas of risk and improvement.

Recommendation 3. Province Should Update the Municipal Elections Act. 16 unmet directives directly pertain to the province's lack of a legislative framework for e-voting. Numerous others exist indirectly as a consequence.

Recommendation 4. Make Information About E-Voting Policies, Procedures and Protections More Widely Available. The SEV is clear: Information on the functioning of an e-voting system shall be made publicly available [1]. We could not assess 32 directives because necessary information was unavailable.

Recommendation 5. Make Election Results Evidence-Based. As the CoE explains, independent verification is needed to build public confidence, which is a "prerequisite for holding e-elections" [1]. Independent verification such as cryptographic end-to-end verification (E2E-V) would address many unmet directives.

A   Summary of Analysis

#	Paraphrasing	Score
1	UI should be easy to use	$\odot^a$
1(a)	Easy to interpret voting options	$\odot^a$
1(b)	Voters involved in design	$\otimes$
1(c)	System compatibility	$\odot^a$
2	Independence for disabled voters	$\odot^a$
2(a)	Special voting interfaces	$\odot^a$
2(b)	WCAG 2.0 AA compliance	$\odot^a$
3	Other voting channels available if e-voting not universally accessible	$\odot^a$
4	Live election interface is explicit	●
5	Voting info presented uniformly	●
5(a)	No superfluous info on ballot	●
5(b)	No biased info about candidates	●
6	Secure aggregation across channels	$\otimes$
7	Voters uniquely identifiable	◐^{i}
8	Voters authenticated	◐^{i}
9	One vote per voter...	◐^{h}
9(a)	...even if multiple casts allowed	$\odot^b$
9(b)	...even if multiple channels	$\odot^b$
9(c)	Multiple casts prevented otherwise	◐^{i}
10	Voting system is protected	○^{d}
10(a)	Voter taught to verify connection	○^{e}
10(b)	Only official information on ballot	◐^{h}
10(c)	Cast ballots are tamper-resistant	○^{f}
10(d)	Coercion resistance	○^{e}
11	Procedures ensure authentic ballot	○^{e}
12	Proper voter intent-capture	●
12(a)	Ballot modifiable before casting	●
13	Voters can cast an abstain vote	$\otimes$
14	Voters are advised of invalid votes	$\otimes$
15	Individual verifiability	◐^{h}
15(a)	Paper copies of votes at polls	$\odot^c$
15(b)	Statistical audits (e.g. RLAs)	$\odot^c$
16	Confirm of cast ballot	●
17	Can verify *all* valid votes incl.	○^{f}
18	Can verify *only* valid votes incl.	○^{f}
19	Ballot secrecy	○^{e}
19(a)	Voter list separated from voting components	●
20	Data minimization	$\otimes$
21	Authentication data is protected	○^{f}
21(a)	Authentication uses cryptography	○^{d}
22	Voter list has access control	●
23	No transferable proof of cast vote	○^{f}
23(a)	Paper-based proofs	$\odot^c$
23(b)	No residual info after casting	◐^{h}
23(c)	Voters informed of ballot secrecy risks and mitigations	○^{f}
23(d)	Voters taught to remove traces from devices	○^{e}
24	No disclosure of premature results	○^{d}
25	Pre-cast selections also secret	◐^{h}
26	Voters anonymous during count	○^{e}
26(a)	Voter identity and choice separated	$\otimes$
26(b)	Ballots decoded ASAP after close	●
26(c)	Confidentiality during auditing	●
27	Gradual introduction of e-voting	○^{e}
27(a)	Public feasibility study beforehand	○^{e}
27(b)	Early pilots	○^{e}
27(c)	Final system tested before election	$\otimes$
27(d)	Comprehensive pilots	○^{e}
28	Legislation enacted beforehand	○^{g}
28(a)	Law: Implement/operate/count	○^{g}
28(b)	Law: Vote validity	○^{g}
28(c)	Law: Discrepancies in verification	○^{g}
28(d)	Law: Data destruction	○^{g}
28(e)	Law: Domestic/int'l observers	○^{g}
28(f)	Law: Timelines	○^{g}
28(g)	No voting before voting period	●
28(h)	E-voting before in-person allowed	●
28(i)	No voting after voting period	$\odot^b$
28(j)	System delays don't invalidate vote	$\otimes$
28(k)	System inaccessible after election	●
29	EMB has control over system	○^{f}
29(a)	Transparent procurement	◐^{h}

Continued on next page...

●: Fully met   ◐: Partially met   ○: Not met $\otimes$: Info not available $\odot$ Not applicable

[a] Not evaluated (outside expertise)
[b] Not applicable to Ontario case
[c] Not applicable to online voting
[d] Some meaningfully attempt
[e] Almost all cities failing
[f] No cities attempt
[g] Provincial failure
[h] Some cities fully meet
[i] Nearly all cities attempt

#	Paraphrasing	Score
	...Continued from previous page	
29(b)	Limit conflicts of interest	◑^h
29(c)	Separation of duties	⊗
29(d)	Not unduly dependent on vendor	○^f
30	Observability of the count	○^f
30(a)	Records of vote-counting process	⊗
30(b)	Evidence-based vote counts	○^f
30(c)	Accuracy features are verifiable	○^f
30(d)	Availability/integrity of ballot box	⊗
31	Transparency	○^f
31(a)	Published list of software used	○^f
31(b)	Public access to source code, docs	○^f
32	Voters provided info about election	●
32(a)	Docs and support how to vote	●
32(b)	Voter info widely available	●
32(c)	Public demo of e-voting system	◑^h
33	Disclosure of system components	○^f
33(a)	Detailed/reliable observation data	○^f
33(b)	Observers have access to docs	○^f
33(c)	Docs in common language	⊙^b
33(d)	Observers trained by cities	⊗
33(e)	Observable hardware and software testing	○^f
33(f)	Observable certification process	○^f
34	Observable election	○^f
35	Component interoperability	○^f
36	Standards must exist for e-voting	○^f
36(a)	Certification aims and methods 36	○^f
37	Independent review of compliance	○^f
37(a)	Certification costs determined	○^f
37(b)	Certification bodies receive relevant info and get sufficient time	○^f
37(c)	Certification mandate regularly reviewed	○^f
37(e)	Certification reports are self-explanatory	○^f
37(f)	Disclosure of certification docs	○^f
38	Certified system is immutable	○^f
39	Open and comprehensive auditing	◑^i
39(a)	Detailed auditing requirements	⊗
39(b)	Components have synchronized time sources	⊗
39(c)	Audit conclusions considered in future elections	⊗
40	Municipality is responsible for compliance, availability, reliability, usability, and security.	○^f
40(a)	No downtime	◑^h

#	Paraphrasing	Score
40(b)	Inform voters of incidents	◑^h
40(c)	No eligible voters excluded	◑^h
40(d)	Cast votes are accessible, secure, and accurate	⊗
40(e)	No data loss when technical problems occur	⊗
40(f)	Security mechanisms consider usability	⊙^a
40(g)	System uptime regularly checked	⊗
40(h)	E-voting infrastructure is secure	⊗
40(i)	Disaster recovery plans exist	◑^h
40(j)	Possible to check state of protection of voting equipment	⊗
40(k)	Permanent backup plans available	⊗
40(l)	Incident response protocols available to staff	⊗
40(m)	Post-election securely stored	⊗
41	Only authorized people have access to infrastructure	○^f
41(a)	System access limited to necessary function	⊗
41(b)	Two-person rule, mandatory reporting and monitoring during voting	⊗
41(c)	Two-person rule for other critical technical activity	⊗
42	Deployed voting system is genuine and operates correctly	○^f
42(a)	Equipment checked before each election	○^d
43	Software updates are re-certified	○^f
43(a)	Infrastructure deployment procedures	⊗
44	Vote immutable once cast	◑^h
45	No info released about votes and voters before counting commences	●
46	Secure handling of cryptographic material by electoral body	○^e
46(a)	Cryptographic key generation ceremony open to public	○^f
47	Integrity incidents are reported	⊗
47(a)	Integrity threats specified in advance	○^e
47(b)	Incident mitigations specified	◑^h
48	Integrity of voter/candidate lists	⊗
48(a)	Security of printing process for voter cards	⊗
49	System identifies irregular votes	⊗
49(a)	System determine if votes cast within time limit	⊗

●: Fully met ◐: Partially met ○: Not met ⊗: Info not available ⊙ Not applicable

^a Not evaluated (outside expertise)   ^d Some meaningfully attempt   ^g Provincial failure
^b Not applicable to Ontario case   ^e Almost all cities failing   ^h Some cities fully meet
^c Not applicable to online voting   ^f No cities attempt   ⁱ Nearly all cities attempt

References

1. Legal, Operational and Technical Standards for E-Voting, Recommendation Rec (2004) 11. Committee of Ministers of the Council of Europe (2004)
2. Explanatory Memorandum to Recommendation CM/Rec(2017) 5 of the Committee of Ministers to member States on standards for e-voting. Council of Europe Ad hoc Committee of Experts on Legal, Operational and Technical Standards for e-voting (2017). https://search.coe.int/cm/Pages/result_details.aspx?ObjectID=090000168071bc84
3. Guidelines on the implementation of the provisions of Recommendation CM/Rec(2017) 5 on standards for e-voting. Council of Europe Ad hoc Committee of Experts on Legal, Operational and Technical Standards for e-voting (2017). https://search.coe.int/cm/Pages/result_details.aspx?ObjectID=0900001680726c0b
4. Recommendation CM/Rec(2017) 5 of the Committee of Ministers to member States on standards for e-voting. Council of Europe Ad hoc Committee of Experts on Legal, Operational and Technical Standards for e-voting (2017). https://search.coe.int/cm/Pages/result_details.aspx?ObjectID=0900001680726f6f
5. Simply voting security information package (2018). https://www.pertheast.ca/en/about-our-community/resources/2018-Election-Simply-Voting-Security-Information.pdf
6. Voluntary Voting System Guidelines VVSG 2.0. US Election Assistance Commission (2021)
7. Alonso, L.P., Gasco, M., del Blanco, D.Y.M., Alonso, J.Á.H., Barrat, J., Moreton, H.A.: E-voting system evaluation based on the council of Europe recommendations: Helios voting. IEEE Trans. Emerg. Top. Comput. **9**(1), 161–173 (2018)
8. del Blanco, D.Y.M., Duenas-Cid, D.: E-voting system evaluation based on the council of Europe recommendations: nvotes. In: E-VOTE-ID, pp. 147–166 (2020)
9. Brunet, J., Pananos, A.D., Essex, A.: Review your choices: when confirmation pages break ballot secrecy in online elections. In: Krimmer, R., Volkamer, M., Duenas-Cid, D., Ronne, P., Germann, M. (eds.) Electronic Voting. LNCS, vol. 13553, pp. 36–52. Springer, Cham (2022). https://doi.org/10.1007/978-3-031-15911-4_3
10. Cardillo, A., Akinyokun, N., Essex, A.: Online voting in Ontario municipal elections: a conflict of legal principles and technology? In: Krimmer, R., et al. (eds.) E-Vote-ID 2019. LNCS, vol. 11759, pp. 67–82. Springer, Cham (2019). https://doi.org/10.1007/978-3-030-30625-0_5
11. Cardillo, A., Essex, A.: The threat of SSL/TLS stripping to online voting. In: Krimmer, R., et al. (eds.) E-Vote-ID 2018. LNCS, vol. 11143, pp. 35–50. Springer, Cham (2018). https://doi.org/10.1007/978-3-030-00419-4_3
12. Central Huron: Bylaw 37–2018 (2018). https://centralhuron.civicweb.net/document/50603/

13. City of Markham: How to vote online in the 2022 municipal election. YouTube video, October 2022. https://www.youtube.com/watch?v=zXUgEfs5gEQ
14. Clark, J., Essex, A.: Internet Voting for Persons with Disabilities - Security Assessment of Vendor Proposals. City of Toronto FOI Request 2014–01543 (2014). https://verifiedvoting.org/wp-content/uploads/2020/07/Canada-2014-01543-security-report.pdf
15. Government of Ontario: Municipal elections act, 1996, s.o. 1996, c. 32, sched. (1996). https://www.ontario.ca/laws/statute/96m32
16. Joseph, S.: Advanced voting down in Markham, despite added day. Webpage, October 2014. https://www.yorkregion.com/news/municipal-elections/advanced-voting-down-in-markham-despite-added-day/article_4a239e02-009c-562b-9913-70e6c4634559.html
17. Klymenko, V.: How successfully run your first online election: Interview with CEO of Neuvote Matthew Heuman. Webpage, 20 January 2023. https://news.neuvote.com/how-successfully-run-your-first-online-elections-interview-with-ceo-of-neuvote-matthew-heuman/
18. Latkowski, B.: New dates set for catholic school board trustee election in Cambridge, November 2022. https://kitchener.citynews.ca/local-news/new-dates-set-for-catholic-school-board-trustee-election-in-cambridge-6055907/
19. Manton, D., Shaw, J.: Alternative voting methods update - 2022 municipal & school board election. Technical report 21–319(CRS), City of Cambridge (2021). https://www.cambridge.ca/en/elections/resources/Alternative-Voting-Methods-Update.pdf
20. Markham: Bylaw 2017–20 (2017). https://pub-markham.escribemeetings.com/filestream.ashx?documentid=9670
21. Ontario Superior Court of Justice: Cusimano V. Toronto (city), 2011 ONSC 2527 (canlii) (2011). http://canlii.ca/t/fl5pg
22. The Corporation of the Municipality of Central Huron: Bylaw 32–2017 (2017). https://centralhuron.civicweb.net/document/45563/
23. Vis, M.: An online ballot error affects 2 ward contests in thunder bay's municipal election. CBC News (2022). https://www.cbc.ca/news/canada/thunder-bay/online-ballot-error-affects-two-thunder-bay-ward-races-1.6609868

Coercion Mitigation for Voting Systems with Trackers: A Selene Case Study

Kristian Gjøsteen[1], Thomas Haines[2], and Morten Rotvold Solberg[1(✉)]

[1] Norwegian University of Science and Technology, Trondheim, Norway
{kristian.gjosteen,mosolb}@ntnu.no
[2] Australian National University, Canberra, Australia
thomas.haines@anu.edu.au

Abstract. An interesting approach to achieving verifiability in voting systems is to make use of tracking numbers. This gives voters a simple way of verifying that their ballot was counted: they can simply look up their ballot/tracker pair on a public bulletin board. It is crucial to understand how trackers affect other security properties, in particular privacy. However, existing privacy definitions are not designed to accommodate tracker-based voting systems. Furthermore, the addition of trackers increases the threat of coercion. There does however exist techniques to mitigate the coercion threat. While the term *coercion mitigation* has been used in the literature when describing voting systems such as Selene, no formal definition of coercion mitigation seems to exist. In this paper we formally define what coercion mitigation means for tracker-based voting systems. We model Selene in our framework and we prove that Selene provides coercion mitigation, in addition to privacy and verifiability.

Keywords: E-voting · Coercion mitigation · Selene

1 Introduction

Electronic voting has seen widespread use over the past decades, ranging from smaller elections within clubs and associations, to large scale national elections as in Estonia. It is therefore necessary to understand the level of security that electronic voting systems provide. In this paper, we define precisely what verifiability, privacy and coercion mitigation means for voting systems using so-called *trackers*, and we prove that Selene provides these properties.

Verifiability is an interesting voting system property, allowing a voter to verify that their particular ballot was counted and that the election result correctly reflects the verified ballots. One example of a system with verifiability is Helios [2], which is used in the elections of the International Association for Cryptologic Research [1], among others. However, the Benaloh challenges used to achieve verifiability in Helios are hard to use for voters [26].

Schneier [33] proposed using human-readable *tracking numbers* for verifiability. Each voter gets a personal tracking number that is attached to their ballot.

© The Author(s) 2023
M. Volkamer et al. (Eds.): E-Vote-ID 2023, LNCS 14230, pp. 69–86, 2023.
https://doi.org/10.1007/978-3-031-43756-4_5

At the end of the election, all ballots with attached trackers are made publicly available. A voter can now trivially verify that their ballot appears next to their tracking number, which gives us verifiability as long as the trackers are unique. Multiple voting systems making use of tracking numbers have been proposed and deployed. Two notable examples are sElect [27] and Selene [31]. Tracking numbers intuitively give the voters a simple way of verifying that their ballot was recorded and counted. However, other security properties must also be considered. In particular, it is necessary to have a good understanding of how the addition of tracking numbers affects the voters' *privacy*.

Verifiable voting may exacerbate threats such as *coercion*, in particular for remote electronic voting systems (e.g. internet voting) where a coercer might be present to "help" a coerced voter submit their ballot. *Coercion resistant* voting systems [9,25] have been developed. Coercion resistance typically involves voters re-voting when the coercer is not present, but this often complicates voting procedures or increases the cost of the tallying phase. Furthermore, re-voting might not always be possible and may even be prohibited by law.

Like verifiability in general, tracking numbers may make coercion simpler: if a coercer gets access to a voter's tracker, the coercer may also be able to verify that the desired ballot was cast. While tracking numbers complicate coercion resistance, it may be possible to *mitigate* the threat of coercion. For instance, if the voter only learns their tracking number after the result (ballots with trackers) has been published, as in Selene, they may lie to a coercer by observing a suitable ballot-tracker pair. *Coercion mitigation* is weaker than coercion resistance, but may be appropriate for low-stakes elections or where achieving stronger properties is considered to be impractical.

1.1 Related Work

Privacy. Bernhard *et al.* [6] analysed then-existing privacy definitions. They concluded that previous definitions were either too weak (there are real attacks not captured by the definitions), too strong (no voting system with any form of verifiability can be proven secure under the definition), or too narrow (the definitions do not capture a wide enough range of voting systems).

The main technical difficulty compared to standard cryptographic privacy notions is that the result of the election must be revealed to the adversary. Not only could the result reveal information about individual ballots, but it also prevents straight-forward cryptographic real-or-random definitions from working. Roughly speaking, there are two approaches to defining privacy for voting systems, based on the two different questions: "Does anything leak out of the casting and tallying prosesses?" *vs.* "Which voter cast this particular ballot?" The first question tends to lead to simulation-based security notions, while the second question can lead to more traditional left-or-right cryptographic definitions.

Bernhard *et al.* [6] proposed the BPRIV definition, where the adversary plays a game against a challenger and interacts with two worlds (real and fake). The adversary first specifies ballots to be cast separately for each world. In the real world, ballots are cast and then counted as usual. In the fake world, the specified ballots are cast, but the ballots from the left world are counted and any tally proofs are simulated. The adversary then gets to see one of the worlds and must decide which world it sees. The idea is that for any secure system, the result in the fake world should be identical to what the result would have been in the real world, proving that – up to the actual result – the casting and tallying processes do not leak anything about the ballots cast, capturing privacy in this sense.

Bernhard et al. [6] proposed MiniVoting, an abstract scheme that models many voting systems (e.g. Helios), and proved that it satisfies the BPRIV definition. Cortier et al. [10] proved that Labelled-MiniVoting, an extension of MiniVoting, also satisfies BPRIV. Belenios [13] also satisfies BPRIV [11].

The original BPRIV definition does not attempt to model corruption in any part of the tally process. Cortier et al. [15] proposed mb-BPRIV which models adversarial control over which encrypted ballots should go through the tally process. Drăgan et al. [18] proposed the du-mb-BPRIV model which also covers systems where verification happens after tallying.

The other approach to privacy is a traditional left-or-right game, such as Benaloh [4], where the adversary interacts with the various honest components of a voting system (voters, their computers, shuffle and decryption servers, etc.), all simulated by an experiment. Privacy is captured by a left-or-right query, and the adversary must determine if the left or the right ballots were cast. The game becomes trivial if the left and the right ballots would give different tallies, so we require that the challenge queries taken together yield the same tally for left and right. In the simplest instantiation, the left and right ballots contain distinct permutations of the same ballots, so showing that they cannot be distinguished shows that the election processes do not leak who cast which ballots. Smyth [36] and Gjøsteen [20] provide examples of this definitional style. As far as we know, no definition in this style captures tracker-based voting systems.

The advantage of the traditional cryptographic left-or-right game relative to the BPRIV approach is that it is easier to model adversarial interactions with all parts of the protocol, including the different parts of the tally process, though authors before Gjøsteen [20] do not seem to do so. In principle, the BPRIV requirement that the tally process be simulatable is troublesome, since such simulators cannot exist in the plain model, which means that the definition itself technically exists in some unspecified idealised model (typically the random oracle model). In practice, this is not troublesome. Requiring balanced left and right ballots is troublesome for some systems with particular counting functions, but not if the system reveals plaintext ballots.

Verifiability. Verifiability intuitively captures the notion that if a collection of voters verify the election, the result must be consistent with their cast ballots. For voters that do not verify or whose verification failed, we make no guarantees.

Several definitions of verifiability have appeared in the literature, see e.g. [12] or [37] for an overview. Furthermore, the verifiability properties of Selene have been thoroughly analysed both from a technical point of view (e.g. [3,31]) and with respect to the user experience (e.g. [17,38]).

Coercion. Coercion resistance models a coercer that controls the voter for a period of time. We refer to Smyth [35] for an overview of definitions. A weaker notion is receipt-freeness, where the coercer does not control the voter, but asks for evidence that the voter cast the desired ballot. This was introduced by Benaloh and Tuinstra [5], while Chaidos *et al.* [7] gave a BPRIV-style security definition. Selene, as generally instantiated, is not receipt-free. *Coercion mitigation* is a different notion, where we assume that the coercer is not present during vote casting and is somehow not able to ask the voter to perform particular operations (such as revealing the randomness used to encrypt). This could allow the voter to fake information consistent with following the coercer's demands. While the term coercion mitigation has been used to describe the security properties provided by Selene (e.g. in [23,31,38]), there seems to be no formal definition of coercion mitigation in the literature.

Selene. Selene as a voting system has been studied previously, in particular with respect to privacy [18]. But a study of the complete protocol, including the tally phase, is missing. The coercion mitigation properties of Selene have also been extensively discussed [23,31], but have not received a cryptographic analysis.

1.2   Our Contribution

We define security for cryptographic voting systems with trackers, capturing privacy, verifiability and coercion mitigation. An experiment models the adversary's interaction with the honest players through various queries.

To break privacy, the adversary must decide who cast which ballot. Our definition is based on a similar definition by Gjøsteen [20, p. 492], adapted to properly accommodate voting systems using trackers. To break verifiability, the adversary must cause verifying voters to accept a result that is inconsistent with the ballots they have cast (similar to Cortier *et al.* [12]). To break coercion mitigation, the adversary is allowed to reveal the verification information of coerced voters and must decide if the coerced voter lied or not. Selene is vulnerable to collisions among such lies; e.g. multiple coerced voters claim the same ballot. We want to factor this attack out of the cryptographic analysis, so we require that the coercer organises the voting such that collisions do not happen. For schemes that are not vulnerable, we would remove the requirement.

Our definitions are easy to work with, which we demonstrate by presenting a complete model of Selene (expressed in our framework) and prove that Selene satisfies both privacy, verifiability and coercion mitigation. Selene has seen some use [32], so we believe these results are of independent interest.

We developed our definitions with Selene in mind, but they also accommodate other tracker based voting systems such as Hyperion [30] and (with some modifications to accomodate secret key material used in the shuffles) sElect [27]. Furthermore, our models also capture voting systems that do not use trackers.

2   Background

2.1   Notation

We denote tuples/lists in bold, e.g. $\mathbf{v} = (v_1, \ldots, v_n)$. If we have multiple tuples, we denote the jth tuple by $\mathbf{v}_j$ and the ith element of the jth tuple by $v_{j,i}$.

2.2   Cryptographic Building Blocks

We briefly introduce some cryptographic primitives we need for our work. Due to space constraints we omit much of the details.

To protect voters' privacy, ballots are usually encrypted. Selene makes use of the ElGamal public key encryption system [19], which is used to encrypt both ballots and trackers. Throughout this paper, we will denote an ElGamal ciphertext by $(x, w) := (g^r, m \cdot \mathsf{pk}^r)$, where g is the generator of the cyclic group $\mathbb{G}$ (of prime order q) we are working in, m is the encrypted message, $\mathsf{pk} = g^{\mathsf{sk}}$ is the public encryption key (with corresponding decryption key sk) and r is a random element in $\mathbb{Z}_q$ (the field of integers modulo q).

Cryptographic voting systems typically make use of zero-knowledge proofs to ensure that certain computations are performed correctly. We refer to [16] for general background on zero-knowledge proofs. In particular, we use *equality of discrete logarithm* proofs and correctness proofs for *shuffles* of encrypted ballots. The former ensures correctness of computations. The latter preserves privacy by breaking the link between voters and their ballots. It is necessary that the shuffles are *verifiable* to ensure that no ballots are tampered with in any way. We refer to [22] for an overview of verifiable shuffles. In Selene it is necessary to shuffle two lists of ciphertexts (ballots and trackers) in parallel. Possible protocols are given in [29] and we detail a convenient protocol in the full version [21].

Furthermore, in Selene, the election authorities make use of Pedersen-style commitments [28] to commit to tracking numbers.

3   Voting Systems with Trackers

We model a voting protocol as a simple protocol built on top of a cryptographic voting scheme in such a way that the protocol's security properties can be easily inferred from the cryptographic voting scheme's properties. This allows us to separate key management (who has which keys) and plumbing (who sends which message when to whom) from the cryptographic issues, which simplifies analysis.

Due to space limitations, we model a situation with honest setup and tracker generation, as well as a single party decrypting. The former would be handled using a bespoke, verifiable multi-party computation protocol (see [31] for a suitable protocol for Selene), while the latter is handled using distributed decryption.

3.1   The Syntax of Voting Systems with Trackers

A verifiable voting system $\mathcal{S}$ consists of the following algorithms (extending Gjøsteen [20]):

- Setup: takes as input a security parameter and returns a pair $(\mathsf{pk}, \mathsf{sk})$ of election public and secret keys.
- UserKeyGen: takes as input an election public key pk and returns a pair $(\mathsf{vpk}, \mathsf{vsk})$ of voter public and secret keys.
- TrackerGen: takes as input an election public key pk and a list $(\mathsf{vpk}_1, \ldots, \mathsf{vpk}_n)$ of voter public keys and returns a list $\mathbf{t}$ of trackers, a list $\mathbf{et}$ of ciphertexts, a list $\mathbf{ct}$ of commitments, a list $\mathbf{op}$ of openings and a permutation π on the set $\{1, \ldots, n\}$.
- ExtractTracker: takes as input a voter secret key vsk, a tracker commitment ct and an opening op and returns a tracker t.
- ClaimTracker: takes as input a voter secret key vsk, a tracker commitment ct and a tracker t and returns an opening op.
- Vote: takes as input an election public key pk and a ballot v and returns a ciphertext ev, a ballot proof Π^v and a receipt ρ.
- Shuffle: takes as input a public key pk and a list $\mathbf{evt}$ of encrypted ballots and trackers, and returns a list $\mathbf{evt}'$ and a proof Π^s of correct shuffle.
- DecryptResult: takes as input a secret key sk and a list $\mathbf{evt}$ of encrypted ballots and trackers and returns a result res and a result proof Π^r.
- VoterVerify: takes as input a receipt ρ, a tracker t, a list $\mathbf{evt}$ of encrypted ballot/tracker pairs, a result res and a result proof Π^r and returns 0 or 1.
- VerifyShuffle: takes as input a public key pk, two lists $\mathbf{evt}, \mathbf{evt}'$ of encrypted ballots and trackers and a shuffle proof Π^s and returns 0 or 1.
- VerifyBallot: takes as input a public key pk, a ciphertext ev and a ballot proof Π^v and returns 0 or 1.
- VerifyResult: takes as input a public key pk, a list $\mathbf{evt}$ of encrypted ballots and trackers, a result res and a result proof Π^r and returns 0 or 1.

We say that a verifiable, tracker-based voting system is (n_v, n_s)-*correct* if for any $(\mathsf{pk}, \mathsf{sk})$ output by Setup, any $(\mathsf{vpk}_1, \mathsf{vsk}_1), \ldots, (\mathsf{vpk}_{n_v}, \mathsf{vsk}_{n_v})$ output by UserKeyGen, any lists $\mathbf{t}, \mathbf{et}, \mathbf{ct}, \mathbf{op}$ and permutations $\pi \colon \{1, \ldots, n_v\} \to \{1, \ldots, n_v\}$ output by TrackerGen$(\mathsf{pk}, \mathsf{sk}, \mathsf{vpk}_1, \ldots, \mathsf{vpk}_{n_v})$, any ballots $v_1, \ldots, v_{n_v}$, any (ev_i, Π_i^v, ρ_i) output by Vote$(\mathsf{pk}, v_i), i = 1, \ldots, n_v$, any sequence of n_s sequences of encrypted ballots and trackers $\mathbf{evt}_i$ and proofs Π_i^s output by Shuffle$(\mathsf{pk}, \mathbf{evt}_{i-1})$, and any (res, Π^r) possibly output by DecryptResult$(\mathsf{sk}, \mathbf{evt}_{n_s})$, the following hold:

- DecryptResult$(\mathsf{sk}, \mathbf{evt}_{n_s})$ did not output $\perp$,
- VoterVerify$(\rho_i, t_i, \mathbf{evt}_{n_s}, \mathsf{res}, \Pi^r) = 1$ for all $i = 1, \ldots, n_v$,
- VerifyShuffle$\big(\mathsf{pk}, \mathbf{evt}_{j-1}, \mathbf{evt}_j, \Pi_j^s\big) = 1$ for all $j = 1, \ldots, n_s$,
- VerifyResult$(\mathsf{pk}, \mathbf{evt}_{n_s}, \mathsf{res}, \Pi^r) = 1$,
- VerifyBallot$(\mathsf{pk}, ev_i, \Pi_i^v) = 1$ for all $i = 1, \ldots, n_v$, and

for any voter key pair $(\mathsf{vpk}, \mathsf{vsk})$, ct in $\mathbf{ct}$ and tracker t in $\mathbf{t}$, we have that

$$\mathsf{ExtractTracker}(\mathsf{vsk}, ct, \mathsf{ClaimTracker}(\mathsf{vsk}, ct, t)) = t.$$

We will describe later how Selene fits into our framework, but we note that this framework also captures voting systems that do not use trackers for verification. Such protocols are simply augmented with suitable dummy algorithms for $\mathsf{TrackerGen}$, $\mathsf{ExtractTracker}$ and $\mathsf{ClaimTracker}$.

3.2 Defining Security

We use a single experiment, found in Fig. 1, to define privacy, integrity and coercion mitigation. Verifiability is defined in terms of integrity. The experiment models the cryptographic actions of honest parties.

The test query is used to model integrity. The challenge query is used to define privacy. The coerce and coercion verification queries are used to model coercion, again modified by freshness. The coerce query specifies two voters (actually, two indices into the list of voter public keys) and two ballots. The first voter is the coerced voter. The first ballot is the coerced voter's intended ballot, while the second ballot is the coercer's desired ballot. The second voter casts the opposite ballot of the coerced voter. In the *coercion verification query*, the coerced voter either reveals an opening to their true tracker, or an opening to the tracker corresponding to the coercer's desired ballot, cast by the second voter, thereby ensuring that the coerced voter can lie about its opening without risking a collision (as discussed in Sect. 1.2). We note that this does not capture full coercion resistance, as that would require that the adversary is able to see exactly which ciphertext the coerced voter submitted (as, for example in [14]). In our definition, however, the adversary gets to see two ciphertexts, where one is submitted by the coerced voter, but he receives no information about which of the two ciphertexts the coerced voter actually submitted.

We make some restrictions on the order and number of queries (detailed in the caption of Fig. 1), but the experiment allows the adversary to make combinations of queries that do not correspond to any behaviour of the voting protocol. Partially, we do so because we can, but also in order to simplify definitions of certain cryptographic properties (such as uniqueness of results).

The adversary decides which ballots should be counted. We need to recognise when the adversary has organised counting such that it results in a trivial win. We say that a sequence $\mathbf{evt}$ of encrypted ballots and trackers is *valid* if

- L_s contains a sequence of tuples $(\mathbf{evt}_{j-1}, \mathbf{evt}_j, \Pi_j^s)_{j=1}^{n_s}$, not necessarily appearing in the same order in L_s, with $\mathbf{evt}_{n_s} = \mathbf{evt}$;
- L_v contains tuples

$$(i_1, j_1, v_{0,1}, v_{1,1}, ev_1, \Pi_1^v, \rho_1), \ldots, (i_{n_c}, j_{n_c}, v_{0,n_c}, v_{1,n_c}, ev_{n_c}, \Pi_{n_c}^v, \rho_{n_c})$$

such that $\mathbf{evt}_0 = (ev_1, \ldots, ev_{n_c})$; and

The experiment proceeds as follows:

- $\boxed{\text{Sample } b, b'' \xleftarrow{\text{r}} \{0,1\}.}$ Let L_r, L_v, L_s, L_d be empty lists.
  We denote by $(\mathsf{vpk}_i, \mathsf{vsk}_i)$ the ith entry in L_r.
- Compute $(\mathsf{pk}, \mathsf{sk}) \leftarrow \mathsf{Setup}$ and send pk to the adversary.
- On a *register query*, compute $(\mathsf{vpk}, \mathsf{vsk}) \leftarrow \mathsf{UserKeyGen}(\mathsf{pk})$, append $(\mathsf{vpk}, \mathsf{vsk})$ to L_r and send vpk to the adversary.
- On a *chosen voter key query* vpk, append $(\mathsf{vpk}, \perp)$ to L_r.
- On a *tracker generation query*, compute
  $(\mathbf{t}, \mathbf{et}, \mathbf{ct}, \mathbf{op}, \pi) \leftarrow \mathsf{TrackerGen}(\mathsf{pk}, \mathsf{vpk}_1, \ldots, \mathsf{vpk}_{n_r})$ where $\mathsf{vpk}_1, \ldots, \mathsf{vpk}_{n_r}$ are the public keys from L_r, and send $(\mathbf{t}, \mathbf{et}, \mathbf{ct})$ to the adversary.
  We denote by t_i, et_i, ct_i and op_i the ith entries in the corresponding lists.
- On a *chosen ciphertext query* (i, ev, Π^v), if $\mathsf{VerifyBallot}(ev, \Pi^v) = 1$, append $(i, \perp, \perp, \perp, ev, \Pi^v, \perp)$ to L_v.
- $\boxed{\boxed{\begin{array}{l}\text{On a } \textit{challenge query } (i, v_0, v_1), \text{ compute } (ev, \Pi^v, \rho) \leftarrow \mathsf{Vote}(\mathsf{pk}, v_b), \text{ append} \\ (i, \perp, v_0, v_1, ev, \Pi^v, \rho) \text{ to } L_v \text{ and send } (ev, \Pi^v) \text{ to } \mathcal{A}.\end{array}}}$
- $\overline{\begin{array}{l}\text{On a } \textit{coerce query } (i, j, v_0, v_1), \text{ compute } (ev_i, \Pi_i^v, \rho_i) \leftarrow \mathsf{Vote}(\mathsf{pk}, v_b) \\ \text{and } (ev_j, \Pi_j^v, \rho_j) \leftarrow \mathsf{Vote}(\mathsf{pk}, v_{1-b}), \text{ append } (i, j, v_0, v_1, ev_i, \Pi_i^v, \rho_i) \text{ and} \\ (j, i, v_1, v_0, ev_j, \Pi_j^v, \rho_j) \text{ to } L_v, \text{ and send } (ev_i, \Pi_i^v) \text{ and } (ev_j, \Pi_j^v) \text{ to } \mathcal{A}.\end{array}}$
- On a *shuffle query* $\mathbf{evt}$, compute $(\mathbf{evt}', \Pi^s) \leftarrow \mathsf{Shuffle}(\mathsf{pk}, \mathbf{evt})$, append $(\mathbf{evt}, \mathbf{evt}', \Pi^s)$ to L_s and send $(\mathbf{evt}', \Pi^s)$ to $\mathcal{A}$.
- On a *chosen shuffle query* $(\mathbf{evt}, \mathbf{evt}', \Pi^s)$, if $\mathsf{VerifyShuffle}(\mathbf{evt}, \mathbf{evt}', \Pi^s) = 1$, append the query to L_s.
- On a *result query* $\mathbf{evt}$, compute $(\mathbf{res}, \Pi^r) \leftarrow \mathsf{DecryptResult}(\mathsf{sk}, \mathbf{evt})$, send $(\mathbf{res}, \Pi^r)$ to $\mathcal{A}$ and append $(\mathbf{evt}, \mathbf{res}, \Pi^r)$ to L_d.
- On a *voter verification query* $(k, \mathbf{evt}, \mathbf{res}, \Pi^d)$ with $(i, \perp, v_0, v_1, ev, \Pi^v, \rho)$ being the kth entry in L_v, compute $t \leftarrow \mathsf{ExtractTracker}(\mathsf{vsk}_i, op_i, ct_i)$ and $d \leftarrow \mathsf{VoterVerify}(\rho_i, t, \mathbf{evt}, \mathbf{res}, \Pi^r)$ and send d to $\mathcal{A}$.
- $\overline{\begin{array}{l}\text{On a } \textit{coercion verification query } k, \text{ with } (i, j, \ldots) \text{ being the } k\text{th entry} \\ \text{in the } L_v \text{ list, then if } b = 0 \text{ send } op_i \text{ to } \mathcal{A}, \text{ otherwise compute } op \leftarrow \\ \mathsf{ClaimTracker}(\mathsf{vsk}_i, ct_i, t_{\pi(j)}) \text{ and send } op \text{ to } \mathcal{A}.\end{array}}$
- On a *test query* $(\mathbf{evt}, \mathbf{res}, \Pi^r)$, compute $d \leftarrow \mathsf{VerifyResult}(\mathbf{evt}, \mathbf{res}, \Pi^r)$ and send d to $\mathcal{A}$.
- On a *voter key reveal query* i, send $(\mathsf{vpk}_i, \mathsf{vsk}_i)$ to $\mathcal{A}$.
- On a *tracker reveal query* i, compute $t \leftarrow \mathsf{ExtractTracker}(\mathsf{vsk}_i, ct_i, op_i)$ and send t to $\mathcal{A}$.
- On a *receipt reveal query* k, where the kth entry of L_v is $(\cdot, \cdot, \cdot, \cdot, \cdot, \cdot, \rho_k)$, send ρ_k to $\mathcal{A}$.
- On an *election key reveal query*, send sk to $\mathcal{A}$.

Eventually, the adversary outputs a bit b'.

Fig. 1. Security experiment for privacy, integrity and coercion mitigation. The bit b'' is not used in the experiment, but simplifies the definition of advantage. The adversary makes register and chosen voter key queries, followed by a single tracker generation query, followed by other queries. Queries in $\boxed{\text{framed boxes}}$ are only used for privacy and coercion mitigation. Queries in $\overline{\underline{\text{dashed boxes}}}$ are only used for coercion mitigation. Queries in $\boxed{\boxed{\text{doubly framed boxes}}}$ are only used for privacy and integrity (with b fixed to 0). Queries in shaded boxes are only used for integrity.

- for any $k, k' \in \{1, \ldots, n_c\}$ with $k \neq k'$, we have $i_k \neq i_{k'}$ (only one ballot per voter public key).

In this case, we also say that **evt** *originated* from $\mathbf{evt}_0$, alternatively from

$$(i_1, j_1, v_{0,1}, v_{1,1}, ev_1, \Pi_1^v, \rho_1), \ldots, (i_{n_c}, j_{n_c}, v_{0,n_c}, v_{1,n_c}, ev_{n_c}, \Pi_{n_c}^v, \rho_{n_c}).$$

Furthermore, we say that a valid sequence **evt** is *honest* if at least one of the tuples $(\mathbf{evt}_{j-1}, \mathbf{evt}_j, \Pi_j^s)$ comes from a shuffle query. A valid sequence is *balanced* if the ballot sequences $(v_{0,1}, \ldots, v_{0,n_c})$ and $(v_{1,1}, \ldots, v_{1,n_c})$ are equal up to order.

An execution is *fresh* if the following all hold:

- If a voter secret key, a receipt or a tracker is revealed, then any challenge query for that voter contains the same ballot on the left and the right side.
- For any result query **evt** that does not return $\bot$, **evt** is balanced and honest.
- For any voter verification query $(j, \mathbf{evt}, \mathsf{res}, \Pi^r)$, **evt** contains an encryption of $v_{b,j}$ and $\mathsf{VerifyResult}(\mathsf{pk}, \mathbf{evt}, \mathsf{res}, \Pi^r)$ evaluates to 1.
- For any encrypted ballot returned by a coerce query, if it is in an origin of any result query, the other encrypted ballot returned by the coerce query is also in the same origin of the same result query.
- There is no election key reveal query.

We define the joint privacy and coercion mitigation event E_p to be the event that after the experiment and an adversary has interacted, the execution is fresh and $b' = b$, or the execution is not fresh and $b' = b''$. In other words, if the adversary makes a query that results in a non-fresh execution of the experiment, we simply compare the adversary's guess to a random bit, giving the adversary no advantage over making a random guess.

In the integrity game, the adversary's goal is to achieve inconsistencies:

- The *count failure* event F_c is that a result query for a valid sequence of encrypted ballots and trackers results in $\bot$.
- The *inconsistent result* event F_r is that a test query $(\mathbf{evt}, \mathsf{res}, \Pi^r)$ evaluates to 1, **evt** originated from

$$(i_1, \cdot, v_{0,1}, v_{1,1}, ev_1, \Pi_1^v, \rho_1), \ldots, (i_{n_c}, \cdot, v_{0,n_c}, v_{1,n_c}, ev_{n_c}, \Pi_{n_c}^v, \rho_{n_c})$$

and there is no permutation π on $\{1, \ldots, n_c\}$ such that for $i = 1, \ldots, n_c$, either $v_{b,i} = \bot$ or $\mathsf{Dec}(\mathsf{sk}, ev_{\pi(i)}) = v_{b,i}$.
- The *no unique result* event F_u is that two test queries $(\mathbf{evt}, \mathsf{res}_1, \Pi_1^r)$ and $(\mathbf{evt}', \mathsf{res}_2, \Pi_2^r)$ both evaluate to 1, **evt** and **evt**' have a common origin, and res_1 and res_2 are not equal up to order.
- The *inconsistent verification* event F_v is that a sequence of voter verification queries $\{(k_j, \mathbf{evt}, \mathsf{res}, \Pi^r)\}_{j=1}^n$ all return 1, **evt** is valid, and with $L_v = ((i_1, \bot, v_{0,1}, v_{1,1}, ev_1, \Pi_1^v, \rho_1), \ldots, (i_{n_c}, \bot, v_{0,n_c}, v_{1,n_c}, ev_{n_c}, \Pi_{n_c}^v, \rho_{n_c}))$ there is no permutation π on $\{1, \ldots, n_c\}$ such that $\mathsf{Dec}(\mathsf{sk}, ev_{\pi(k_j)}) = v_{b,k_j}$ for all $j = 1, \ldots, n$, i.e. that all the specified voters think their ballots are included in the tally, but at least one of the ballots is not.

We define the advantage of an adversary $\mathcal{A}$ against a voting system $\mathcal{S}$ to be

$$\mathsf{Adv}_{\mathcal{S}}^{\mathsf{vote}-\mathsf{x}}(\mathcal{A}) = \begin{cases} 2 \cdot |\Pr[E_p] - 1/2| & x = \mathsf{priv} \text{ or } x = \mathsf{c-mit}, \text{ or} \\ \Pr[F_c \vee F_r \vee F_u \vee F_v] & x = \mathsf{int}. \end{cases}$$

3.3 The Voting Protocol

The different parties in the voting protocol are the n_v voters and their devices, a trusted *election authority* (EA) who runs setup, registration, tracker generation and who tallies the cast ballots, a collection of n_s shuffle servers, one or more auditors, and a public append-only bulletin board BB. There are many simple variations of the voting protocol.

In the *setup phase*, the EA runs Setup to generate election public and secret keys pk and sk. The public key pk is posted to BB.

In the *registration phase*, the EA runs UserKeyGen(pk) to generate per-voter keys (vpk, vsk) for each voter. The public key vpk is posted to BB and the secret key vsk is sent to the voter's device.

In the *tracker generation phase*, the EA runs TrackerGen(pk, sk, $\mathsf{vpk}_1, \ldots, \mathsf{vpk}_{n_v}$) to generate trackers, encrypted trackers, tracker commitments and openings to the commitments. To break the link between voters and their trackers, the trackers are encrypted and put through a re-encryption mixnet before they are committed to. Each encrypted tracker and commitment is assigned to a voter public key and posted to BB next to this key. Plaintext trackers are also posted to BB.

In the *voting phase*, a voter instructs her device on which ballot v to cast. The voter's device runs the Vote algorithm to produce an encrypted ballot ev and a proof of knowledge Π^v of the underlying plaintext. The encrypted ballot and the proof are added to the web bulletin board next to the voter's public key, encrypted tracker and tracker commitment.

In the *tallying phase*, the auditors first verify the ballot proofs Π_i^v, subsequently ignoring any ballot whose ballot proof does not verify. The pairs (ev_i, et_i) of encrypted ballots and trackers are extracted from the bulletin board and sent to the first shuffle server. The first shuffle server uses the shuffle algorithm Shuffle on the input encrypted ballots and trackers, before passing the shuffled ballots on the next shuffle server, which shuffles the ballots again and sends the shuffled list to the next shuffle server, and so on. All the shuffle servers post their output ciphertexts and shuffle proofs on the bulletin board, and the auditors verify the proofs. If all the shuffles are correct, the EA runs DecryptResult on the output from the final shuffle server, to obtain a result res and a proof Π^r. The auditors verify this too and add their signatures to the bulletin board.

In the *verification phase*, the EA tells each voter which tracker belongs to them (the exact details of how this happens depends on the underlying voting system). The voters then run VoterVerify to verify that their vote was correctly cast and counted. For voting systems without trackers (such as Helios [2] and Belenios [13]), voters simply run VoterVerify without interacting with the EA.

Security Properties. It is easy to see that we can simulate a run of the voting protocol using the experiment. It is also straight-forward for anyone to verify, from the bulletin board alone, if the list of encrypted ballots and trackers that is finally decrypted in a run of the protocol is valid.

For simplicity, we have assumed trusted setup (including tracker generation) and no distributed decryption. We may also assume that any reasonable adversary against the voting scheme has negligible advantage.

It follows, under the assumption of trusted tracker generation, that as long as the contents of the bulletin board verifies, we have verifiability in the sense that the final result is consistent with the ballots of voters that successfully verify. (Though we have not discussed this, one can also verify eligibility by verifying the bulletin board against the electoral roll. When Selene is used without voter signatures, it does not protect against voting on behalf of abstaining honest voters, though such voters could detect this.)

If at least one of the shuffle servers is honest and the election secret key has not been revealed, and the adversary does not manage to organise the voting to get a trivial win, we also have *privacy* and *coercion mitigation*.

4   The Selene Voting System

We provide a model of Selene and analyse it under our security definition. Relative to the original Selene paper, there are three interesting differences/choices: (1) We do not model distributed setup and tracker generation, nor distributed decryption. (2) The voter proves knowledge of the ballot using an equality of discrete logarithm proof. (3) We assume a particular shuffle described in the full version [21] is used. The latter two simplify the security proof by avoiding rewinding. The first is due to lack of space (though see [31] for distributed setup protocols, and [20] for how to model distributed decryption).

4.1   The Voting System

Let $\mathbb{G}$ be a group of prime order q, with generator g. Let $\mathsf{E} = (\mathsf{Kgen}, \mathsf{Enc}, \mathsf{Dec})$ be the ElGamal public key encryption system. Let $\Sigma_{dl} = (\mathcal{P}_{dl}, \mathcal{V}_{dl})$ be a proof system for proving equality of discrete logarithms in $\mathbb{G}$ (e.g. the Chaum-Pedersen protocol [8]). We abuse notation and let $\Sigma_s = (\mathcal{P}_s, \mathcal{V}_s)$ denote both a proof system for shuffling ElGamal ciphertexts and a proof system for shuffling pairs of ElGamal ciphertexts. Our instantiation of Selene works as follows:

- Setup: sample $h_v \xleftarrow{\text{r}} \mathbb{G}$ and compute $(\mathsf{pk}_v, \mathsf{sk}_v) \leftarrow \mathsf{Kgen}(1^\lambda)$ and $(\mathsf{pk}_t, \mathsf{sk}_t) \leftarrow \mathsf{Kgen}(1^\lambda)$. The election public key is $\mathsf{pk} = (\mathsf{pk}_v, \mathsf{pk}_t, h_v)$ and the election secret key is $\mathsf{sk} = (\mathsf{sk}_v, \mathsf{sk}_t)$.
- UserKeyGen(pk): compute $(\mathsf{vpk}, \mathsf{vsk}) \leftarrow \mathsf{Kgen}(1^\lambda)$.
- TrackerGen($\mathsf{pk}, \mathsf{vpk}_1, \ldots, \mathsf{vpk}_n$): set $\mathbf{t} \leftarrow (1, \ldots, n)$. Choose a random permutation π on the set $\{1, \ldots, n\}$. For each i, choose random elements $r_i, s_i \xleftarrow{\text{r}} \{0, \ldots, q-1\}$, compute ElGamal encryptions $et_i \leftarrow (g^{r_{\pi(i)}}, \mathsf{pk}_t^{r_{\pi(i)}} g^{t_{\pi(i)}})$ and

commitments $ct_i \leftarrow \mathsf{vpk}_i^{s_i} \cdot g^{t_{\pi(i)}}$. Set $op_i = g^{s_i}$. The public output is the list of trackers $\mathbf{t}$, the list of encrypted trackers $\mathbf{et}$ and the list of tracker commitments $\mathbf{ct}$. The private output is the list of openings $\mathbf{op}$ to the commitments and the permutation π.

- ExtractTracker(vsk, ct, op): compute $g^t \leftarrow ct \cdot op^{-\mathsf{vsk}}$.
- ClaimTracker(vsk, ct, g^t): compute $op \leftarrow (ct/g^t)^{1/\mathsf{vsk}}$.
- Vote(pk, v): sample $r \xleftarrow{\text{r}} \{0, \ldots, q-1\}$ and compute $x \leftarrow g^r$, $\hat{x} \leftarrow h_v^r$ and $w \leftarrow \mathsf{pk}_v^r v$. Compute a proof $\Pi^{dl} \leftarrow \mathcal{P}_{dl}((g, h_v, x, \hat{x}), r)$ showing that $\log_g x = \log_{h_v} \hat{x} = r$. Output $c = (x, w)$, $\Pi^v = (\hat{x}, \Pi^{dl})$ and $\rho = v$.
- Shuffle($\mathsf{pk}, \mathbf{evt}$): sample two lists $\mathbf{r}_v, \mathbf{r}_t \xleftarrow{\text{r}} \{0, \ldots, q-1\}^n$ and a random permutation on the set $\{1, \ldots, n\}$. For each $((x_{v,i}, w_{v,i}), (x_{t,i}, w_{t,i})) \in \mathbf{evt}$, compute $x'_{v,i} \leftarrow g^{r_{v,\pi(i)}} x_{v,\pi(i)}, w'_{v,i} \leftarrow \mathsf{pk}_v^{r_{v,\pi(i)}} w_{v,\pi(i)}, x'_{t,i} \leftarrow g^{r_{t,\pi(i)}} x_{t,\pi(i)}$ and $w'_{t,i} \leftarrow \mathsf{pk}_t^{r_{t,\pi(i)}} w_{t,\pi(i)}$. Compute a proof $\Pi^s \leftarrow \mathcal{P}_s((\mathbf{evt}, \mathbf{evt}'), (\mathbf{r}_v, \mathbf{r}_t, \pi))$ of correct shuffle and output $(\mathbf{evt}', \Pi^s)$.
- DecryptResult($\mathsf{sk}, \mathbf{evt}$): for each $((x_{v,i}, w_{v,i}), (x_{t,i}, w_{t,i})) \in \mathbf{evt}$, compute $v_i \leftarrow \mathsf{Dec}(\mathsf{sk}_v, (x_{v,i}, w_{v,i}))$, $t_i \leftarrow \mathsf{Dec}(\mathsf{sk}_t, (x_{t,i}, w_{t,i}))$ and proofs $\Pi_{v,i}^{dl} \leftarrow \mathcal{P}_{dl}((g, x_{v,i}, \mathsf{pk}_v, w_{v,i}/v_i), \mathsf{sk}_v)$ and $\Pi_{t,i}^{dl} \leftarrow \mathcal{P}_{dl}((g, x_{t,i}, \mathsf{pk}_t, w_{t,i}/t_i), \mathsf{sk}_t)$, proving that $\log_g \mathsf{pk}_v = \log_{x_{v,i}}(w_{v,i}/v_i) = \mathsf{sk}_v$ and $\log_g \mathsf{pk}_t = \log_{x_{t,i}}(w_{t,i}/t_i) = \mathsf{sk}_t$. Set $\mathbf{res} \leftarrow \mathbf{v}$ and $\Pi^r \leftarrow (\{\Pi_{v,i}^{dl}\}, \{\Pi_{t,i}^{dl}\}, \mathbf{t})$ and output $(\mathbf{res}, \Pi^r)$.
- VoterVerify($\rho, t, \mathbf{evt}, \mathbf{v}, \Pi^r$): parse Π^r as $(\{\Pi_{v,i}^{dl}\}, \{\Pi_{t,i}^{dl}\}, \mathbf{t})$ and check if $\rho \in \mathbf{v}$, and $t \in \mathbf{t}$, and that if $t = t_i$ then $\rho = v_i$, i.e. the ballot appears next to the correct tracker.
- VerifyShuffle($\mathsf{pk}, \mathbf{evt}, \mathbf{evt}', \Pi^s$): compute $d \leftarrow \mathcal{V}_s(\mathsf{pk}, \mathbf{evt}, \mathbf{evt}', \Pi^s)$.
- VerifyBallot(pk, ev, Π^v): parse Π^v as $(\hat{x}, \Pi^{dl})$ and compute $d \leftarrow \mathcal{V}_{dl}((g, h, x, \hat{x}), \Pi^{dl})$.
- VerifyResult($\mathsf{pk}, \mathbf{evt}, \mathbf{res}, \Pi^r$): parse Π^r as $(\{\Pi_{v,i}^{dl}\}, \{\Pi_{t,i}^{dl}\}, \mathbf{t})$ and compute $d_{v,i} \leftarrow \mathcal{V}_{dl}((g, x_{v,i}, \mathsf{pk}_v, w_{v,i}/v_i), \Pi_{v,i}^{dl})$ and $d_{t,i} \leftarrow \mathcal{V}_{dl}((g, x_{t,i}, \mathsf{pk}_t, w_{t,i}/t_i), \Pi_{t,i}^{dl})$ for all $i = 1, \ldots, n$, where $((x_{v,i}, w_{v,i}), (x_{t,i}, w_{t,i})) \in \mathbf{evt}$, $v_i \in \mathbf{res}$, $t_i \in \mathbf{t}$.

The correctness of Selene follows from the correctness of ElGamal, the completeness of the verifiable shuffles and the straight-forward computation

$$\mathsf{ExtractTracker}(\mathsf{vsk}, ct, \mathsf{ClaimTracker}(\mathsf{vsk}, ct, g^t)) = ct \cdot \left(\left(ct/g^t\right)^{1/\mathsf{vsk}}\right)^{-\mathsf{vsk}} = g^t.$$

Note that in the original description of Selene [31], the exact manner of which the voters prove knowledge of their plaintext in the voting phase is left abstract. However, several different approaches are possible. One may, for example, produce a Schnorr proof of knowledge [34] of the randomness used by the encryption algorithm. We choose a different approach, and include a check value $\hat{x}$ and give a Chaum-Pedersen proof that $\log_{h_v} \hat{x} = \log_g x$. Both are valid approaches, however our approach simplifies the security proof by avoiding rewinding.

4.2 Security Result

We say that an adversary against a voting scheme is *non-adaptive* if every voter key reveal query is made before the tracker generation query.

Theorem 1. *Let $\mathcal{A}$ be a non-adaptive $(\tau, n_v, n_c, n_d, n_s)$-adversary against Selene, making at most n_v registration and chosen voter key queries, n_c challenge and coerce queries, n_d chosen ciphertext queries, and n_s shuffle/chosen shuffle queries, and where the runtime of the adversary is at most τ. Then there exist a τ_1'-distinguisher $\mathcal{B}_1$, a $\tau_{2,1}'$-distinguisher $\mathcal{B}_{2,1}$, a $\tau_{2,2}'$-distinguisher $\mathcal{B}_{2,2}$ and a τ_3'-distinguisher $\mathcal{B}_3$, all for DDH, $\tau_1', \tau_{2,1}', \tau_{2,2}', \tau_3'$ all essentially equal to τ, such that*

$$\mathsf{Adv}^{\mathsf{vote}-\mathsf{x}}_{\mathsf{Selene}}(\mathcal{A}) \leq \mathsf{Adv}^{\mathsf{ddh}}_{\mathbb{G},g}(\mathcal{B}_1) + 2n_s(\mathsf{Adv}^{\mathsf{ddh}}_{\mathbb{G},g}(\mathcal{B}_{2,1}) + \mathsf{Adv}^{\mathsf{ddh}}_{\mathbb{G},g}(\mathcal{B}_{2,2}))$$
$$+ \mathsf{Adv}^{\mathsf{ddh}}_{\mathbb{G},g}(\mathcal{B}_3) + \textit{negligible terms},$$

where $\mathsf{x} \in \{\mathsf{priv}, \mathsf{c}-\mathsf{mit}, \mathsf{int}\}$.

(Better bounds in the theorem are obtainable, but these are sufficient.)

4.3   Proof Sketch

We begin by analysing the integrity events. *Count failures* cannot happen. If we get an inconsistent result, then either the equality of discrete logarithm proofs used by the decryption algorithm or the shuffle proofs are wrong. The soundness errors of the particular proofs we use are negligible (and unconditional), so an *inconsistent result* happens with negligible probability. The same analysis applies to *non-unique results* as well as *inconsistent verification*.

We now move on to analysing the privacy event. The proof is structured as a sequence of games. We begin by simulating the honestly generated non-interactive proofs during ballot casting. This allows us to randomize the check values $\hat{x}_v$ in honestly generated ballot proofs, so that we afterwards can embed a trapdoor in h_v. The trapdoors allow us to extract ballots from adversarially generated ciphertexts. The shuffle we use also allows us to extract permutations from adversarially generated shuffles by tampering with a random oracle. This allows us to use the ballots from chosen ciphertext queries to simulate the decryption, so we no longer use the decryption key. The next step is to also simulate the honest shuffles, before randomising the honestly generated ciphertexts (including encrypted trackers) and the re-randomisations of these ciphertexts. Finally, we sample tracker commitments at random and compute the openings from tracker generation using the ClaimTracker algorithm. This change is not observable, and makes the computation of tracker commitments and openings independent of the challenge bit. This makes the entire game independent of the challenge bit, proving that the adversary has no advantage.

The complete security proof can be found in the full version [21].

5   Other Variants of Selene

There are [30,31] some challenges tied to the use of trackers in Selene. First, if the coercer is also a voter, there is a possibility that a coerced voter points to the coercer's own tracker when employing the coercion evasion strategy. Second, publishing the trackers in the clear next to the ballots might affect the voters' *perceived* privacy, and some might find this troublesome.

To address the first challenge, the authors of Selene have proposed a variant they call Selene II. Informally, the idea is to provide each voter with a set of alternative (or dummy) trackers, one for each possible candidate, in a way that the set of alternative trackers is unique to each voter. This way, it is not possible for a coerced voter to accidentally point to the coercer's tracker. However, trackers are still published in the clear.

Both challenges are also addressed by Ryan *et al.* [30], who have proposed a voting system they call Hyperion. The idea is to only publish commitments next to the plaintext ballots, rather than plaintext trackers. Furthermore, to avoid the issue that voters might accidentally point to the coercer's own tracker, each voter is given their unique view of the bulletin board.

For both Selene II [31] and Hyperion [30], we refer to the original papers for the full details of the constructions, but we briefly describe here how these systems fit into our framework. We first remark that in Selene II, it is necessary that the encryption system used to encrypt the ballots supports *plaintext equivalence tests* (PETs). As in the original description of Selene, we use ElGamal encryption to encrypt the ballots, so PETs are indeed supported (see e.g. [24]).

For Selene II, we need to change the TrackerGen algorithm so that it outputs $c+1$ trackers for each voter, where c is the number of candidates, and c "dummy" ciphertexts, one ciphertext for each candidate. We let the last tracker be the one that is sent to the voter to be used for verification. By construction, for all voters there will be an extra encrypted ballot for each candidate. Thus, the DecryptResult algorithm works similarly as for Selene, except that it needs to subtract n_v votes for each candidate, where n_v is the number of voters. The *voting protocol* must also be changed. Before notifying the voters of their tracking numbers, the EA must now perform a PET between each voter's submitted ciphertext, and each of the "dummy" ciphertexts belonging to the voter, before removing the ciphertext (and the corresponding tracker) containing the same candidate as the voter voted for. This way, all voters receive a set of trackers, each pointing to a different candidate, which is unique to them. The opening to their real trackers is transmitted as usual, and thus the ExtractTracker algorithm works as in Selene. The ClaimTracker algorithm also works exactly as in Selene, except that voters now can choose a tracker from their personal set of dummy trackers, thus avoiding the risk of accidentally choosing the coercer's tracker.

For Hyperion, the modification of the TrackerGen algorithm is straight forward: we simply let it compute tracker commitments as described in [30], namely by (for each voter) sampling a random number r_i and computing the commitment as $\mathsf{vpk}_i^{r_i}$. At the same time, an opening is computed as $op_i \leftarrow g^{r_i}$. The Shuffle algorithm still shuffles the list of encrypted ballots and tracker commitments in parallel, in the sense that they are subjected to the same permutation. However, the encrypted ballots are put through the same re-encryption shuffle as before, but the tracker commitments are put through an *exponentiation mix*, raising all commitments to a common secret power s. The DecryptResult algorithm now performs additional exponentiation mixes to the commitments, one mix for each voter (by raising the commitment to a secret power s_i, unique to each voter), giving the voters their own unique view of the result. For each voter, it also computes the final opening to their commitments, as $op_i \leftarrow g^{r_i \cdot s \cdot s_i}$. Again, we need to change the voting protocol, this time so that each voter actually receives their own view of the bulletin board. The ExtractTracker algorithm raises the opening op_i to the voter's secret key and loops through the bulletin board to find a matching commitment. The ClaimTracker algorithm uses the voter's secret key to compute an opening to a commitment pointing to the coercer's desired ballot.

Acknowledgments. We thank the anonymous reviewers at E-Vote-ID for their helpful comments. This work was supported by the Luxembourg National Research Fund (FNR) and the Research Council of Norway (NFR) for the joint project SURCVS (FNT project ID 11747298, NFR project ID 275516). Thomas Haines is the recipient of an Australian Research Council Australian Discovery Early Career Award (project number DE220100595).

References

1. Final report of IACR electronic voting committee. https://www.iacr.org/elections/eVoting/finalReportHelios_2010-09-27.html. Accessed 05 May 2023
2. Adida, B.: Helios: web-based open-audit voting. In: van Oorschot, P.C. (ed.) USENIX Security 2008, pp. 335–348. USENIX Association (2008)
3. Baloglu, S., Bursuc, S., Mauw, S., Pang, J.: Election verifiability in receipt-free voting protocols. In: 2023 2023 IEEE 36th Computer Security Foundations Symposium (CSF) (CSF), pp. 63–78. IEEE Computer Society, Los Alamitos (2023). https://doi.org/10.1109/CSF57540.2023.00005
4. Benaloh, J.: Verifiable Secret-Ballot Elections. Ph.D. thesis (September 1987). https://www.microsoft.com/en-us/research/publication/verifiable-secret-ballot-elections/
5. Benaloh, J.C., Tuinstra, D.: Receipt-free secret-ballot elections (extended abstract). In: 26th ACM STOC, pp. 544–553. ACM Press (1994). https://doi.org/10.1145/195058.195407
6. Bernhard, D., Cortier, V., Galindo, D., Pereira, O., Warinschi, B.: A comprehensive analysis of game-based ballot privacy definitions. Cryptology ePrint Archive, Report 2015/255 (2015). https://eprint.iacr.org/2015/255
7. Chaidos, P., Cortier, V., Fuchsbauer, G., Galindo, D.: BeleniosRF: a non-interactive receipt-free electronic voting scheme. In: Weippl, E.R., Katzenbeisser, S., Kruegel, C., Myers, A.C., Halevi, S. (eds.) ACM CCS 2016, pp. 1614–1625. ACM Press (2016). https://doi.org/10.1145/2976749.2978337
8. Chaum, D., Pedersen, T.P.: Wallet databases with observers. In: Brickell, E.F. (ed.) CRYPTO 1992. LNCS, vol. 740, pp. 89–105. Springer, Heidelberg (1993). https://doi.org/10.1007/3-540-48071-4_7
9. Clarkson, M.R., Chong, S., Myers, A.C.: Civitas: toward a secure voting system. In: 2008 IEEE Symposium on Security and Privacy, pp. 354–368. IEEE Computer Society Press (2008). https://doi.org/10.1109/SP.2008.32

10. Cortier, V., Dragan, C.C., Dupressoir, F., Schmidt, B., Strub, P.Y., Warinschi, B.: Machine-checked proofs of privacy for electronic voting protocols. In: 2017 IEEE Symposium on Security and Privacy, pp. 993–1008. IEEE Computer Society Press (2017). https://doi.org/10.1109/SP.2017.28

11. Cortier, V., Dragan, C.C., Dupressoir, F., Warinschi, B.: Machine-checked proofs for electronic voting: privacy and verifiability for Belenios. In: Chong, S., Delaune, S. (eds.) CSF 2018 Computer Security Foundations Symposium, pp. 298–312. IEEE Computer Society Press (2018). https://doi.org/10.1109/CSF.2018.00029

12. Cortier, V., Galindo, D., Küsters, R., Mueller, J., Truderung, T.: SoK: verifiability notions for E-voting protocols. In: 2016 IEEE Symposium on Security and Privacy, pp. 779–798. IEEE Computer Society Press (2016). https://doi.org/10.1109/SP.2016.52

13. Cortier, V., Gaudry, P., Glondu, S.: Belenios: a simple private and verifiable electronic voting system. In: Guttman, J.D., Landwehr, C.E., Meseguer, J., Pavlovic, D. (eds.) Foundations of Security, Protocols, and Equational Reasoning. LNCS, vol. 11565, pp. 214–238. Springer, Cham (2019). https://doi.org/10.1007/978-3-030-19052-1_14

14. Cortier, V., Gaudry, P., Yang, Q.: Is the JCJ voting system really coercion-resistant? Cryptology ePrint Archive, Report 2022/430 (2022). https://eprint.iacr.org/2022/430

15. Cortier, V., Lallemand, J., Warinschi, B.: Fifty shades of ballot privacy: privacy against a malicious board. In: Jia, L., Küsters, R. (eds.) CSF 2020 Computer Security Foundations Symposium, pp. 17–32. IEEE Computer Society Press (2020). https://doi.org/10.1109/CSF49147.2020.00010

16. Damgård, I.: Commitment schemes and zero-knowledge protocols. In: Damgård, I.B. (ed.) EEF School 1998. LNCS, vol. 1561, pp. 63–86. Springer, Heidelberg (1999). https://doi.org/10.1007/3-540-48969-X_3

17. Distler, V., Zollinger, M.L., Lallemand, C., Roenne, P.B., Ryan, P.Y.A., Koenig, V.: Security - visible, yet unseen? CHI '19, pp. 1–13. Association for Computing Machinery, New York (2019). https://doi.org/10.1145/3290605.3300835

18. Dragan, C.C., et al.: Machine-checked proofs of privacy against malicious boards for Selene & co. In: CSF 2022 Computer Security Foundations Symposium, pp. 335–347. IEEE Computer Society Press (2022). https://doi.org/10.1109/CSF54842.2022.9919663

19. ElGamal, T.: A public key cryptosystem and a signature scheme based on discrete logarithms. In: Blakley, G.R., Chaum, D. (eds.) CRYPTO'84. LNCS, vol. 196, pp. 10–18. Springer, Heidelberg (Aug (1984). https://doi.org/10.1007/3-540-39568-7_2

20. Gjøsteen, K.: Practical Mathematical Cryptography. Chapman and Hall/CRC, Boca Raton (2023)

21. Gjøsteen, K., Haines, T., Solberg, M.R.: Coercion mitigation for voting systems with trackers: a Selene case study. Cryptology ePrint Archive, report 2023/1102 (2023). https://eprint.iacr.org/2023/1102

22. Haines, T., Müller, J.: SoK: techniques for verifiable mix nets. In: Jia, L., Küsters, R. (eds.) CSF 2020 Computer Security Foundations Symposium, pp. 49–64. IEEE Computer Society Press (2020). https://doi.org/10.1109/CSF49147.2020.00012

23. Iovino, V., Rial, A., Rønne, P.B., Ryan, P.Y.A.: Using Selene to verify your vote in JCJ. In: Brenner, M., et al. (eds.) FC 2017 Workshops. LNCS, vol. 10323, pp. 385–403. Springer, Heidelberg (Apr (2017). https://doi.org/10.1007/978-3-319-70278-0_24

24. Jakobsson, M., Juels, A.: Mix and match: secure function evaluation via cipher-texts. In: Okamoto, T. (ed.) ASIACRYPT 2000. LNCS, vol. 1976, pp. 162–177. Springer, Heidelberg (2000). https://doi.org/10.1007/3-540-44448-3_13

25. Juels, A., Catalano, D., Jakobsson, M.: Coercion-resistant electronic elections. Cryptology ePrint Archive, Report 2002/165 (2002). https://eprint.iacr.org/2002/165

26. Karayumak, F., Olembo, M.M., Kauer, M., Volkamer, M.: Usability analysis of Helios-an open source verifiable remote electronic voting system. In: EVT/WOTE, vol. 11, no. 5 (2011)

27. Küsters, R., Müller, J., Scapin, E., Truderung, T.: sElect: a lightweight verifiable remote voting system. In: Hicks, M., Köpf, B. (eds.) CSF 2016 Computer Security Foundations Symposium, pp. 341–354. IEEE Computer Society Press (2016). https://doi.org/10.1109/CSF.2016.31

28. Pedersen, T.P.: Non-interactive and information-theoretic secure verifiable secret sharing. In: Feigenbaum, J. (ed.) CRYPTO 1991. LNCS, vol. 576, pp. 129–140. Springer, Heidelberg (1992). https://doi.org/10.1007/3-540-46766-1_9

29. Ramchen, K.: Parallel shuffling and its application to Prêt à voter. In: EVT/WOTE (2010)

30. Ryan, P.Y.A., Rastikian, S., Rønne, P.B.: Hyperion: an enhanced version of the Selene end-to-end verifiable voting scheme. E-Vote-ID 2021, 285 (2021)

31. Ryan, P.Y.A., Rønne, P.B., Iovino, V.: Selene: voting with transparent verifiability and coercion-mitigation. In: Clark, J., Meiklejohn, S., Ryan, P.Y.A., Wallach, D., Brenner, M., Rohloff, K. (eds.) FC 2016. LNCS, vol. 9604, pp. 176–192. Springer, Heidelberg (2016). https://doi.org/10.1007/978-3-662-53357-4_12

32. Sallal, M., et al.: VMV: augmenting an internet voting system with Selene verifiability (2019)

33. Schneier, B.: Applied Cryptography: Protocols, Algorithms, and Source Code in C, 2nd edn. John Wiley & Sons Inc, Hoboken (1995)

34. Schnorr, C.P.: Efficient identification and signatures for smart cards. In: Brassard, G. (ed.) CRYPTO 1989. LNCS, vol. 435, pp. 239–252. Springer, New York (1990). https://doi.org/10.1007/0-387-34805-0_22

35. Smyth, B.: Surveying definitions of coercion resistance. Cryptology ePrint Archive, Report 2019/822 (2019). https://eprint.iacr.org/2019/822

36. Smyth, B.: Ballot secrecy: security definition, sufficient conditions, and analysis of Helios. J. Comput. Secur. 29(6), 551–611 (2021). https://doi.org/10.3233/JCS-191415

37. Smyth, B., Clarkson, M.R.: Surveying definitions of election verifiability. Cryptology ePrint Archive, Report 2022/305 (2022). https://eprint.iacr.org/2022/305

38. Zollinger, M.L., Distler, V., Rønne, P., Ryan, P., Lallemand, C., Koenig, V.: User experience design for E-voting: how mental models align with security mechanisms (2019). https://doi.org/10.13140/RG.2.2.27007.15527

Verifiability Experiences in Ontario's 2022 Online Elections

Nicole Goodman[1] ⓘ, Iuliia Spycher-Krivonosova[1,2](✉) ⓘ, Aleksander Essex[3] ⓘ, and James Brunet[3] ⓘ

[1] Brock University, St. Catharines, Canada
nicole.goodman@brocku.ca, iuliia.spycher@kpm.unibe.ch
[2] University of Bern, Bern, Switzerland
[3] Western University, London, Canada

Abstract. Despite being one of the biggest international users of online voting with two decades of use, Canada has tended to use non-verifiable online voting systems. This has prompted concern about the verification of election results and potential impacts on public and administrator confidence in elections and democracy. In the 2022 Ontario municipal elections, however, about 9% of municipalities offered the option of individual verifiability to online voters. This article draws upon the experiences of two local governments of different sizes, resources, capacity, and online voting histories - Ignace and Markham - and their vendors to understand the considerations and challenges that come with the introduction of verifiability mechanisms in local elections. We identify deterrents to implementation and possible solutions to see an increase in uptake and improve the integrity of local elections.

Keywords: Verifiability · Online Voting · Election Administration · Canada · Municipal Elections

1 Introduction

As democratic elections increasingly become 'cyber elections', calls for measures to safeguard election outcomes and promote electoral integrity are growing [34, 27]. Voting technologies are of particular concern, given potential security vulnerabilities and possibilities for hacking or interference. Online voting systems attract notable attention because they are touted as offering the greatest benefits to voters in terms of access and convenience [14, 35], but pose the greatest risks to compromise election outcomes or public confidence should something go awry [36]. To counteract such effects, there are increasing calls from scholars and practitioners [3, 9, 26] that online voting systems used in binding elections be verifiable, notably meeting the requirements of end-to-end verifiability (E2EV) - a concept which ensures that voters can verify that their votes have been correctly cast and recorded (known as individual verifiability [22]) and any member of the public can verify the final tally of votes (known as universal verifiability [15]). Such mechanisms are regarded as "a revolutionary new paradigm to enable secure and transparent elections" that could enhance confidence in election outcomes [37].

© The Author(s) 2023
M. Volkamer et al. (Eds.): E-Vote-ID 2023, LNCS 14230, pp. 87–105, 2023.
https://doi.org/10.1007/978-3-031-43756-4_6

In response, many jurisdictions around the world have sought to adopt verifiable online voting systems [37]. In the Netherlands, for example, an online voting system with individual verifiability was used in the 2004 elections of the "waterschappen" in Rijnland and Dommel [23]. Likewise, in Norway, the online voting system used in the 2011 and 2013 local elections was said to be individually and universally verifiable [24]. In Estonia, the option of individual verifiability has been available since 2013 and the option of universal verifiability since 2017 [15]. Finally, Switzerland, which has one of the longest-running online voting programs, now legally requires an online voting system to provide "complete verifiability" [20]. Despite these examples and a commonly shared perception that E2EV is the future of online elections [33] however, verification mechanisms continue to be regarded as "new and novel concepts" [2].

A glaring example of a jurisdiction where verification is regarded as nascent is in Ontario, Canada. Ontario is one of the longest and largest adopters of online voting (based on the frequency of elections and the number of voters eligible to cast online ballots). Yet, most deployments are not verifiable. They are either conducted by systems without verifiability or election administrators opt out of enabling the mechanism. Online voting activity in Canada is concentrated at the local level without intervention from higher orders of government. Most countries that offer online voting have involvement from national governments leading the charge for systems with enhanced security. In Ontario, however, decisions about whether to use online voting, the type of system and its features are at the sole discretion of local governments.

In this article, we draw upon focus group data collected from a large (City of Markham) and small (Township of Ignace) municipality in Ontario, Canada as well as their vendors to better understand municipal experiences with advanced online voting systems and the considerations that affect adoption and deployment. Both municipalities introduced verifiable online voting systems for the first time in 2022 with very different resources, capacity, and history of use. Their experiences help explain why verifiable voting systems are not more readily used in Canada.

We use the term 'verifiable voting' to refer to online voting systems that offered individual verifiability to voters. This article is a part of an interdisciplinary research project focused on examining administrator perceptions towards, and experiences with, verifiable online voting systems, including E2EV, in Canada. While this article focuses on municipal experiences deploying individual verifiability, a second contribution systematically addresses the barriers to municipal uptake of verifiable voting via a province-wide survey with municipal administrators.

By examining the election experiences of Markham and Ignace we accomplish three goals. First, we explore factors that prompt the adoption of verifiable voting at the local level and those that may deter governments from using them in both large and small municipalities. Second, we consider the benefits and challenges of using verifiable voting in lower-level elections. When local governments use advanced voting technologies are they satisfied? Do they see improvements in security, fraud or voter confidence? Would they opt to use such technologies again? Does municipal size make a difference? Finally, we discuss how to overcome barriers to the implementation of verifiable online voting systems to improve electoral integrity in lower-level elections.

The Ontario Case. Online voting in Canada is most frequently deployed by municipal governments for local elections, but it is also used by Indigenous communities, unions, political parties, and by some provincial and territorial election agencies in more limited capacities [38]. Currently used by municipalities in the provinces of Ontario and Nova Scotia, adoption in Ontario is by far the greatest given the number of municipalities that run elections (49 in Nova Scotia compared to 414 in Ontario) and the longest-standing history of implementation, commencing in 2003. About 3.8 million voters were eligible to cast an online ballot in the 2022 Ontario municipal elections.

Online voting implementation in Ontario happens contrary to common drivers of usage [17]. Many cities have sizable senior populations and lack robust internet infrastructure. Majority of municipalities drop paper ballots [36]. Under Canada's multi-level governance structure, the sub-national governments (provinces and territories) are responsible for writing the acts that govern local elections. In Ontario, the Municipal Elections Act includes a provision to deploy alternative forms of voting and gives municipalities autonomy to make their own decisions about which voting methods to use. This discretion has resulted in implementation approaches that differ on the period in which online voting is available, the process to authenticate voters, the voting modes used, the types of online voting systems (e.g., blockchain) and their abilities to verify election results. This latter consideration is our main interest in this article.

The first five election cycles (2003–2018) where online voting was offered were largely characterized by the use of relatively 'generic' technology, which relied upon web-based platforms without verification capabilities. The 2022 municipal elections, however, saw an increasing number of municipalities introduce individual verifiability (see Table 1). To the best of our knowledge, such systems were offered by four of six vendors that provided services to 102 municipalities (out of 222 in total that used online voting). Two vendors - Scytl and Neuvote/ Smartmatic - offered individual verifiability by way of a downloadable application where verification was available for a limited time after casting a ballot. Two other vendors - Simply Voting and Voatz - offered web-based verification after the close of the polls. With Voatz, voters also had the option to verify their ballots in the voting application.

Case Information. Markham and Ignace chose vendors with verification applications. The process involved downloading the application from the App Store or Google Play to their mobile device. Upon casting their ballot, voters had 30 min to verify that their vote was cast as intended. For Scytl's Verify app voters were required to scan the QR code on their voting confirmation screen and enter their voter PIN and date of birth to access a secure preview of their ballot and confirm that their selections matched how they voted [32]. In the case of Neuvote/Smartmatic's TIVI Verifier app voters scanned a QR code on the voter confirmation screen to review their selections and confirm their correctness, however, no additional credential was required.

The City of Markham was the largest of twelve municipalities in Ontario to first adopt online voting in 2003. At the time, Markham housed IBM Canada's headquarters, which led many to view the community as a technical leader [40]. The city has continued to be a leader in online voting by forming community partnerships, surveying voters, and trialing new technologies to improve voter experiences and innovate elections. The decision to use a verifiable online voting system was motivated by increasing global public skepticism around elections, notably disinformation. Officials saw it as a means to strengthen the integrity of the vote. Online voting in Markham's 2022 election was available from October 14 to 24, while paper ballots were offered at select polls from October 20 to 22. Paper ballots and touchscreen voting were also available at the returning office the entire voting period. To cast an online ballot, voters input a 16-digit numeric code from their Voter Information Letter (VIL) and date of birth.

Table 1: Ontario municipalities with individual verifiability in the 2022 elections*

Municipality name	Population	Vendor	# online ballots cast	# online ballots verified
Arnprior	7504	Voatz	3064	27
Atikokan	2753	Scytl	1140	0
Baldwin	620	Scytl	220	0
Blind River	3472	Scytl	383	0
Centre Wellington	28191	Scytl	9130	0
Greater Madawaska	5232	Voatz	1617	20
Grimsby	23981	Voatz	6096	149
Huron Shores	1664	Scytl	830	0
Ignace	1202	Neuvote/ Smartmatic	725	N/A
LaSalle	30180	Scytl	6868	8
Manitouwadge	1937	Scytl	841	0
Marathon	3273	Scytl	1044	0
Markham	328966	Scytl	64864	2504
McNab/ Braeside	6786	Voatz	2629	25
Quinte West	46560	Simply Voting	10587	N/A
Red Lake	1260	Simply Voting	1730	N/A
Sables-Spanish River	3214	Scytl	1093	0
West Lincoln	12559	Voatz	2467	72
West Perth	6963	Voatz	2761	14
Woolwich	25006	Scytl	5283	2
Vaughan	306233	Scytl	36641	617

* Neuvote/Smartmatic and Simply Voting reported not tracking the number of verified ballots so we are unable to collect verification data for those municipalities.

The Township of Ignace, by comparison, used online voting for the first time in 2022. Administrators became interested in verifiability since they were expecting a contested election. Allegations on social media suggested that someone may hack the election, and administrators liked the additional assurance that verification gave voters in the election outcome. The administration had limited experience with online voting and "no knowledge of the logistics involved", however, the township had run an all-mail election in 2014. Online voting was the only voting option in Ignace's 2022 municipal election, available from October 11 to 24. To vote online, voters input a 25-digit alphanumeric code from their VIL and date of birth as a second credential.

2 Literature Review

Choosing Verifiable Voting (or not) and Low-Stakes Elections. Previous research on verifiability of online voting has explored "why election organizers still largely opt for systems that are not verifiable and how this could be changed" [41, p.555]. Research suggests that it is easier for election administrators to decide in favor of "black-box solutions that are directly advertised by the vendors" [41, p.559]. This assumes that vendors do not offer verification mechanisms by default, and that administrators do not necessarily have the capacity to actively request them from vendors. The reasons why vendors do not offer online voting systems with verification mechanisms, according to [41], has to do with costs of developing them, lack of promotion by the market, and their profitability. This explanation suggests that municipalities may not opt for verifiable voting systems. We explore this below in the context of Ontario.

Further insight into municipal rationales for adopting online voting systems with verifiability (or not) can be found in the literature differentiating low- and high-stakes elections. This strand of literature suggests that if online voting is ever acceptable, then it should only be in the context of low-stakes elections [6, 13]. While research on online voting claims that no binding public elections can be considered low-stakes [6, 13], elections research frequently defines local elections as such [5, 30]. Scholars argue that unlike in high-stakes elections, the financial costs of an online voting system is of particular concern for low-stakes elections [11, 16]. Furthermore, in terms of security, "a weaker threat model is [seen as being] suitable" [16]. E2EV studies, in particular, have established that economic feasibility can impact system uptake [2]. Scholars argue that despite benefits, verifiability "obviously raises the price" of an online voting system [10]. Thus, the costs of verifiable online voting systems may be a deterrent for municipal adoption, especially since many cities have small budgets. An additional deterrent related to security is the perception that verifiable systems increase the risk of voter coercion such as vote-buying [42] or provide voters with an ability to prove to others how they voted (see [8] for more on receipt-freeness). Municipalities might be hesitant to introduce verifiability if they believe it can increase the risks of vote-buying.

Another consideration involves the perceived costs of voting in low-stakes elections. Studies show that voters are more willing to forgo their ballots in lower-level elections, seeing them as low-stakes [4]. On this basis, municipalities may be less inclined to opt for verifiable online voting systems because they may not see the purpose of deploying additional security. Furthermore, the public policy and political economy theory assumes that in democracies it is not only public institutions and politicians that define policies, but also voters, who "tend to focus on the direct effects of the policy change and underappreciate the indirect effects" [7, p.3]. Thus, it is possible that voters do not demand verifiable online voting because they might focus on the direct effects of the policy change (like increased costs and complexity) and underappreciate indirect effects (like increased security). Based on this another explanation for municipal adoption (or lack thereof) may be voter demand and/or enhanced public confidence.

Government Perceptions, Benefits, and Challenges. To date little is known about government experiences with and perceptions of verifiable voting systems. Most verifiable voting implementation has been driven by higher order governments and analyses of these deployments have been conducted by computer scientists focusing on system security [10, 12, 29] or usability [18]. Few contributions are situated in the social sciences [24] and none of which we are aware address election administrators' rationales for adopting verifiable systems nor their perspectives on the outcomes of these trials. Moynihan & Lavertu [19] suggest looking at administrators' technology preferences. They find that election administrators' decision-making regarding technology is frequently shaped by biases. Due to these biases municipalities may be less inclined to try something new (like a verifiable online voting system) because they prefer systems that they have already tried. Similarly, there could be information gaps wherein some local bureaucrats may not understand the meaning of E2EV and the benefits it offers. On the flip side, the "faith in technology bias", is a potential driver for using verifiable systems as the most advanced ones.

Administrators' experience is important because, at least in Canada, officials play a key role in deciding whether verifiability will be implemented. To enhance the security of online elections we need to understand what stops administrators from implementing verifiability, challenges faced with introduction, and how to mitigate these obstacles. This article addresses these gaps by providing empirical evidence of administrators' perceptions of verifiability and their experiences implementing it. Highlighting these experiences can help address barriers to greater uptake in Ontario and elsewhere.

3 Case Selection, Data and Approach

Case Selection. This article primarily draws upon focus group data collected from two municipalities - the City of Markham and Township of Ignace - that used a voter verification application for the first time in 2022. Focus groups were conducted with municipal administrators and online voting service providers. We used a most-different case selection approach [28] to select the municipalities, which differ by size, urbanity, geography, population characteristics, internet infrastructure, online voting history, and vendor. Markham tendered services from Scytl, who has been providing online voting services in Canada since 2014, including in Markham. Ignace, by contrast, selected a newer company (Neuvote) who formed a partnership with an international corporation (Smartmatic) to provide online voting for the first time in an Ontario municipal election.

The Township of Ignace is the only municipality that used the Neuvote/Smartmatic TIVI Verifier application. It has a population of 1,200 persons, is based in the north and predominantly rural, has a sizable senior population (30 percent) which includes many seasonal residents, has poor digital infrastructure, and had not used online voting before. Selecting among other municipalities that provided individual verifiability but were served by another vendor, the City of Markham fit the criteria of the most-different case selection approach. In comparison to Ignace, Markham is a large municipality with a population of 328,000, is located centrally, classified as urban/suburban, has a balanced population in terms of age, excellent digital infrastructure, and has used online voting in five previous elections. The City of Markham also had the highest number of verified ballots of all municipalities based on available data.

The selected cases represent two distinct paths that municipalities in Ontario can take to move away from generic online voting systems to verifiable ones. One example is a municipality that has not used online voting before and tries a verifiable system for their first deployment, while the other has a history of use and transitioned to a verifiable system.

Data and Approach. As noted, this article is part of a larger study focused on understanding voter and administrator perceptions toward, and experiences using, verifiable voting systems. In this article we primarily draw upon focus group data obtained from municipal administrators and private sector vendors. To supplement and enhance this information, we also reference interview data with other municipalities that used verifiable voting. Four focus groups were conducted between November 4, 2022 and March 21, 2023: with election administrators in Markham (6 officials) and Ignace (3 officials) and with Scytl (3 officials) and Neuvote/Smartmatic (3 officials). Each focus group lasted between 1.5 and 2 h and followed semi-structured guides (one for municipal administrators and one for vendors) that were provided to participants in advance. All groups were structured around three themes: (1) the 2022 experience with verifiable voting; (2) barriers, and (3) solutions to E2EV adoption. Focus groups were recorded with participant consent and notes were taken. Some documents and additional information were shared by participants afterward via email.

We chose focus groups because the group environment allowed us to communicate with a wider range of stakeholders representing the public (e.g., clerks, treasurers, IT personnel, and election managers) and the private sectors (e.g., CIOs, product managers and IT staff). We performed note-based analysis [21], with video recordings allowing us to verify quotations. For analyzing focus group notes we applied qualitative text analysis techniques. We coded the text along the three predefined themes - drivers and barriers, benefits and challenges, and solutions - that guided the focus groups.

Finally, to better understand why so few ballots were verified in the other municipalities that adopted verifiable voting we administered a short questionnaire between July 4 to 19 to those cities and towns. All municipalities were contacted by email and asked to either take part in a 30-min interview by phone or Microsoft Teams or submit written responses. Seven of thirteen responded. Five municipalities answered our questions in an interview format, while two submitted responses via email.

4   Findings

Drivers and Barriers to the use of Verifiable Online Voting. What factors prompt municipal adoption of verifiable voting? Likewise, which considerations may deter local governments from using them? Focus groups with election administrators in Markham and Ignace and their vendors identified several drivers and barriers (see Table 2 for the summary). Interviews with other municipal officials confirmed them.

In line with the literature, both election administrators and vendors in Ignace and Markham noted ambiguity regarding *the meaning of E2EV and verifiability* as key barriers to uptake. In the administrator focus groups, even members of the same election team assigned different meanings to verifiability. One official saw it as "an extra step in building confidence, increasing transparency and accountability", while another highlighted its "added complexity" for stakeholders. A vendor further highlighted the knowledge gap by noting that of the 100 + clerks they spoke with, only around 20 percent understood the difference between E2EV and generic online voting systems. Confusion of verifiable voting was further seen in interviews with municipalities that used the service but did not have any verified ballots. One administrator observed that they used the verifiable option "by default", unaware that they could have opted out. Another official, where ballots were verified, remarked that a "better understanding of processes" would have helped implementation.

A second related barrier is *the absence of a definition of E2EV or verifiability*. This gap was felt by both the first-time online voting user (Ignace) and long-time adopter (Markham). As an election administrator from Markham noted, "[we] still try to understand E2EV better". Another election administrator from Markham remarked that their definition of verifiability has changed over the years, stating, "in previous elections we said that our elections were verifiable, but our definition evolved." Without definitions of these terms uptake in the municipal sector is likely to remain low.

Third, administrators cited concerns of many administrators that verifiable voting systems present *a higher risk of vote buying* since voters can show their unencrypted ballot to third parties. They noted that this was a reason many chose to opt out of the feature. Among other barriers, vendors cited the *higher cost of verifiable systems, election administrators' preferences for systems they have already tried, and a lack of external pressure from voters, candidates, the media, and higher levels of government to implement verifiable online voting*. As one vender representative remarked, "Generic solutions are low cost. They [administrators] do not necessarily understand and value the differences in the systems. Some people just do not want a change. And nobody told them that they need to". This correlates with the literature findings on the "status-quo bias" and "own judgment bias" defining the choice of technological solutions by election administrators [19]. Another official further emphasized that "a lot of times the low price is what matters the most" and is a key factor that decides RFPs.

It is surprising that election administrators from both Ignace and Markham did not identify cost as a barrier to verifiable voting adoption as the literature suggests [2, 10], despite the fact that the financial resources of these two municipalities vary significantly. Cost was also not raised as a factor in any interviews we conducted with other municipalities that offered individual verifiability. Typically larger municipalities can have election budgets upwards of $500,000 whereas some small towns have budgets of less than $25,000. Additional input from vendors clarified why cost may not have come up. One employee noted that another vendor offered all of their municipal clients the option of using an application for individual verification at no extra cost. This business strategy could have affected election administrators' perceptions of price.

Finally, an additional barrier is the need to review and re-write processes and policies when introducing verification mechanisms. This perception came out in the focus groups and interviews with larger municipalities. Many administrators in small towns did not see a need to revisit policies so long as testing of the verification mechanisms was conducted beforehand. Some did not even require testing. Our discussions suggest that small and large municipalities approach the need for revised policies differently, increasing the adoption effort for large places, albeit those cities have more staff to facilitate updates.

Moving on to consider drivers that motivate verifiable voting use in local elections, *education* was identified as driving early uptake. A vendor representative remarked that the diffusion of verifiable voting systems in Ontario happened, at least partially, due to their efforts to educate the market by disseminating videos and hosting webinars for the municipal sector. The other vendor and the municipal administrators echoed these comments. While large municipalities in our study already knew about verifiability, some smaller towns learned about it via a vendor open house hosted by Markham.

A second driver is *the expectation of a contested election*. As noted, the evidence-based aspect of online voting systems with verifiability mechanisms was of particular importance for Ignace as a precautionary measure given the allegations that someone may try to hack their election. Likewise, interviews with other municipal users echoed this sentiment as one official commented, "[We used it to] lend more validity and trust to people's vote." This was a common theme across municipalities of all sizes.

Finally, *administrators' preference for the most technologically advanced systems* was identified as a third driver. When describing their system, one vendor referred to it as "revolutionary" and "slightly ahead of the curve". This presentation may encourage adoption among municipalities looking to innovate with the latest technology - what the literature called the "faith in technology bias" [19]. It could also act as a barrier in more risk-averse cities. This sentiment of innovation was communicated by both the smallest and largest municipalities we spoke with.

Benefits and Challenges of Using Verifiable Online Voting for Local Governments. What are the perceived benefits and challenges local governments observe deploying verifiable voting systems? Do they perceive improvements in security, fraud, or voter confidence? Likewise, are they satisfied, and would they use a verifiable system in a future election? Overall, several challenges and benefits were reported. Not surprisingly, there were differences in reported benefits and challenges based on municipal size, resources, and previous experience with online voting.

One challenge identified by election administrators in Markham and confirmed in interviews with other larger municipalities that used verifiable voting is *the need to review processes when introducing verification mechanisms combined with the lack of established procedures*. This perception came out in the focus groups and interviews with larger municipalities whose comments focused on the need for procedures relating to dispute resolution and handling ballot challenges. While vendors often offer policy suggestions to support wording changes to municipal legislation, 2022 was the first time that the vendors who participated in our focus groups used verification applications in government elections in Canada which meant that some supports were not in place like they are for other areas of online voting. As one administrator remarked, "The vendor came with the [verification] tool but not the processes of how to use it in Canada [...].

We needed to do our own research [...]. We created the processes [for the Canadian context]". This example highlights the challenges associated with early implementation of a technology and the work needed to ensure processes are in place to support deployment. The need for internal capacity was further emphasized from an administrator when stating, "I do not know if I would do it [introduce verifiable online voting], if not for my team [IT-skilled people]. It is uncomfortable". As an administrator in Markham noted, "...we had to understand the process for how the system would enable us to cancel a ballot [if challenged after verification] and then how to reissue the voter new credentials to vote. And we had to figure out how to handle those in real time." In an interview another larger municipality noted that they were unclear on what would happen should a voter select the "not my selections" button on the verification app. The administrator remarked, ""What would happen if someone clicked that button? I wasn't entirely sure." Having more knowledge to work through these processes would enable greater municipal confidence.

A second challenge is *the complexity of deploying the verification application* and communication of information between vendors and local governments. Any new component in election deployment adds complexity working through and testing the new aspects [43]. This sentiment was observed by both municipal administrators, albeit to different extents, due to differences in resources, previous experience, and perhaps even vendor selection. Testing and proactively devising solutions to potential problems took time and additional care. Ensuring adequate testing was particularly challenging for Ignace, albeit it was less about the complexity of procedures encountered by larger cities. The Apple version of the verification application used in Ignace was only in French. Despite contacting Apple, a change was not made prior to the election ending, which may have affected uptake among English speaking voters. This challenge may be linked to a lack of previous experience with online voting on the part of the election administration or the vendor who offered the service in a municipal election in Canada for the first time. Some, but not all, small municipalities we interviewed also did less testing. "I maybe checked two of them [ballots]" remarked one official. By comparison, testing was less of an issue for larger cities. As a Markham official pointed out, the added benefit of having experience and an IT team was conducting numerous tests: "We did test it really thoroughly beforehand. I think we conducted four or five rounds of user testing, [and] ran several 100 test cases involving the app." The experiences of Ignace and Markham testing the verification applications before deployment were quite different. These experiences were associated with differences in resources, previous experience, and perhaps even vendor selection.

Educating voters about the verification application was a challenge for both Markham and Ignace, however, it seemed to be a bigger obstacle for smaller municipalities. While Markham had the greatest number of verified ballots (4% of voters), Ignace reported challenges, despite education efforts. The voluntary nature of individual verifiability and the fact that it was separate from the voting process was unclear to some Ignace voters and affected their voting experience. As one administrator remarked, "the app should have been brought up even before we brought up the online voting process. They [voters] thought it was mandatory but it wasn't." In addition, some voters were unsure whether their vote had been successfully cast when seeing the additional instructions and QR code. In comparison to Markham, which is urban, has a balanced population in terms of age, and excellent digital infrastructure, Ignace provided some insights for other jurisdictions that are rurally based, have poor digital infrastructure, and greater proportions of elderly voters. Many Ignace voters cast online ballots from public laptops at polling stations because they required assistance. Most voters did not have a device to download and use the verification application in the 30-min timeframe.

Municipalities that took part in interviews confirmed these sentiments noting that they would handle voter education differently next time. In many cases places with few to no verified ballots used one or two channels to communicate verification with voters, and in some cases, information was not circulated until part way through the election. One small municipality, for example, educated voters about verifiability via a public information session that was recorded and posted on the municipal website. All municipalities with verified ballots posted information on social media and dedicated election pages. They also embedded videos explaining the process. Markham's approach to include verification details on the voter card seemed to have the best conversion.

A final challenge that affected smaller municipalities to a greater degree was *the acclimation of races*. It is customary in many small towns to have some contests acclaimed, meaning that there is no challenger and no need for an election for that race. One municipality we interviewed had all races acclaimed except for the school board position, which is often perceived as a lower salience contest. The clerk attributed the low number of verified ballots to the fact that voters were less concerned about checking the accuracy of the ballot since the bigger ticket races were not included. It is likely that competition for bigger ticket races drives verification. This could be tested in future research.

Moving on to benefits, Markham highlighted that they received *far fewer inquiries about election security and integrity* than in previous contests. While the verification application could have contributed to this, it could also be explained in part as a spillover effect from additional communication efforts undertaken by the city. Based on election administrators' observation that either using, or learning about, the application, contributed to the "sharp decline in the number of inquiries", it may be that use of verifiable systems improves voter perceptions of election security and integrity, however, confirmation of this hypothesis would require further testing.

Other identified benefits were *greater transparency and security, as a result, the expectation for improved trust in the election and its outcomes*: "[with verification mechanisms] you don't need to trust our results, you can check everything yourself". Some officials felt that this contributed to the absence of an election challenge, even though one was expected. Likewise, it was observed by administrators in Markham and Ignace and their vendors that verifiability mechanisms provided benefits for dispute resolution by generating evidence for potential disputes: "when using online voting systems without verification, election administrators do not have any evidence to prove the correctness of the election results in case they are challenged, and sooner or later the election results will be challenged". These sentiments were felt equally among the large and small municipalities we spoke to in follow-up interviews. Transparency and security were the primary reasons cited for implementation. As one clerk commented, "we did it for security". Another echoed that it was to "lend more validity and trust to people's vote." These remarks highlight two questions worth future examination. First, whether the use of verifiable online voting increases voter trust and confidence; and second, whether it decreases the number of electoral disputes.

Thinking about the future, Markham and Ignace were asked about the likelihood of future use. Both municipalities took different positions. Ignace encountered additional challenges, the extent of which are not fully outlined above because some were attributable to implementing an online voting system for the first time or going all online, and not necessarily related to the verification application. The combination of issues arising from these circumstances makes it difficult to isolate feelings about verifiability in general. That said, there was a consensus among Ignace administrators that while they would be open to using online voting in the future it would not be the sole channel and it would probably not include verification, despite its benefits. As one administrator remarked, "I would get rid of the verification, because you already get a message [from the system], your vote has been cast, what else would you need? It created much more confusion. Less is more sometimes." If they were to use it in a future election it would require more voter education and clearer explanations early on.

Markham, by contrast, was more positive about using verifiable online voting again, including working to expand their definition of verifiability. As one official remarked, "…we definitely had some lessons learned about how we are going to approach this in the future, but it will be a mandatory element of any kind of election system that we're offering." Based on the perceived success of the trial there was also a sense that continued use of verifiable voting was now an expectation to ensure electoral integrity. Another official commented, "…verifiability is ultimately in service of trying to assure voters, candidates and all other interested parties that our election is being run with the same integrity that they would expect of a, you know, let's say, a more conventional voting channel." For Markham, using verifiability is now a foregone conclusion.

The differences in opinion in Markham and Ignace seemed to be related to their unique circumstances rather than an issue of municipal size. Of the municipalities that took part in follow up interviews, some with populations half the size of Ignace indicated that they would offer the verification application again. Despite having no verified ballots in one town a clerk commented, "Oh my gosh yes. I want to do it again." The focus from most municipalities was on improving communications to promote voter uptake. However, a couple of cities commented on useability, noting they would need to evaluate future use. One noted issue was *accessibility*. Voters were required to have a second device to verify their ballots, and this was less accessible to some, notably elderly voters in smaller rural communities. Navigating a QR code could also be difficult if digital literacy was an issue for voters. It was observed that this likely disproportionately affected certain groups of voters.

Another issue was that verification happened differently in municipalities depending on the online voting approach used. Cities that offered only online voting or that had a composite ballot had one code that could be used to verify a vote, however, places without composite ballots that offered multi-channel voting (where voters could switch between internet and telephone voting) had one code for each race. This meant that there was a verification code for up to four races: mayor, councilor, school board, and, if applicable, a regional position. Having multiple codes was communicated as a deterrent for voters since it made the verification process more complex and lengthier. One clerk commented, "We would use it again if it were a bit more user friendly. Now that we have more information you could set-up a printer and people could print their own." Using one code to verify the entire ballot would be a recommendation for future use.

Solutions for the Greater Adoption of Online Voting Systems with E2EV. Having identified the barriers to uptake of verifiable online voting systems and the challenges municipalities face in their deployment, we turn to possible solutions to encourage local governments to pursue verifiable systems. Our research provides some initial answers that are of interest to scholars, private vendors, and public and policy communities.

One noted challenge, communicated by both vendors and municipalities, is the lack of verifiable online voting systems on the Canadian market. However, most vendors offer some version of verifiability. This suggests that a key solution is *communication across vendors, across municipalities, and between them*. Notably, vendors should spend more time talking to each other and educating about verifiability.

A second dimension that came from speaking with vendors was the notion of *E2EV as a competitive advantage*. One vendor noted that their decision to invest in verifiability was "a conscious business decision", which, in their opinion, proved to be successful, given the number of municipalities they attracted as customers. Another vendor highlighted that the costs of E2EV development creates "huge barriers" for others to enter the market. This narrative of verifiable systems as a competitive advantage might encourage other vendors that currently do not offer the service to develop it over time. With more options, uptake among municipalities may grow. However, if local governments continue to opt out of verifiability, having a verifiable system could perversely become a competitive disadvantage for a vendor given the costs to develop and maintain it, especially in the context of lower salience elections.

There is also a need for an established, widely shared and "acceptable" *definition of verifiability and specifically E2EV* to "help election administrators and vendors to build it". In the absence of such a definition, municipalities are left to come up with their own interpretation or ignore it altogether. As one official remarked, "There's no one understanding, or definition of verifiability so municipal returning officers aren't prioritizing this feature as part of their procurement." Additionally, both election administrators and vendors emphasized the importance of establishing *standards* for online voting use, which could provide a forum for a definition. While there are no online voting standards in force for Canadian municipalities currently, some are in development. Should the published standard include verifiability, it could, in the words of one administrator, "pressure" vendors to develop systems with E2EV and election officials to use them. In addition to a clear definition and standards, an administrator in one of our cases highlighted the importance of building a "collective understanding" of the meaning and purpose of verifiability for administrators who write the RFPs and the vendors who provide the services. This understanding is important for municipalities of all sizes, capacities and history of implementation.

Similarly, election administrators in Markham and Ignace identified the need for "a collaborative environment across municipalities" to counter barriers in municipal education and offer lessons learned. One major gap identified was that many municipalities were unaware that their vendor had systems with verifiability. When one municipality called a meeting of other cities with the same vendor, they were surprised that "a number of municipalities didn't even know that they had the verify app available". This user group was effective at informing all clients of one vendor, but municipal clients of other vendors may have been unaware of the option. This example highlights the importance of *horizontal cooperation among municipalities*. Municipal cooperation has been an effective strategy for addressing other election delivery challenges including (1) drafting joint RFPs to lower the administrative burden; (2) conducting joint audits of candidates' financial statements; or (3) organizing user group meetings for municipalities working with the same vendor. Furthermore, municipalities in Canada have a vast experience in intermunicipal contracting and other forms of horizontal cooperation [31], which can be fruitful if applied to election delivery.

In addition, administrators in our focus groups pointed to *greater involvement from academia* to support uptake of verifiable voting systems. As one administrator put it, "Right now you have only our municipality saying it [verifiability] is good. Having the academic support would be great and having a review from the academic community is also helpful". Vendors also emphasized the importance of ensuring that online voting systems are transparent to the academic community to facilitate research and system scrutiny. One vendor remarked, "Right now the basics of that don't even exist". Greater vendor transparency and collaboration with scholars could educate the municipal sector about the benefits of verifiability in low-stakes elections. Likewise, one vendor emphasized the importance of creating online voting roundtables with experts, vendors, administrators, and regulators to promote inter-stakeholder cooperation.

To address challenges with *voter education* the City of Markham highlighted their willingness to share lessons learned with other municipalities. Markham had the largest proportion of voters verify their online ballots, pointing to the success of their voter education strategy. As noted, officials included information about the verification application on the VIL, but were careful not to use a QR code to facilitate voting, which caused confusion in other municipalities. As one official commented, "We...decided we're going all in on this. So we promoted it in our voter information letter and pretty much anywhere else that we could promote it." Inclusion on the VIL was not used in Ignace or any other municipalities that offered verifiability. Based on Markham's conversion it is a key solution to educate voters in future elections. Instructions on the VIL could clarify the voluntary nature of individual verifiability and the need for a second device. In addition, sharing information via social media and on municipal election pages and including demonstration videos were other strategies used by municipalities that were successful in getting voters to verify their ballots.

In addition to voter education, one vendor concluded that improving the usability of verification mechanisms could promote uptake. The vendor acknowledged that installing a one-time use app is a barrier for some voters. Municipal clerks that took part in interviews echoed that downloading an application may not be desirable or usable for all voters. In addition, the 30-min time limit and need for an additional device to facilitate verification were communicated as issues that deterred use. Finally, municipalities that offered multi-channel voting commented that having one code for verification rather than four would be more user friendly and encourage uptake. This latter point has more to do with the approach used, rather than the application itself. However, some municipalities that offered both internet and telephone voting got around this by only allowing verification for internet ballots. This meant that voters had one code for their entire ballot. Enhanced usability of verification mechanisms might motivate uptake and likewise encourage voters and candidates to request such features.

Table 2: Summary of findings

Drivers to uptake:	Barriers to uptake:
– market education; – expectation of a contested election and being able to generate evidence for dispute resolution; – administrators' preference for the most advanced systems	– no clear meaning of verifiability – no clear definition; – higher risk of vote buying; – higher development cost; – administrators' preference for systems they have already tried; – lack of stakeholder pressure
Implementation benefits:	**Implementation challenges:**
– fewer inquiries about election security and integrity; – greater transparency and security, and as a result, the expectation for improved trust in the election and its outcomes	– lack of established procedures; – need to review processes; – complexity of deploying and testing the verification application (includes communication with vendors); – educating voters; – a lack of motivation to verify ballots in low salience and acclaimed contests; – usability of verification mechanisms

Solutions:
– communication across vendors, municipalities, and between them
– perception of E2EV as a competitive advantage;
– an established, widely shared definition of verifiability, specifically E2EV, and standards for online voting use;
– horizontal cooperation among municipalities;
– greater academic involvement;
– voter education;
– improving the usability of verification mechanisms

5   Discussion and Conclusion

This article identifies factors that motivate and discourage use of verifiable online voting systems at the local level. Barriers such as a lack of voter pressure for verifiable online voting systems and drivers like market education have not been observed by previous research. We also consider the challenges and benefits of implementation and whether the deployment experiences of our cases were perceived as successes. Our analysis of Markham and Ignace's experiences point to mixed reviews. They also highlight the complexity of using verifiability in local elections. Despite education efforts, the problems identified by administrators supports previous research that online voting systems with verifiability can have low use and satisfaction due to complexity [1]. The low number of verified ballots in most municipalities that used it suggests that online elections in Ontario are at best verifiable but not verified. This raises questions regarding whether being verifiable but not verified is enough [39]. "If the system is verifiable but not verified it may not produce the evidence trail that it was designed to build" [25, p.341]. Involvement from academics to build a common understanding of the meaning and the purpose of verification in online elections and collaboration across academic, public, and private sector communities can build awareness among administrators and voters to encourage the importance of ballot verification.

Another recommendation that can be drawn from this research is for governments to take slow, small steps to build online voting programs and not try to do everything at once. Using online voting for the first time, going all online, and trialing a verifiability app may be too much. Likewise, introducing individual verifiability before universal verifiability may be a stepwise plan to develop sufficient processes, testing, and education to ensure success of implementation.

Municipal capacity and resources also play a role in the ease and success of verifiable online voting implementation. While large and small municipalities face many of the same barriers, drivers, challenges and benefits, there are subtle differences that could affect uptake and implementation. Larger cities spent more time re-tooling policies and procedures compared to smaller places which integrated verification without the additional work. The level of testing undertaken also varied by municipal size and community. Some small municipalities did numerous tests, while others tried the verification application a couple of times. Finally, based on our conversations, education, acclaimed races, and digital literacy and access (e.g., having a second device and navigating a QR code) seemed to impact smaller municipalities to a greater extent.

Leveling the playing field across small and large municipalities requires horizontal cooperation, resource sharing, and municipal collaboration on RFPs and testing. Tiered price offerings based on municipal size is something vendors might consider. Likewise, academics could partner with smaller cities to support implementation and evaluation. As Gebhardt et al. [10, p.32] note: "Procuring an E2E verifiable electronic voting system is not a simple task. This is a question of having the right resources available, both in terms of money and personnel." Collaboration presents a way forward here.

Future research should assess whether there is a relationship between verifiable online voting use and voter satisfaction and trust. It may be that certain types of technology have positive or negative effects on voter attitudes and orientations. Comparative work could also assess whether the same drivers, barriers, challenges, benefits, and solutions are replicated in other country contexts and what this means for the future of online elections. Finally, studies could assess the opinions of other election stakeholders toward E2EV such as candidates and the media.

Overall, most municipalities that used online voting in the 2022 municipal elections did not offer verification despite having the option to do so. Our data also show that offering verification mechanisms does not necessarily mean that voters will utilize them. However, a key part of usership involves education and communication, which municipalities agree could be more robust in future elections. The solutions presented in this article provide a way forward to encourage vendor development and municipal uptake, contributing to improved electoral integrity in Canada's online elections.

Acknowledgments. We extend our sincere thanks to the municipalities who supported this research by sharing their experiences - Ignace and Markham for participating in our focus groups - and to Baldwin, Blind River, Centre Wellington, Huron Shores, LaSalle, Woolwich, and Vaughan for taking part in interviews or completing our questionnaire. Thank you also to the vendors - Neuvote, Scytl and Smartmatic for taking part in focus groups and to Simply Voting and Voatz for taking the time to explain their online voting systems. Without the support of vendors and municipalities this research would not be possible. We are grateful to Mihkel Solvak for graciously shepherding our paper and to the blind reviewers for their helpful comments. Special thanks to Carlie Pagliacci and Noah Nickel who provided invaluable research support throughout the study. This research was financially supported by the Social Sciences and Humanities Research Council of Canada, Grant No. 892-2022-1079.

References

1. Acemyan, C.Z., Kortum, P., Byrne, M.D., Wallach, D.S., Schneider, S., Teague, V.: Usability of voter verifiable, end-to-end voting systems: baseline data for Helios, Prêt à Voter, and scantegrity {II}. In: 2014 Electronic Voting Technology Workshop/Workshop on Trustworthy Elections (EVT/WOTE 14) (2014)

2. Ali, S.T., Murray, J.: An overview of end-to-end verifiable voting systems. In: Hao, F., Ryan, P.Y.A. (ed.) Real-World Electronic Voting, pp. 189–234. CRC Press, Taylor & Francis Group (2016)

3. Benaloh, J., Rivest, R., Ryan, P.Y., Stark, P., Teague, V., Vora, P.: End-to-end verifiability (2014). arXiv preprint arXiv:1504.03778

4. Blais, A.: To vote or not to vote?: The merits and limits of rational choice theory. University of Pittsburgh Press, Pittsburgh (2000)

5. Bracco, E., Revelli, F.: Concurrent elections and political accountability: evidence from Italian local elections. J. Econ. Behav. Organ. **148**, 135–149 (2018)

6. Cortier, V., Gaudry, P., Glondu, S.: Belenios: a simple private and verifiable electronic voting system. In: Guttman, J.D., Landwehr, C.E., Meseguer, J., Pavlovic, D. (eds.) Foundations of Security, Protocols, and Equational Reasoning: Essays Dedicated to Catherine A. Meadows, pp. 214–238. Springer International Publishing, Cham (2019). https://doi.org/10.1007/978-3-030-19052-1_14

7. Dal Bó, E., Dal Bó, P., Eyster, E.: The demand for bad policy when voters underappreciate equilibrium effects. Rev. Econ. Stud. **85**(2), 964–998 (2018)

8. Dzieduszycka-Suinat, S., et al.: The future of voting end-to-end verifiable internet voting specification and feasibility assessment study internet voting today no guarantees end-to-end verifiability E2e-viv. US Vote Foundation (2015)

9. Election Assistance Commission. Voluntary Voting System Guidelines VVSG 2.0. (2021). https://www.eac.gov/sites/default/files/TestingCertification/Voluntary_Voting_System_Gui delines_Version_2_0.pdf Accessed 14 May 2023

10. Gebhardt Stenerud, I. S., Bull, C.: When reality comes knocking: Norwegian experiences with verifiable electronic voting. In: 5th International Conference on Electronic Voting (EVOTE) (2012)

11. Haines, T., Müller, J.: A novel proof of shuffle: exponentially secure cut-and-choose. In: Baek, J., Ruj, S. (eds.) Information Security and Privacy. ACISP 2021. LNCS, vol. 13083, pp. 293–308. Springer, Cham (2021). https://doi.org/10.1007/978-3-030-90567-5_15

12. Halderman, J.A., Teague, V.: The new South Wales iVote system: Security failures and verification flaws in a live online election. In: E-Voting and Identity: 5th International Conference (VoteID), pp. 35–53 (2015)

13. Hall, T.: Electronic voting. Electronic democracy, pp. 153–176 (2012)

14. Hall, T.: Internet voting: the state of the debate. In: Coleman, S., Freelon, D. (eds.) Handbook of digital politics, pp. 103–117. Edward Elgar Publishing, Cheltenham (2015)

15. Heiberg, S., Martens, T., Vinkel, P., Willemson, J.: Improving the verifiability of the Estonian internet voting scheme. In: Krimmer, R., Volkamer, M., Barrat, J., Benaloh, J., Goodman, N., Ryan, P.Y.A., Teague, V. (eds.) E-Vote-ID 2016. LNCS, vol. 10141, pp. 92–107. Springer, Cham (2016). https://doi.org/10.1007/978-3-319-52240-1_6

16. Hirschi, L., Schmid, L., Basin, D.: Fixing the achilles heel of e-voting: the bulletin board. In: 2021 IEEE 34th Computer Security Foundations Symposium, pp. 1–17, June 2021

17. Licht, N., Duenas-Cid, D., Krivonosova, I., Krimmer, R.: To i-vote or Not to i-vote: drivers and barriers to the implementation of internet voting. In: Krimmer, R., et al. (ed.) Electronic Voting. E-Vote-ID 2021. LNCS, vol. 12900, pp. 91–105. Springer, Cham (2021). https://doi.org/10.1007/978-3-030-86942-7_7

18. Marky, K., Kulyk, O., Renaud, K., Volkamer, M.: What did I really vote for? On the usability of verifiable e-voting schemes. In: Proceedings of the 2018 CHI Conference on Human Factors in Computing Systems, pp. 1–13, April 2018

19. Moynihan, D.P., Lavertu, S.: Cognitive biases in governing: technology preferences in election administration. Public Adm. Rev. **72**(1), 68–77 (2012)

20. OEV. Federal chancellery ordinance on electronic voting (2022)

21. Onwuegbuzie, A.J., Dickinson, W.B., Leech, N.L., Zoran, A.G.: A qualitative framework for collecting and analyzing data in focus group research. Int. J. Qual. Methods **8**(3), 1–21 (2009)

22. Pereira, O.: Individual verifiability and revoting in the Estonian internet voting system. Cryptology ePrint Archive (2021)

23. Pieters, W.: Verifiability of electronic voting: between confidence and trust. In: Gutwirth, S., Poullet, Y., De Hert, P. (eds.) Data Protection in a Profiled World, pp. 157–175. Springer, Dordrecht (2010) https://doi.org/10.1007/978-90-481-8865-9_9

24. Puiggalí, J., Cucurull, J., Guasch, S., Krimmer, R.: Verifiability experiences in government online voting systems. In: Krimmer, R., Volkamer, M., Braun Binder, N., Kersting, N., Pereira, O., Schürmann, C. (eds.) Electronic Voting. E-Vote-ID 2017. LNCS, vol. 10615, pp. 248–263. Springer, Cham (2017). https://doi.org/10.1007/978-3-319-68687-5_15

25. Ryan, P. Y., Schneider, S., Teague, V.: Prêt à voter—the evolution of the species. In: Real-World Electronic Voting, pp. 325–358. Auerbach Publications (2016)

26. Ryan, P.Y., Schneider, S., Teague, V.: End-to-end verifiability in voting systems, from theory to practice. IEEE Secur. Priv. **13**(3), 59–62 (2015)

27. Schneider, M.K.: Election security: increasing election integrity by improving cybersecurity. In: Brown, M., Hale, K., King, B. (eds.) The Future of Election Administration. Elections, Voting, Technology, pp. 243–259. Palgrave Macmillan, Cham (2020). https://doi.org/10.1007/978-3-030-14947-5_14

28. Seawright, J., Gerring, J.: Case selection techniques in case study research: a menu of qualitative and quantitative options. Polit. Res. Q. **61**(2), 294–308 (2008)

29. Springall, D., et al.: Security analysis of the Estonian internet voting system. In: Proceedings of ACM SIGSAC Conference, pp. 703–715 (2014)

30. Söderlund, P., Wass, H., Blais, A.: The impact of motivational and contextual factors on turnout in first-and second-order elections. Elect. Stud. **30**(4), 689–699 (2011)

31. Spicer, Z.: Delivery by Design: Intermunicipal Contracting, Shared Services, and Canadian Local Government. University of Toronto Press, Toronto (2022)

32. Verify Your Vote- City of Markham. City of Markham. https://www.electionsmarkham.ca/en/voting/verify-your-vote/. Accessed 10 May 2023

33. Zagórski, F., Carback, R.T., Chaum, D., Clark, J., Essex, A., Vora, P.L.: Remotegrity: design and use of an end-to-end verifiable remote voting system. In: Jacobson, M., Locasto, M., Mohassel, P., Safavi-Naini, R. (eds.) Applied Cryptography and Network Security. ACNS 2013. LNCS, vol. 7954, pp. 441–457. Springer, Berlin (2013). https://doi.org/10.1007/978-3-642-38980-1_28

34. Garnett, H.A., James, T.S.: Cyber elections in the digital age: threats and opportunities of technology for electoral integrity. Election Law J. **19**(2), 111–126 (2020)

35. Goodman, N., Pammett, J.H., DeBardeleben, J.: Internet voting: the Canadian municipal experience. Can. Parliamentary Rev. **33**(3), 13–21 (2010)

36. Hayes, H.A., Goodman, N., McGregor, R.M., Spicer, Z., Pruysers, S.: The effect of exogenous shocks on the administration of online voting: evidence from Ontario, Canada. In: Krimmer, R., Volkamer, M., Duenas-Cid, D., Rønne, P., Germann, M. (eds.) Electronic Voting. E-Vote-ID 2022. LNCS, vol. 13553, pp. 70–89. Springer, Cham (2022). https://doi.org/10.1007/978-3-031-15911-4_5

37. Haq, H.B., Ali, S.T., McDermott, R.: End-to-end verifiable voting for developing countries--what's hard in Lausanne is harder still in Lahore. arXiv preprint (2022)

38. Goodman, N., Gabel, C.: Internet voting: Strengthening Canadian democracy or weakening it. Digital Politics in Canada: Promises and Realities, pp. 90–111 (2020)

39. Teague, V.: Democracy, security and evidence let's have all three. ASIACRYPT (2018)

40. Goodman, N., Spicer, Z.: Administering elections in a digital age: online voting in Ontario municipalities. Can. Public Adm. **62**(3), 369–392 (2019)

41. Kirsten, M., Volkamer, M., Beckert, B.: Why Is online voting still largely a black box?. In: Katsikas, S., et al. Computer Security. ESORICS 2022 International Workshops. ESORICS 2022. LNCS, vol. 13785, pp. 555–567. Springer, Cham (2023). https://doi.org/10.1007/978-3-031-25460-4_32

42. Juels, A., Catalano, D., Jakobsson, M.: Coercion-resistant electronic elections. In Proceedings of the 2005 ACM Workshop on Privacy in the Electronic Society, pp. 61–70 (2005)

43. Spycher-Krivonosova, I.: The impact of internet voting on election administration: Directing implementation towards a blessing or a curse (Doctoral dissertation, Doctoral thesis, Tallinn University of Technology] (2022). https://digikogu.taltech.ee/en/Download/83043625-5340-46c1-a2f1-998f6323876d

Pretty Good Strategies for Benaloh Challenge

Wojciech Jamroga[(✉)]

Interdisc. Centre on Security, Reliability and Trust, SnT, University of Luxembourg
Institute of Computer Science, Polish Academy of Sciences, Warsaw, Poland
`wojciech.jamroga@uni.lu`

Abstract. Benaloh challenge allows the voter to audit the encryption of her vote, and in particular to check whether the vote has been represented correctly. An interesting analysis of the mechanism has been presented by Culnane and Teague. The authors propose a natural game-theoretic model of the interaction between the voter and a corrupt, malicious encryption device. Then, they claim that there is no "natural" rational strategy for the voter to play the game. In consequence, the authorities cannot provide the voter with a sensible auditing strategy, which undermines the whole idea.

Here, we claim the contrary, i.e., that there exist simple rational strategies that justify the usefulness of Benaloh challenge.

1   Introduction

Benaloh challenge [3,4] aims to give the voter the possibility to audit the encryption of her vote, and in particular to check whether the vote has been represented correctly. More precisely, the device that encrypts and sends the ballot must first commit to a representation of the vote. After that, the voter decides whether to cast it or "spoil" it, i.e., open the encryption and check its correctness. Intuitively, this should reduce the risk of altering the value of the vote by a malfunctioning or corrupt machine when it casts the ballot on the voter's behalf.

An interesting analysis of the mechanism has been presented in [6]. The authors propose a natural game-theoretic model of the interaction between the voter and a corrupt, malicious encryption device. Then, they claim that there is no "natural" rational strategy for the voter to play the game. More precisely, they claim that: (1) only randomized voting strategies can form a Nash equilibrium, (2) for audit sequences with bounded length, the voter gets cheated in all Nash equilibria, and (3) the Nash equilibria in the infinite game do not form an easy pattern (e.g., Bernoulli trials). In consequence, the voter cannot be provided with a sensible auditing strategy, which undermines the whole method.

In this paper, we claim that – on the contrary – there exist simple auditing strategies that justify the usefulness of Benaloh challenge. This follows from three important observations. First, we show that there *are* Nash equilibria in bounded strategies where the voter casts her intended vote with high probability. Based on this observation, we focus on a small subset of randomized strategies, namely the ones where the voter spoils the ballot with probability p in the first round,

M. Volkamer et al. (Eds.): E-Vote-ID 2023, LNCS 14230, pp. 106–122, 2023.
https://doi.org/10.1007/978-3-031-43756-4_7

and in the second round always casts. Secondly, we point out that the rationality of strategies in Benaloh challenge is better captured by Stackelberg equilibrium, rather than Nash equilibrium. Thirdly, a sensible Stackelberg strategy does not have to be optimal; it suffices that it is "good enough" for whatever purpose it serves. Fourthly, we prove that the Stackelberg equilibrium in the set of such strategies does not exist, but the voter can get arbitrarily close to the upper limit of the Stackelberg payoff. To show this, we formally define the concept of *Stackelberg value*, and show that it is always higher than the value of Nash equilibrium in the set of randomized strategies for the voter.

Related Work. Game-theoretic analysis of voting procedures that takes into account the economic or social incentives of the participants has been scarce. In [5], two voting systems were compared using zero-sum two-player games based on attack trees, with the payoffs representing the success of coercion. In [12], a simple game-theoretic model of preventing coercion was proposed and analyzed using Nash equilibrium, maxmin, and Stackelberg equilibrium. The authors of [22] applied Stackelberg games to prevent manipulation of elections, focussing on the computational complexity of preventing Denial of Service attacks. The research on *security games* [19], using Stackelberg equilibrium to design anti-terrorist and anti-poaching policies, is of some relevance, too.

2 Benaloh Challenge and Benaloh Games

We start by a brief introduction of Benaloh challenge. Then, we summarize the game-theoretic analysis of the challenge, proposed in [6].

2.1 Benaloh Challenge

Benaloh challenge [3,4] is a "cut-and-choose" technique for voter-initiated encryption audits, which proceeds as follows:
1. An empty ballot is generated and provided to the voter.
2. The voter fills in the ballot and transmits it to the encryption device;
3. The device encrypts the ballot with the election public key, and makes the encrypted vote available to the voter;
4. The voter decides to cast the encrypted vote, or to open and audit the encryption. If the encryption is opened, the ballot is discarded, and the voter proceeds back to step 1.

Benaloh challenge is meant to counter the threat of a malicious encryption device that falsely encrypts the ballot, e.g., in favor of another election candidate. Importantly, this should be done without compromising receipt-freeness of the voting protocol. In a broader perspective, the challenge can be applied in any communication scenario where the encryption mechanism is not trustworthy and plausible deniability is required on the side of the sender.

The idea behind the technique is that, if the voters audit the encryption from time to time, corrupt devices will be exposed and investigated. Thus, it does not pay off to tamper with the encryption in the long run, and the perpetrator would have little incentive to do that. At its core, this is a game-theoretic argument.

Condition	Voter payoff $u_V(n_{cast}, n_{cheat})$	Device payoff $u_D(n_{cast}, n_{cheat})$	Comment
$n_{cast} < n_{cheat}$	$Succ_V - (n_{cast} - 1)c_{audit}$	0	Voter votes as intended
$n_{cast} = n_{cheat}$	$-Fail_V - (n_{cast} - 1)c_{audit}$	$Succ_D$	Device successfully cheats
$n_{cast} > n_{cheat}$	$-n_{cheat} \cdot c_{audit}$	$-Fail_D$	Voter catches cheating device

Fig. 1. Inspection game for Benaloh challenge [6, Fig. 2]

2.2 Benaloh Challenge as Inspection Game

Intuitively, the interaction in Benaloh challenge can be seen as a game between the voter V and the encryption device D – or, more accurately, between the voter and the malicious party that might have tampered with the device. We will use the term *Benaloh game* to refer to this aspect of Benaloh challenge. In each round, the voter can choose between casting her intended vote (action *cast*) and auditing the encryption (action *audit*). At the same time, the device chooses to either encrypt the vote truthfully (action *true*) or cheat and encrypt another value of the vote (action *false*). Both players know exactly what happened in the previous rounds, but they decide what to do without knowing what the other player has selected in the current round.

A very interesting analysis has been presented by Chris Culnane and Vanessa Teague in [6]. The authors model the interaction as an *inspection game* [2]. The idea is very simple: V chooses the round n_{cast} in which she wants to cast the vote, and D chooses the round n_{cheat} when it will fake the encryption for the first time. Consequently, the voter's plan is to audit the encryption in all rounds $n < n_{cast}$, and similarly the device encrypts truthfully for all $n < n_{cheat}$. The players choose their strategies before the game, without knowing the opponent's choice. Their payoffs (a.k.a. utilities) are presented in Fig. 1, with the parameters interpreted as follows:

- $Succ_i$: the reward of player i for succeeding with their task (i.e., casting the vote as intended for V, and manipulating the vote for D);
- $Fail_i$: player i's penalty for failing (i.e., getting cheated for V, and getting caught with cheating for D);
- c_{audit}: the cost of a single audit; essentially, a measure of effort and time that V needs to invest into encrypting and spoiling a spurious ballot;

It is assumed that $Succ_i, Fail_i, c_{audit} > 0$. Also, $c_{audit} < Fail_V$, i.e., the voter cares about what happens with her vote enough to audit at least once.

There are two variants of the game: finite, where the number of rounds is bounded by a predefined number $n_{max} \in \mathbb{N}_{\geq 1}$, and infinite, where the game can proceed forever. In the finite variant, the voter chooses $n_{cast} \in \{1, \dots, n_{max}\}$, and the device selects $n_{cheat} \in \{1, \dots, n_{max}, \infty\}$, with $n_{cheat} = \infty$ meaning that it always encrypts truthfully and never cheats. In the infinite variant, the voter and the device choose respectively $n_{cast} \in \mathbb{N}_{\geq 1}$ and $n_{cheat} \in \mathbb{N}_{\geq 1} \cup \{\infty\}$. The structure of the game is common knowledge among the players.

Discussion. One might consider a slightly richer game by allowing the voter to refuse participation ($n_{cast} = 0$) or to keep auditing forever ($n_{cast} = \infty$). Also, we could include a reward $Catch_V$ that the voter gets when detecting an attack and reporting it to the authorities. In this paper, we stick to the game model of [6], and leave a proper analysis of the richer game for the future.

2.3 Are There Simple Rational Strategies to Cast and Audit?

Culnane and Teague make the following claims about their model (and, by implication, about the game-theoretic properties of Benaloh challenge):

1. There is no Nash equilibrium in deterministic strategies [6, Lemma 1]. Thus, a rational voter must use *randomized strategies* in Benaloh challenge.[1]
2. A Nash equilibrium in the *finite Benaloh game* can only consist of the voter casting right away and the device cheating right away; the argument proceeds by backward induction [6, Lemma 2 and its proof]. Thus, by [6, Lemma 1], there are no Nash equilibria in the finite Benaloh game, and a rational voter should use *infinite audit strategies*.
3. In the *infinite Benaloh game*, there is no Nash equilibrium in which the voter executes a Bernoulli process, i.e., randomizes in each round with the same probability r whether to audit or cast [6, Theorem 2]. Quoting the authors, "this prevents authorities from providing voters with a sensible auditing strategy." In other words, there are no "easy to use" rational strategies for the voter in Benaloh challenge.

The above claims have two controversial aspects: a technical one and a conceptual one. First, while claims (1) and (3) are correct, claim (2) is not. By Nash's theorem [15], every finite game has a Nash equilibrium in randomized strategies, and this one cannot be an exception. We look closer at the issue in Sect. 4, show why backward induction does *not* work here, and demonstrate that a clever election authority can design the procedure so that the voters do have a simple Nash equilibrium strategy to cast and audit.

Secondly, the authors of [6] implicitly assume that "sensible strategies" equals "simple Nash equilibrium strategies." As we discuss in Sect. 5, Nash equilibrium is not the only concept of rationality that can be applied here. In fact, Stackelberg equilibrium [20] is arguably a better fit for the analysis of Benaloh challenge. Following the observation, we prove that generalized Stackelberg equilibrium [13] for the voter in the set of randomized strategies does not exist, but V can get arbitrarily close to the upper limit of the Stackelberg payoff function. Moreover, there is always a Bernoulli strategy for the voter whose Stackelberg value is higher than the payoff in Nash equilibrium. In sum, Stackelberg games better capture rational interaction in Benaloh challenge, provide the voter with simple strategies, and obtain higher payoffs for V than Nash equilibria.

---

[1] A concise explanation of game-theoretic terms is presented in Sects. 3 and 5.1.

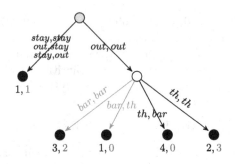

Alice \ Bob	bar	theater
bar	3, 2	1, 0
theater	4, 0	2, 3

Fig. 2. A variation on the Battle of the Sexes game. The only Nash equilibrium is indicated by the black frame. Stackelberg equilibrium for Alice is set on yellow background. The players' best responses to the opponent's strategies are underlined (Color figure online)

Fig. 3. Multi-step Battle of the Sexes. The initial state is filled with yellow, and terminal states with black. Transitions corresponding to dominated choices are shown in grey (Color figure online)

3   Intermezzo: Game Theory Primer, Part One

Here, we present a compressed summary of the relevant game-theoretic notions. For a detailed introduction, see e.g. [16,18].

Strategic Games. A *strategic game* consists of a finite set of *players* (or *agents*), each endowed with a finite set of *actions*. A tuple of actions, one per player, is called an *action profile*. The *utility function* $u_i(\alpha_1, \ldots, \alpha_n)$ specifies the *utility* (often informally called the *payoff*) that agent i receives after action profile $(\alpha_1, \ldots, \alpha_n)$ has been played. In the simplest case, we assume that each player plays by choosing a single action. This kind of choice represents a *deterministic strategy* (also called *pure strategy*) on the part of the agent.

The payoff table of an example strategic game is shown in Fig. 2. Two players, Alice and Bob, decide in parallel whether to go to the local bar or to the theater. The strategies and utilities of Bob are set in grey for better readability.

Rationality Assumptions. The way rational players choose their behaviors is captured by *solution concepts*, formally represented by a subset of strategies or strategy profiles. In particular, *Nash equilibrium (NE)* selects those strategy profiles σ which are stable under unilateral deviations, i.e., no player i can improve its utility by changing its part of σ while the other players stick to their choices. Equivalently, σ is a Nash equilibrium if each σ_i is a best response to the choices of the other players in σ. In our example, *(theater,theater)* is the only Nash equilibrium. Another solution concept (Stackelberg equilibrium) will be introduced in Sect. 5.1.

Multi-step Games. To model multi-step interaction, we use *concurrent extensive form games*, i.e., game trees where the players proceed in rounds, and choose their actions simultaneously in each round. The agents' payoffs are defined for each *play*, i.e., maximal path from the root to a leaf of the tree. A multi-step variant of the Battle of the Sexes, where Alice and Bob first veto-vote on whether to go out and then decide on where to go, is shown in Fig. 3. In such games, a deterministic strategy of player i is a conditional plan that maps the nodes in the tree to i's actions. Each strategy profile determines a unique play.

Nash equilibrium is defined analogously to strategic games. Additionally, σ is a *subgame-perfect Nash equilibrium (SPNE)* if it is a Nash equilibrium in each subtree obtained by fixing another starting point for the game. *Backward induction* eliminates choices that are *weakly dominated*, i.e., ones for which there is another choice obtaining a better vector of payoffs. Backward induction preserves subgame-perfect Nash equilibria, and can be used to reduce the game tree if the agents are assumed to play SPNE. For example, Alice's strategy *bar* obtains payoff vector $\boxed{3}\boxed{1}$, while *theater* obtains $\boxed{4}\boxed{2}$. Thus, the former strategy is dominated by the latter, and can be removed from the game three.

Randomized Play. Randomization makes it harder for the opponents to predict the player's next action, and to exploit the prediction. Moreover, Nash equilibrium is guaranteed to exist for randomized strategy profiles (Nash's theorem). In multi-step games, players can randomize in two ways. A *mixed strategy* for player i is a probability distribution over the pure strategies of i, with the idea that the player randomizes according to that distribution, and then duly executes the selected multi-step strategy. A *behavioral strategy* assigns each game node with a probability distribution over the *actions* of i, with the idea that i randomizes freshly before each subsequent move. By Kuhn's theorem, every mixed strategy has an outcome-equivalent behavioral strategy and vice versa in games with perfect recall. Note that deterministic strategies can be seen as a special kind of randomized strategies that use only Dirac distributions, i.e., $s_i(\alpha) = 1$. In that case we will write $s_i = \alpha$ as a shorthand.

4 Benaloh According to Nash

In this section, we look closer at the claims of [6].

4.1 Deterministic Audit Strategies in Benaloh Games

The first claim is that Benaloh games have no Nash equilibrium where the voter plays deterministically [6, Lemma 1]. This is indeed true. To see that, consider any strategy profile (n_{cast}, s_D) where V deterministically chooses a round n_{cast} to cast her vote, and D chooses n_{cheat} according to probability distribution s_D. If $s_D \neq n_{cast}$, then the device increases its payoff by responding with $s_D = n_{cast}$, i.e., cheating with probability 1 at round n_{cast}; hence, (n_{cast}, s_D) is not a Nash equilibrium. Conversely, if $s_D = n_{cast}$, then the voter increases her payoff by changing her mind and casting at round $n_{cast} - 1$ earlier (if $n_{cast} > 1$) or at round $n_{cast} + 1$ (otherwise); hence (n_{cast}, n_{cast}) is not a Nash equilibrium either.

Ultimately, V must use randomized strategies, so that D cannot precisely predict in which round the vote will be cast.

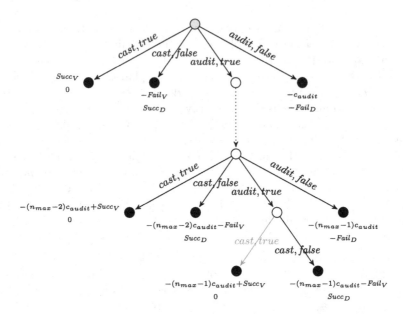

Fig. 4. Game tree for Benaloh challenge. V's payoffs are in black, D's payoffs in red (Color figure online)

4.2   The Rise and Fall of Backward Induction

Now, we turn to randomized voting strategies in Benaloh games with finite horizon n_{max}. It was claimed in [6, proof of Lemma 2] that all V's strategies where the voter does not cast immediately cannot be part of a Nash equilibrium. The argument goes by backward induction: D knows that V must cast in round $n = n_{max}$, so it can safely cheat in that round. Thus, the voter should cast in rounds $1, \ldots, n_{max} - 1$ to avoid being cheated, in which case the device can actually safely cheat in round $n_{max} - 1$, and so on. Unfortunately (or fortunately from the voters' point of view), the argument is incorrect.

To begin with, backward induction *cannot* be applied to games in strategic form nor to inspection games; it requires a proper representation of the sequential nature of the game. We propose the concurrent EF game in Fig. 4 as a model of Benaloh challenge with horizon n_{max}. Each level in the game tree corresponds to a subsequent round of the game. The players choose their actions simultaneously; if V casts, or V audits and D submits false encryption, then the game ends and the payoffs are distributed. If V audits and D encrypts truthfully, the game proceeds to the next round. At $n = n_{max}$, the voter can only cast.

Let us start with the final round of the procedure (i.e., the lowest level in the tree). D has two available choices: *true* and *false*, promising the payoff vectors of $\boxed{0}$ and $\boxed{Succ_D}$, respectively. Indeed, the choice to encrypt truthfully is dominated and can be removed from the tree, leaving only the right-hand branch. We can also propagate the payoffs from the remaining leaf to its parent (i.e., $-(n_{max} - 1)c_{audit} - Fail_V$ for V, and $Succ_D$ for D).

Consider now the second-to-last level of the tree. Again, the device has two choices: *true* promising $\boxed{0}\ \boxed{Succ_D}$, and *false* promising $\boxed{Succ_D}\ \boxed{-Fail_D}$. It is easy to see that none of them dominates the other: *false* works strictly better if the opponent decides to cast, whereas *true* obtains better payoff if the opponent does *audit*. Also the voter has now two available choices: *cast* with the payoff vector $\boxed{-(n_{max}-2)c_{audit}+Succ_V}\ \boxed{-(n_{max}-2)c_{audit}-Fail_V}$ and *audit* with $\boxed{-(n_{max}-1)c_{audit}-Fail_V}\ \boxed{-(n_{max}-1)c_{audit}}$. Clearly, the former vector obtains better payoff in the first dimension, but strictly worse in the second one. Thus, no choice of the voter is dominated. Since we cannot eliminate any choices, the backward induction stops already at that level.

Why is the intuitive argument in [6] wrong? After all, if the voter assigns a positive probability p to auditing in the round $n_{max}-1$, she knows she will be cheated (in the final round) with exactly that probability. The problem is, if she sets $p=0$, she is sure to get cheated right away! Thus, the voter should use p to keep the opponent uncertain about her current action, which is the usual purpose of randomizing in strategies.

4.3 Mixed Nash Equilibria in Finite Benaloh Games

We know from Sect. 4.2 that backward induction does *not* eliminate randomized audit strategies in finite Benaloh games. The next question is: what Nash equilibria do we obtain? We start with *mixed strategies*, i.e., ones represented by probability distributions $s_V = [p_1^V, \cdots, p_{n_{max}}^V]$ and $s_D = [p_1^D, \cdots, p_\infty^D]$, where p_n^V is the probability that the voter casts her vote in round n, and p_n^D is the probability that the device cheats for the first time in round n.

Support sets of Nash Strategies. First, observe that there are no subgames outside of the main path in the game tree. Thus, all Nash equilibria are subgame perfect. Moreover, backward induction eliminates the possibility that the device encrypts truthfully in the last round, hence $p_\infty^D = 0$ in any Nash equilibrium. Consequently, we can represent s_D by $[p_1^D, \cdots, p_{n_{max}}^D]$.

Secondly, all the other probabilities must be nonzero, see the following lemma.[2]

Lemma 1. *If $s_V = [p_1^V, \cdots, p_{n_{max}}^V]$ and $s_D = [p_1^D, \cdots, p_{n_{max}}^D]$ form a Nash equilibrium, then for all $i = V, D$ and $n = 1, \ldots, n_{max}$ we have $p_n^i > 0$.*

Calculating the Audit Probabilities. We compute $p_1^V, \ldots, p_{n_{max}}^V$ using the standard necessary condition for Nash equilibrium in mixed strategies [16, Lemma 33.2]. If (s_V, s_D) is a Nash equilibrium with $p_n^V > 0$ and $p_n^D > 0$ for all $n = 1, \ldots, n_{max}$, then the following conditions must hold:

1. Every deterministic strategy of V obtains the same payoff against s_D, in other words: $\forall n_{cast}, n'_{cast} \in \{1, \ldots, n_{max}\}$. $u_V(n_{cast}, s_D) = u_V(n'_{cast}, s_D)$

---

[2] The proofs of the formal results can be found in the extended version of the paper [11].

2. Every deterministic strategy of D obtains the same payoff against s_V, in other words: $\forall n_{cheat}, n'_{cheat} \in \{1, \ldots, n_{max}\} \cdot u_D(s_V, n_{cheat}) = u_D(s_V, n'_{cheat})$

Consider condition (2). Using the payoffs in Fig. 1, we get:

Lemma 2. *If* $s_V = [p_1^V, \cdots, p_{n_{max}}^V]$ *is a part of Nash equilibrium then* $p_{n+1}^V = \frac{Succ_D}{Succ_D + Fail_D} p_n^V$ *for every* $n \in \{1, \ldots, n_{max} - 1\}$.

Theorem 1. *The mixed voting strategy* $s_V = [p_1^V, \cdots, p_{n_{max}}^V]$ *is a part of Nash equilibrium iff, for every* $n \in \{1, \ldots, n_{max}\}$:

$$p_n^V = \frac{(1-R)R^{n-1}}{1 - R^{n_{max}}}, \qquad where \ R = \frac{Succ_D}{Succ_D + Fail_D}.$$

Indeed, the mixed equilibrium strategy s_V provides no *simple* recipe for the voter. This is evident when we consider concrete payoff values.

Example 1. Take $n_{max} = 5$ and assume $Succ_D = 1$, $Fail_D = 4$, i.e., the opponent fears failure four times more than he values success. Then, $R = 0.2$, and hence $s_V = [0.8, 0.16, 0.032, 0.006, 0.001]$ is the unique equilibrium strategy for the voter. In other words, the voter should cast immediately with probability 0.8, audit once and cast in round 2 with probability 0.16, and so on.

4.4   Towards Natural Audit Strategies

So far, we have considered *mixed strategies* for the voter. That is, the voter draws n_{cast} before the game according to the probability distribution s_V, and then duly follows the outcome of the draw. An alternative is to use a *behavioral strategy* $b_V = (b_1^V, \ldots, b_{n_{max}}^V)$, where the voter does a *fresh* Bernoulli-style lottery with probability of success b_n^V in each subsequent round. If successful, she casts her vote; otherwise, she audits and proceeds to the next round.

Behavioral Nash Equilibria. First, we observe that the game in Fig. 4 is a game of *perfect recall*, i.e., the players remember all their past observations (in our case, the outcomes of all the previous rounds). Thus, by Kuhn's theorem, mixed and behavioral strategies are outcome-equivalent. In other words, the same outcomes can be obtained if the players randomize before the game or throughout the game. Below, we characterize the behavioral strategy that corresponds to the mixed strategy of Theorem 1.

Theorem 2. *The behavioral voting strategy* $b_V = [b_1^V, \cdots, b_{n_{max}}^V]$ *is a part of Nash equilibrium iff, for every* $n \in \{1, \ldots, n_{max}\}$:

$$b_n^V = \frac{1-R}{1 - R^{n_{max}-n+1}}, \qquad where \ R = \frac{Succ_D}{Succ_D + Fail_D}.$$

Example 2. The behavioral strategy implementing s_V of Example 1 is $b_V = [0.8, 0.801, 0.81, 0.83, 1]$. That is, the voter casts immediately with probability 0.8, else audits, randomizes again, and casts with probability 0.801, and so on.

n_{cast} \ n_{cheat}	1	2
1	$-Fail_V,\ Succ_D$	$Succ_V,\ 0$
2	$-c_{audit},\ -Fail_D$	$-c_{audit} - Fail_V,\ Succ_D$

n_{cast} \ n_{cheat}	1	2
1	$-3,\ 1$	$2,\ 0$
2	$-1,\ -4$	$-4,\ 1$

Fig. 5. Benaloh game for $n_{max} = 2$: (a) parameterized payoff table; (b) concrete payoff table for the values of Example 4

Behavioral Audit Strategies are Reasonably Simple. At the first glance, the above behavioral strategy seems difficult to execute, too. We cannot expect the voter to randomize with probability *exactly* 0.8, then *exactly* 0.801, etc. On the other hand, b_V can be approximated reasonably well by the following recipe: "in each round before n_{max}, cast with probability close to 0.8, otherwise audit, randomize freshly, and repeat; in the last round, cast with probability 1." This can be generalized due to the following observation.

In Benaloh games, we can usually assume that $Fail_D \gg Succ_D$. First of all, it is important to realize that the opponent of the voter is not the encrypting device, but a human or organizational perpetrator represented by the device. To be more precise, the strategies in the game are defined by the capabilities of the device, but the incentives are those of the perpetrator. Thus, the utility values defined by u_D should not be read as "the payoffs of the device," but rather the utilities of the external party who rigged the device in order to achieve some political, social, or economic goals. Secondly, the scope of the opponent's activity is not limited to the interaction with a single voter and to corrupting a single encryption device. Presumably, they must have tampered with multiple devices in order to influence the outcome of the vote. Consequently, the opponent is in serious trouble if even few devices are caught cheating. This is likely to attract attention and trigger investigation, which may lead to an audit of all the encryption devices, revision or voiding of the votes collected from those that turned out corrupt, and even an arrest and prosecution of the perpetrator. All in all, the penalty for fraud detection ($Fail_D$) is usually much higher than the reward for a successful swap of a single vote ($Succ_D$).

Theorem 3. *If* $\frac{Succ_D}{Fail_D} \to 0$, *then the equilibrium strategy* b_V *of the voter converges to the following behavioral strategy:*

$$\widehat{b_n^V} = \begin{cases} \frac{Fail_D}{Succ_D + Fail_D} & for\ n < n_{max} \\ 1 & for\ n = n_{max} \end{cases}$$

The finite Bernoulli strategy to audit with probability $R = \frac{Fail_D}{Succ_D + Fail_D}$ in each round except last seems reasonably simple. By Theorem 3, it is also reasonably close to the unique Nash equilibrium.

Making Things even Simpler for the Voter. In order to make Benaloh challenge even easier to use, the voting authority can set n_{max} accordingly. In particular, it can fix $n_{max} = 2$, i.e., allow the voter to audit at most once. That does not seem very restrictive, as empirical evidence suggests that voters seldom audit their votes [1,7,21], and even fewer are able to complete it correctly [1,9, 21].[3] The Benaloh game in strategic form for $n_{max} = 2$ is shown in Fig. 5a.

Theorem 4. *For $n_{max} = 2$, the behavioral NE strategy of the voter is:*

$$b_1^V = \frac{Succ_D + Fail_D}{2 Succ_D + Fail_D}, \qquad b_2^V = 1.$$

To make the analysis intuitive, consider the concrete values in Example 1.

Example 3. Take $Succ_D = 1$, $Fail_D = 4$. By Theorem 2, the behavioral Nash equilibrium strategy of the voter is $b_V = [\frac{5}{6}, 1]$. That is, the voter casts immediately with probability $\frac{5}{6}$, otherwise audits and casts in the next round – which is a rather simple strategy.

Also, recall our argument that, typically, $Fail_D \gg Succ_D$. In that case, p_V^1 becomes close to 1. In other words, the voter should *almost always* cast immediately, which is a very simple recipe to follow. Thus, contrary to what Culnane and Teague claim in [6], Benaloh challenge can be designed in a way that admits simple Nash equilibrium strategies of the voter.

4.5   Behavioral Audit Strategies are Simple Enough, but are They Good Enough?

We have just seen that finite Benaloh games do allow for simple and easy to use Nash equilibrium strategies. This seems good news, but what kind of utility do they promise for the voter? That is, how much will the voter benefit from playing NE in Benaloh challenge? For easier reading, we calculate the answer on our running example.

Example 4. Following Example 3, we take $n_{max} = 2$, $Succ_D = 1$, $Fail_D = 4$. Moreover, we assume $Succ_V = 2$, $Fail_V = 3$, $c_{audit} = 1$, i.e., the voter loses slightly more by getting cheated than she gains by casting successfully, and the cost of an audit is half of the gain from a successful vote. The resulting payoff table is presented in Fig. 5b.

We can now compute the Nash equilibrium strategy of the device using Lemma 1 and Condition 1 of Sect. 4.3. Consequently, we get $-3p_1^D + 2(1 - p_1^D) = -p_1^D - 4(1 - p_1^D)$, and thus $s_D = [\frac{3}{4}, \frac{1}{4}]$. Recall that the NE strategy of the voter is $s_V = [\frac{5}{6}, \frac{1}{6}]$. This yields the following expected payoffs of the players:

$$u_V(s_V, s_D) = -3\frac{15}{24} + 2\frac{5}{24} - 1\frac{3}{24} - 4\frac{1}{24} = -\frac{7}{6}$$

$$u_D(s_V, s_D) = 1\frac{15}{24} + 0\frac{5}{24} - 4\frac{3}{24} + 1\frac{1}{24} = \frac{1}{6}.$$

---

[3] In fairness, there is also some evidence that suggests the contrary [8, Section 5.6.1].

So, the voter gets negative expected utility, and would be better off by not joining the game at all! If that is the case, then a considerate election authority should forbid electronic voting *not* because there are no simple NE strategies to audit and vote, but because there is one and it is bad for the voter. The big question is: does Nash equilibrium really provide the right solution concept for rational interaction in Benaloh challenge? We discuss this in Sect. 5.

5   Benaloh According to Stackelberg

Nash equilibrium encodes a particular view of rational decision making. In this section, we discuss its applicability to Benaloh games, suggest that Stackelberg equilibrium is a much better match, and analyze Benaloh challenge through the lens of Stackelberg games.

5.1   Game-Theoretic Intermezzo, Part Two

Every solution concept encodes its own assumptions about the nature of interaction between players and their deliberation processes. The assumptions behind Nash equilibrium in 2-player games can be characterized as follows [17]:

1. Alice and Bob have common belief that each of them plays best response to one another, and
2. Alice believes that Bob has an accurate view of her beliefs, and that Bob believes that Alice has an accurate view of his beliefs,
3. ...and analogously for Bob.

Alternatively, NE can be characterized as a local optimum of strategy search with mutual adaptations. Informally, it represents collective behaviors that can emerge when the agents play the game repeatedly, and adapt their choices to what they expect from the other agents. Thus, it captures the "organic" emergence of behavior through a sequence of strategy adjustments that leads to a point where nobody is tempted to change their strategy anymore.

Is Nash equilibrium the right concept of rationality for Benaloh games? Note that the characterizations of NE are inherently symmetric. In particular, they assume that both players are able to form accurate beliefs about each other's intentions. This is *not* the case in Benaloh challenge. In line with the arguments of [6], the perpetrator has significant technological and motivational advantage over an average voter. For example, he can use opinion polls and statistical methods to get a good view of the voter's preferences. Even more importantly, machine learning techniques can be used to profile the frequencies with which the voter chooses to audit or cast. On the other hand, the voter has neither data nor resources to form accurate predictions w.r.t. the strategy of the encryption device. This seems pretty close to the Stackelberg model of economic interaction.

Stackelberg Equilibrium. *Stackelberg games* [20] represent interaction where the strategy of one player (called the *leader*) is known in advance by the other player (the *follower*). The follower is assumed to play best response to that strategy. The *generalized Stackelberg equilibrium (SE)* [13] prescribes the leader's strategy that maximizes the guaranteed payoff against the follower's best responses. We define and analyze SE for Benaloh games in Sect. 5.2.

5.2   Pretty Good Strategies Against Best Response

For simplicity, we assume that $n_{max} = 2$ throughout this section, i.e., the voter can audit the encryption at most once. Thus, the strategy of the voter can be represented by the probability p_V of casting the vote in the first round. Similarly, the strategy of the device can be represented by the probability p^D of cheating in the first round. We first establish D's best response to any fixed p^V and the voter's guaranteed expected utility against best response. These can be formally defined as follows.

Definition 1. *The* best response *of* D, *given* V*'s strategy represented by* p^V, *returns those strategies* p^D *for which the expected value of* $u_D(p^V, p^D)$ *is maximal:*

$$BR_D(p^V) = \mathrm{argmax}_{p^D \in [0,1]}(Eu_D(p^V, p^D)).$$

Note that a best response always exists, though it does not have to be unique.

Definition 2. *The* generalized Stackelberg equilibrium *for* V *is defined as the strategy that maximizes* V*'s expected payoff against best response. In case of multiple best responses to some* p^V, *we look at the worst case scenario.*

$$SE_V = \mathrm{argmax}_{p^V \in [0,1]} \inf{}_{p^D \in BR_D(p^V)}(Eu_V(p^V, p^D)).$$

For randomized strategies of the leader, the Stackelberg equilibrium does not have to exist (cf. Example 5). To characterize the leader's abilities in such games, we propose the notion of *Stackelberg value*.

Definition 3. *The* Stackelberg value *for* V *is the expected guaranteed payoff that* V *can obtain against best response in the limit:*

$$SVal_V = \sup{}_{p^V \in [0,1]} \inf{}_{p^D \in BR_D(p^V)}(Eu_V(p^V, p^D)).$$

Clearly, $SVal_V$ is always well defined. Moreover, the game has a Stackelberg equilibrium if V obtains the Stackelberg value for some strategy. Finally, for each $\epsilon > 0$, the voter has a strategy that ϵ-approximates the Stackelberg value, i.e., obtains at least $SVal_V - \epsilon$ against best response.

Lemma 3. *The best response of the device to any fixed strategy of the voter is*

$$BR_D(p^V) = \begin{cases} 0 & \text{for } p^V < p^V_{NE} \\ 1 & \text{for } p^V > p^V_{NE} \\ \text{any } p^D \in [0,1] & \text{for } p^V = p^V_{NE} \end{cases}$$

where $p^V_{NE} = \frac{Succ_D + Fail_D}{2Succ_D + Fail_D}$ *is the NE probability of casting in round 1.*

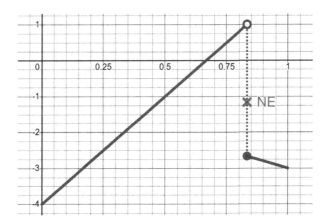

Fig. 6. V's payoffs against best response for the Benaloh game in Fig. 5b. The voter's payoff obtained by Nash equilibrium is shown for comparison

Lemma 4. *The voter's expected utility against best response is:*

$$Eu_V(p^V, BR_D(p^V)) = \begin{cases} p^V Succ_V - (1 - p^V)(c_{audit} + Fail_V) & for\ p^V < p^V_{NE} \\ -p^V Fail_V - (1 - p^V)c_{audit} & for\ p^V \geq p^V_{NE} \end{cases}$$

Example 5. The graph of $Eu_V(p^V, BR_D(p^V))$ for the parameters in Example 4 (i.e., $n_{max} = 2, Succ_D = 1, Fail_D = 4, Succ_V = 2, Fail_V = 3, c_{audit} = 1$) is depicted in Fig. 6. It is easy to see that the function does not reach its optimum, and hence the optimal p^V against best response does not exist. Still, the strategies based on p^V being *slightly smaller* than the Nash equilibrium strategy $p^V_{NE} = \frac{5}{6}$ are quite attractive to the voter, since they obtain payoff that is both positive and strictly higher than the Nash payoff.

The next and final theorem generalizes the example to arbitrary two-round Benaloh games. It shows that the voter has no optimal Stackelberg strategy in the game (point 1), but the value of $SVal_V = \frac{Succ_D(Succ_V - Fail_V - c_{audit}) + Fail_D Succ_V}{2Succ_D + Fail_D}$ can be approximated arbitrarily closely (point 2). That is, for each $\epsilon > 0$, the voter has a strategy that obtains at least $SVal_V - \epsilon$ against best response. Moreover, ϵ-approximating Stackelberg equilibrium is strictly better than playing Nash equilibrium (point 3). Lastly, approximate Stackelberg strategies obtain positive utility for the voter under reasonable assumptions (point 4).

Theorem 5. *The following properties hold for the Benaloh game with $n_{max} = 2$:*

1. *There is no Stackelberg equilibrium for V in randomized strategies.*
2. *The Stackelberg value of the game is $sVal_V = \frac{Succ_D(Succ_V - Fail_V - c_{audit}) + Fail_D Succ_V}{2Succ_D + Fail_D}$.*
3. *$SVal_V > Eu_V(p^V_{NE}, p^D_{NE})$, where (p^V_{NE}, p^D_{NE}) is the Nash equilibrium.*
4. *If $Fail_D \gg Succ_D$ and $Succ_V \geq aFail_V$ for a fixed $a > 0$, then $SVal_V > 0$.*

Thus, Stackelberg games capture the rational interaction in Benaloh games better than Nash equilibrium, and predict strictly higher payoffs for the voter.

6   Conclusions, or What Do We Learn from That?

In this paper, we analyze a simple game-theoretic model of incentives in Benaloh challenge, inspired by [6]. Contrary to [6], we conclude that the voters have at their disposal simple strategies to audit and cast their votes. This is especially the case if encryption audits are limited to at most one audit per voter. In that event, a pretty good strategy for the voter is to almost always (but not *exactly* always!) cast immediately in the first round. Interestingly, this is how voters usually behave in real-life elections, according to empirical evidence.

Moreover, we point out that rational interaction in Benaloh games is better captured by Stackelberg equilibrium, rather than Nash equilibrium. While the optimal Stackelberg strategy is not attainable for the voter, it can be approximated arbitrarily close by casting the vote immediately with probability *slightly lower* than for the Nash equilibrium. This is good news, because Stackelberg strategies (even approximate) promise strictly better payoffs for the voter than Nash strategies. And, under reasonable assumptions, they produce positive utility for V. Thus, using Benaloh challenge *is* beneficial to the voter, after all.

The takeaway advice based on this study can be summarized as follows:

1. Using Benaloh challenge is practical and beneficial to the rational voter.
2. Putting a strict limit on the number of allowed audits makes things easier for the voter. The election authority might design the voting system so that each voter can audit the vote encryption at most once.
3. The voters should not try to adapt to the strategy of the attacker, the way Nash equilibrium prescribes. Instead, they should stick to auditing the votes with a fixed (and rather low) frequency, thus approximating the Stackelberg optimum and putting the opponent on the defensive.

Discussion and Future Work. An obvious limitation of the current study is the assumption of *complete information* about the structure of the game. In particular, it is dubious to assume that the voter knows how much the adversary values the outcomes of the game. In the future, we plan to extend the analysis to an incomplete information game model of Benaloh challenge, e.g., in the form of a Bayesian game [10].

Moreover, the analysis in this paper is performed as a 2-player game between a single voter and the voter's device. It would be interesting to see how this extends to scenarios where the adversary controls multiple devices and plays multiple rounds with different voters. Last but not least, the players' payoffs for either failing or succeeding need further discussion. In particular, we assume that the costs of failure for the opponent are much higher than the benefits of success; this should be better justified or refuted.

Acknowledgments. The author thanks Stanisław Ambroszkiewicz, Peter B. Roenne, Peter Y.A. Ryan, and the anonymous reviewers of E-VOTE-ID for their valuable comments, suggestions, and discussions. The work has been supported by NCBR Poland and FNR Luxembourg under the PolLux/FNR-CORE projects STV (POLLUX-VII/1/

2019 and C18/IS/12685695/IS/STV/Ryan), SpaceVote (POLLUX-XI/14/SpaceVote/2023 and C22/IS/17232062/SpaceVote) and PABLO (C21/IS/16326754/PABLO).

References

1. Acemyan, C.Z., Kortum, P., Byrne, M.D., Wallach, D.S.: Usability of voter verifiable, end-to-end voting systems: baseline data for Helios, Prêt à Voter, and Scantegrity II. In: Proceedings of EVT/VVOTE. USENIX Association (2014)
2. Avenhaus, R., Von Stengel, B., Zamir, S.: Inspection games. In: Handbook of Game Theory **3**, 1947–1987. North-Holland (2000)
3. Benaloh, J.: Simple verifiable elections. In: USENIX Electronic Voting Technology Workshop (2006)
4. Benaloh, J.: Ballot casting assurance via voter-initiated poll station auditing. In: USENIX/ACCURATE Electronic Voting Technology Workshop (2007)
5. Buldas, A., Mägi, T.: Practical security analysis of e-voting systems. In: Miyaji, A., Kikuchi, H., Rannenberg, K. (eds.) IWSEC 2007. LNCS, vol. 4752, pp. 320–335. Springer, Heidelberg (2007). https://doi.org/10.1007/978-3-540-75651-4_22
6. Culnane, C., Teague, V.: Strategies for voter-initiated election audits. In: Zhu, Q., Alpcan, T., Panaousis, E., Tambe, M., Casey, W. (eds.) GameSec 2016. LNCS, vol. 9996, pp. 235–247. Springer, Cham (2016). https://doi.org/10.1007/978-3-319-47413-7_14
7. Ehin, P., Solvak, M., Willemson, J., Vinkel, P.: Internet voting in Estonia 2005–2019: evidence from eleven elections. Gov. Inf. Q. **39**(4), 101718 (2022)
8. Gjøsteen, K.: E-voting in Norway. In: Hao, F., Ryan, P.Y.A. (eds.) Real-World Electronic Voting. Design, Analysis and Deployment. CRC Press (2016)
9. Gjøsteen, K., Lund, A.S.: An experiment on the security of the Norwegian electronic voting protocol. Ann. Telecommun. **71**(7), 299–307 (2016). https://doi.org/10.1007/s12243-016-0509-8
10. Harsanyi, J.C., Selten, R.: A generalized Nash solution for two-person bargaining games with incomplete information. Manage. Sci. **18**(5/2), 80–106 (1972)
11. Jamroga, W.: Pretty good strategies for Benaloh challenge (2023). arXiv:2307.03258, https://arxiv.org/abs/2307.03258
12. Jamroga, W., Tabatabaei, M.: Preventing coercion in e-voting: be open and commit. In: Krimmer, R., et al. (eds.) E-Vote-ID 2016. LNCS, vol. 10141, pp. 1–17. Springer, Cham (2017). https://doi.org/10.1007/978-3-319-52240-1_1
13. Leitmann, G.: On generalized stackelberg strategies. J. Optim. Theory Appl. **26**(4), 637–643 (1978)
14. Marky, K., Kulyk, O., Renaud, K., Volkamer, M.: What did I really vote for? In: Proceedings of the Conference on Human Factors in Computing Systems CHI, p. 176. ACM (2018)
15. Nash, J.F.: Equilibrium points in n-person games. Proc. Nat. Acad. Sci. U.S.A., **36**, 48–49 (1950)
16. Osborne, M., Rubinstein, A.: A Course in Game Theory. MIT Press, Cambridge (1994)
17. Perea, A.: A one-person doxastic characterization of Nash strategies. Synthese **158**(2), 251–271 (2007)
18. Shoham, Y., Leyton-Brown, K.: Multiagent Systems - Algorithmic, Game-Theoretic, and Logical Foundations. Cambridge University Press, Cambridge (2009)

19. Tambe, M.: Security and Game Theory: Algorithms Deployed Systems Lessons Learned. Cambridge University Press, Cambridge (2011)
20. von Stackelberg, H.: The Theory of the Market Economy. Oxford University Press, Oxford (1952)
21. Weber, J.-L., Hengartner, U.: USAB. study of the open audit voting system Helios (2009). http://www.jannaweber.com/wpcontent/uploads/2009/09/858Helios.pdf
22. Yin, Y., Vorobeychik, Y., An, B., Hazon, N.: Optimally protecting elections. In: Proceedings of SECMAS. IFAAMAS (2016)

CAISED: A Protocol for Cast-as-Intended Verifiability with a Second Device

Johannes Müller[1]([⊠]) and Tomasz Truderung[2]

[1] University of Luxembourg, Esch-sur-Alzette, Luxembourg
johannes.mueller@uni.lu
[2] Polyas GmbH, Berlin, Germany

Abstract. Numerous approaches for cast-as-intended verifiability have been proposed in the literature on electronic voting, balancing practical aspects and security guarantees in different ways. One of the well-established methods involves the use of a second device that allows voters to audit their submitted ballots. This approach offers several benefits, including support for flexible ballot and election types and an intuitive user experience. Moreover, solutions based on this approach are generally adaptable to a range of existing voting protocols, rather than being restricted to a particular election scheme. This approach has been successfully implemented in real-life elections, such as in Estonia [18].

In this work, we improve the existing solutions for cast-as-intended verifiability based on the use of a second device. We propose a solution that preserves the advantageous practical properties outlined above, while providing stronger security guarantees. Our method does not increase the risk of vote selling compared to the underlying voting protocol to be augmented, and it requires only comparatively weak trust assumptions to achieve this. It can be combined with various voting protocols, including commitment-based systems that provide everlasting privacy.

Overall, our work offers a new option to strengthen cast-as-intended and end-to-end verifiability for real-world Internet elections.

1 Introduction

Internet voting has been used by many institutions, such as companies, universities or non-governmental organisations, as well as for some remote national elections. The adoption of Internet voting has been driven by several practical advantages of this form of voting, in particular the possibility for all voters to participate regardless of their physical location.

However, Internet voting has its own challenges and risks. One of these risks is the potential for malfunction, which cannot be easily excluded in such complex software/hardware systems. Such problems can be caused by design/programming errors, security vulnerabilities or even deliberate manipulation of the deployed system. In any case, malfunctions can have potentially serious practical consequences. If the final result of an election is accepted even though it does not correspond to the votes cast by the voters, the very purpose of the election is undermined.

© The Author(s) 2023
M. Volkamer et al. (Eds.): E-Vote-ID 2023, LNCS 14230, pp. 123–139, 2023.
https://doi.org/10.1007/978-3-031-43756-4_8

To protect against such risks, modern Internet voting systems strive for so-called *end-to-end verifiability* [8]. This fundamental property requires the system to provide *evidence* that the election result accurately reflects the votes cast by eligible voters. Importantly, this evidence must be independently verifiable.

Individual verifiability is an essential part of end-to-end verifiability. This property guarantees that each individual voter is able to verify that the vote she has cast on her voting machine has actually been counted. Individual verifiability is typically achieved in the following way. First, the voter checks whether her (possibly malfunctioning) voting machine has cast her encrypted vote as she intended; this property is called *cast-as-intended verifiability*. Then the voter checks that the vote she cast is recorded by the authorities; this feature is called *recorded-as-cast*. These features, when combined with universal verifiability (providing *tallied-as-recorded*), allow all individual voters to independently verify that their exact secret votes are counted.

The requirement for end-to-end verifiability in general, and individual verifiability in particular, is not only widely accepted by the research community, but is also becoming part of standard legal requirements and frameworks. The importance of verifiability is, for example, recognised by the Council of Europe in its Recommendation on standards for e-voting [26]. Importantly, the same document specifies that "individual verifiability can be implemented provided adequate safeguards exist to prevent coercion or vote-buying". Requirements for individual verifiability are also postulated for the Swiss elections in *Federal Chancellery Ordinance on Electronic Voting*, for the Estonian elections in *Riigikogu Election Act*, and for non-political elections in Germany [5].

Numerous techniques for cast-as-intended verifiability have been proposed in the literature (see, e.g., [2,4,7,11–15,18,22,27]). Some of them are also employed in real elections, for example [10,18] in the Estonian voting system IVXV, and [2] in the Helios voting system [1]. Each of these techniques provides its own balance between security, trust assumptions, usability, and deployability.

Our Contributions. We propose a method for cast-as-intended verifiability (called CAISED[1]) that offers a new balance between security guarantees and practicality; in particular, it can be used to augment many relevant Internet voting protocols. Our method does not increase the risk of vote selling, when compared to the underlying voting protocol being augmented, which is provided under comparatively weak trust assumptions.

The method proposed in this paper is intended to be an optional feature of the POLYAS 3.0 e-voting platform to ensure cast-as-intended verifiability. Our design choices have therefore been informed by practical considerations and the needs of a wide range of customers and use cases.

More specifically, we have optimised our cast-as-intended mechanism for the following *design goals*. The first four design goals, (DG1)–(DG4), are functional and essentially determine the election scenarios in which the cast-as-intended mechanism can be used; in combination, the functional design goals cover a wide range of real-world elections over the Internet, which is a key requirement for our practice-oriented work. The last two design goals (DG5)–(DG6) express security features that the cast-as-intended mechanism should provide.

---

[1] Cast-As-Intended withe SEcond Device.

- *(DG1) Support for flexible ballot types.* The mechanism should not be limited to certain types of ballots, such as simple ballots with a relatively small number of candidates or simple voting rules. On the contrary, it is desirable that complex ballots are supported, including, for example, ballots with write-in candidates or ranked ballots.
- *(DG2) Low cost.* The mechanism should not significantly increase the cost of the election, for example by requiring special secure printing/distribution facilities.
- *(DG3) No disenfranchisement of voters.* The mechanism should not make unrealistic assumptions about voters' knowledge, skills, and possessions. This rules out mechanisms that require some kind of special hardware. It should also be reasonably intuitive, so that an average voter can understand what to do and why.
- *(DG4) Modularity.* The mechanism can be used to augment a large class of Internet voting protocols, in particular protocols using different types of tallying, and protocols with everlasting privacy. The method should support modular security analysis, where the security properties of the combined scheme can be derived from the security properties of the underlying protocol (without individual verifiability) and the properties of the individual verifiability method.
- *(DG5) No facilitation of vote-selling.* The mechanism should not make it easier to sell votes than in the voting scheme being extended. To be clear, we do not aim to protect the entire voting scheme against vote selling, but we do require that the cast-as-intended mechanism should not additionally provide voters with receipts that they can use to *trivially* prove to a vote buyer how they voted.
- *(DG6) Possibly minimal trust assumptions.* We prioritise solutions that require weaker or more flexible trust assumptions. An example of a trust assumption we want to avoid is relying on some trapdoor values generated by a trusted party, where for the integrity of the individual verifiability method we need to assume that this party is honest (not corrupted) and that the trapdoor value does not leak.

As we discuss in detail in Sect. 2, no existing cast-as-intended verifiability method in the literature satisfies all of our design goals simultaneously. We note, however, that while our solution is optimised for our particular design goals, other methods may be better suited for different election settings that require a different resolution of the security/usability/deployability trade-offs.

Let us now explain at a high level how and why our cast-as-intended mechanism achieves all of our design goals satisfactorily:

- We follow the approach of using a second device, called an *audit device*, which allows voters to verify that the digital ballot submitted on their behalf contains their intended choice. This approach is well established and has already been used in real elections, for example in Estonia [18]. More specifically, in our method, the voter can use a common device, such as a mobile phone or tablet, as an audit device. This audit device needs to be able to scan QR codes, and it also needs to be connected to the internet in order to communicate with the voting system. This way we avoid costly additional infrastructure (DG2) and we do not have to make unrealistic assumptions about what voters have (DG3).
- From the voter's point of view, the audit process is straightforward, as explained next. Once the encrypted ballot has been sent to the voting system, the voting application displays a QR code. The voter uses the audit device to scan this QR code.

The audit device then prompts the voter to authenticate to the election system and, if this authentication is successful, displays the voter's choice in clear text, in the same form as the ballot was displayed on the primary (voting) device. We note that most voters today are used to this or similar checks, for example in the context of secure online banking. Furthermore, the verification step is optional and thus not required for a successful vote. In summary, we make reasonable assumptions about voters' knowledge and skills (DG2).

- On a technical note, our method works well with all possible ballot types, even very complex ones, satisfying (DG1). Moreover, our modular method can be used to augment a large class of relevant Internet voting protocols (DG4), and the computational cost of the ballot auditing computations is very reasonable (DG2).

- Unlike all previous cast-as-intended mechanisms that employ a second device [13, 18], our method simultaneously satisfies (DG5) and (DG6). We achieve this by providing *cryptographic deniability*, without introducing additional trust assumptions. To do this, we employ *interactive* zero-knowledge proofs where, by definition, any party can easily simulate the protocol transcript without knowing the plaintext or the encryption coin. We use well-understood and relatively simple cryptography: our method is essentially based on the interactive zero-knowledge proof of correct re-encryption. This results in simpler security proofs, which is another important factor in building trust.

Technically, the main challenge we had to overcome was caused by the general limitations of QR codes. As described above, the QR codes in our method are used as the only communication channel between the voting application and the audit device. However, QR codes provide very limited communication capacity as they are one-way and have very limited bandwidth. In order to implement an *interactive* zero-knowledge proof in this restricted setting, we split the role of the prover between the voting application and the voting system in such a way that the voting system does not learn anything during the process, while it does most of the 'heavy lifting'. The role of verifier, as usual in such schemes, is played by the second device.

We note that, since the audit device displays the voter's choice, it must be trusted for ballot privacy. This is also the case for all other techniques that deploy a second device [13,18]. In general, cast-as-intended methods based on return or voting codes do not have this disadvantage, but they do fall short of other design goals (see Sect. 2 for more details).

Structure of the Paper. In the next section, we provide more details on the existing approaches for cast-as-intended verifiability. We describe our cast-as-intended mechanism in Sect. 3 and we analyze its security in Sect. 4. In Sect. 5, we embed our cast-as-intended protocol in an example protocol which provides full individual verifiability and state higher-level security properties of this protocol. Finally, in Sect. 6, we discuss some practical cryptographic instantiations of our approach. See the full version of this paper [25] for more details.

2   Related Work

Various mechanisms for individual (cast-as-intended) verifiability have been proposed in the literature, striking different balances between security, usability, and various other practical aspects of the voting process. In this section, we give a brief overview of such mechanisms and explain why none of them provide the security features (DG5)-(DG6) in the real-world elections we are interested in, as determined by (DG1)-(DG4). In particular, we focus here only on methods used for *Internet e-voting* as opposed to on-site voting).

Return Codes. In the return-codes-based approach (see, e.g., [4, 11, 14, 15]), before the voting phase starts, each voter receives a *code sheet* (e.g. via postal mail) listing all the possible voting choices together with corresponding *verification codes*. These codes are unique for each voter and should be kept secret. During the voting phase, the voter, after having cast her ballot, receives (via the voting application or another dedicated channel) the return code corresponding to the selected choice. The voter compares this code to the one listed on the code sheet next to the intended choice.

While this approach may work well and seems intuitive from the voter's point of view, it has several drawbacks. It does not scale well to complex ballots ($\nmid$DG1), such as ballots with many candidates or when voters have the option to select multiple choices, because the code sheets become very big and the user experience quickly degrades (see, e.g., [21]). Another disadvantage is the cost incurred by (secure) printing and delivery of code sheets ($\nmid$DG2). Finally, the printing and delivery facilities must be trusted in this approach: if the verification codes leak to the adversary, the integrity of the process completely breaks (a dishonest voting client can cast a modified choice and return the code corresponding to the voter's intended choices). This trust assumption is rather strong ($\nmid$DG6).

Voting Codes. In this approach, the voter, as above, obtains a voting sheet with voting codes. The difference is that the codes are not used to check the ballot after it has been cast, but instead to prepare/encode the ballot in the first place: in order to vote, the voter enters the code (or scans a QR-code) corresponding to their choice. By construction, the voting client is then only able to prepare a valid ballot for the selected choice and no other ones. This approach is used, for example, in [7], where the voting codes are used not only to provide individual verifiability, but also to protect ballot privacy against dishonest voting client.

This approach, similarly to the return codes, works only for simple ballots ($\nmid$DG1); arguably, the usability issues are even bigger than for return codes, as the voter needs to type appropriated codes or scan appropriate QR-codes in order to correctly cast a ballot, not just compare the returned code with the expected one. As before, it incurs additional costs ($\nmid$DG2) and requires one to trust the printing/delivery facilities ($\nmid$DG6).

Cast-or-Audit. The cast-or-audit approach, used for instance in Helios [1], utilizes the so-called Benaloh Challenge [2] method. In this approach, the voter, after her choice has been encrypted by the voting client, has two options: she can *either* choose to (1) cast this encrypted ballot *or* (2) challenge (i.e., audit) the ballot. If the latter option is chosen, the voting client enables the audit by revealing the randomness used to encrypt the ballot, so that the voter (typically using some additional device or application) can check that it contains the intended choice. The voter then starts the ballot cast process over again, possibly selecting a different choice.

The security of this approach relies on the assumption that the client application (the adversary) does not know beforehand, whether the encrypted vote will be audited or cast. Therefore, if the adversary tries to manipulate the ballot, it risks that this will be detected. Note, however, that the ballot which is actually cast is not the one which is audited. This, unlike most of the other approaches, provides the voter with some (probabilistic) assurance, but not with fully effective guarantees.

This method has the advantage that it does not produce a receipt (the voter can choose different candidates for the audited ballots) and that the audit device does not need to have Internet access for verification (unlike cast-and-audit methods like ours), but it has several usability issues. The studies on usability of this scheme [19,28] conclude that voters tend to not verify their votes and have serious problems with understanding the idea of this type of ballot audit, which make this approach score low on (DG3). The above issues render the cast-or-audit approach ineffective in practice.

Cast-and-*Audit.* The solution presented in this paper belongs to this category. In this approach, the voter audits, typically using a second device, the cast ballot (before or after it is cast). This approach is used by the system deployed for the Estonian elections [18]. In this case, the voters can use a mobile application to scan a QR-code displayed by the voting client application. This QR-code includes the random encryption coin used to encrypt the voter's choice. The audit device fetches the voter's ballot from the ballot box and uses the provided randomness to extract the voter's choice which is then displayed for the voter to inspect.

This method is flexible as it works well also for complex ballot types (DG1) (the audit device conveniently displays the vote in the same way the ballot appeared in the main voting device). The user experience, for this method, is relatively simple (DG3). The method does not incur extra cost (DG2).

The main disadvantage of this method in general is that the additional (audit) device must be trusted for ballot privacy, as it "sees" the voter choice in clear. Also, the fact that the voters need to have an additional device (such as a mobile phone), which is able to scan QR-codes and which has Internet access, can be seen as a disadvantage. However, with the high availability of such devices, this does not seem to be a significant issue in practice. The correctness of the ballot audit process relies on the assumption that one of the devices the voter uses (either the main voting device or the audit device) is not corrupted. In practice, it is therefore desirable that the software programs (apps) run on these two devices were developed and installed independently, ideally by different vendors or trusted third parties (e.g., pro-democratic organizations).

The main idea of the cast-as-intended mechanism proposed in [18] is that the QR-code includes the encryption random coins. Such a coin constitutes a trivial and direct evidence for the plaintext content of the encrypted ballot. As such, the simple cast-as-intended mechanism of [18] does not provide cryptographic *deniability* and may potentially facilitate vote buying/coercion ($\nmid$DG4). Whether this potential for vote buying/coercion becomes an actual threat depends on the overall voting protocol; for instance, the Estonian system allows for vote updating as a measure to mitigate the threat of coercion. The lack of cryptographic deniability remains nevertheless a serious drawback of this method and significantly limits it applicability.

The issue of selling cast-as-intended data as trivial receipts in Internet elections is addressed in [13], where cryptographic deniability is provided using non-interactive zero-knowledge proofs with trapdoors. This solution to the receipt problem has, however, its own issues: the trapdoor (for each voter) is generated by a registrar who therefore needs to be trusted for integrity of this method. This is arguably a strong trust assumption ($\frac{1}{2}$ DG6).

As already mentioned in the introduction, the solution presented in this paper, while also providing cryptographic denialability, does not require such an additional trust assumption (DG6). It also avoids the relatively complex cryptographic machinery of [13], which often is the source of serious programming flaws (see, e.g., [16]).

Custom Hardware Tokens. Some other solutions, such as [12], rely on using dedicated hardware tokens during the cast process. Relying on custom hardware makes these solutions expensive and difficult to deploy in real, big scale elections ($\frac{1}{2}$ DG2), ($\frac{1}{2}$ DG3). Furthermore, [20] demonstrated that [12] suffers from several security issues and concluded that [12] was not yet ready to be deployed.

Tracking Codes. The sElect system [22] achieves cast-as-intended in a simple way: voters are given random tracking numbers as they cast their ballots. After the tally, voters can check that their tracking numbers appear next to their respective votes.

This method is simple and intuitive for the voters, but has the following drawbacks. End-to-end verifiability relies on the voters to perform the checks because there is no universal verifiability process that complements the individual verifiability made by the voters. Also, in [22], the tracking codes were "generated" and entered by the voters. This is somehow problematic both from the usability point of view and because of the poor quality of "random" numbers made up by voters (see, e.g., [3]). Altogether, this method seems to take somehow unrealistic assumptions about the voters: that the voters carry out the process often enough for achieving the desired security level and that they are able to generate decent randomness ($\frac{1}{2}$ DG3). Furthermore, the tracking codes, as used in [22], may allow for simple vote buying ($\frac{1}{2}$ DG5).

The construction presented in Selene [27] also builds upon the idea of tracking codes, but further guarantees receipt-freeness, and thus impedes vote buying, due to a complex cryptographic machinery. The cast-as-intended mechanism is here, however, tightly bound to the e-voting protocol and thus not modular ($\frac{1}{2}$ DG4). In particular, unlike for the method proposed in this paper, it is not immediately obvious how to improve Selene towards everlasting privacy or how to instantiate Selene with practical post-quantum primitives.

3 Cast-As-Intended Verifiability: Generic Protocol

In this section, we present our protocol for cast-as-intended verifiability. We take a modular approach: in Sect. 3.1, we first describe a generic basic ballot submission process *without* cast-as-intended, and then, in Sect. 3.2, we build on this basic process and extend it with cast-as-intended verifiability.

The protocol presented here, with the security result given in Sect. 4, deals only with the core cast-as-intended mechanism. In particular, it does not address the recorded-as-cast aspect of individual verifiability. In Sect. 5, we explain how to (easily) extend our cast-as-intended protocol to achieve full individual verifiability.

3.1 Basic Ballot Submission

We describe now how the basic ballot submission (sub-)protocol of an e-voting protocol without cast-as-intended verifiability works which establishes the starting point for our mechanism, introduced in the next subsection. Doing this, we abstract from some aspects (such as authentication) which are irrelevant for our cast-as-intended protocol.

We provide this explicitly defined basic protocol in order to be able to compare the knowledge the voting server gathers during this process with the knowledge it gathers during the process extended with the cast-as-intended mechanism.

Participants. The basic submission protocol is run among the following participants: the voter V, the voting device VD, and the voting server VS. In what follows, we implicitly assume that the channel from V (via the voting devices) to the voting server VS is authenticated without taking any assumption about how authentication is carried out.[2]

Cryptographic Primitives. In the basic ballot submission protocol, an IND-CPA-secure public-key encryption scheme $\mathcal{E} = (\mathsf{KeyGen}, \mathsf{Enc}, \mathsf{Dec})$ is employed.

Ballot Submission (Basic). We assume that $(pk, sk) \leftarrow \mathsf{KeyGen}$ was generated correctly in the setup phase of the voting protocol and that each party knows pk.[3] The program of the basic submission protocol works in the standard way:

1. Voter V enters plaintext vote v to her voting device VD.
2. Voting device VD chooses randomness $r \xleftarrow{\$} R$, computes ciphertext $c \leftarrow \mathsf{Enc}(pk, v; r)$, and sends c to voting server VS.

We note that the basic protocol may include signing the ballot with voter's private key if a public-key infrastructure (PKI) among the voters is established.[4]

3.2 Cast-as-Intended Verifiable Ballot Submission

We now describe how to extend the basic ballot submission protocol described above for cast-as-intended verifiability.

---

[2] Since the exact method of authentication is not relevant for the purposes of our cast-as-intended protocol, we abstract away from authentication in our presentation. In practice, the voter can use for example a password to log in to VS.

[3] The secret key sk is known only to the talliers of the election who use (their shares of) sk to decrypt the ballots in the tallying phase. The exact method used to verifiably tally the ballots (via, e.g., homomorphic aggregation, or verifiable shuffling) is orthogonal to the cast-as-intended method proposed in this paper.

[4] Since this aspect is independent of our cast-as-intended protocol, we do not assume that voters sign their ballots in our presentation. We note that our protocol also works with ballots signed by voters.

Participants. In addition to the three participants of the basic ballot submission phase (voter V, voting device VD, voting server VS), the extended protocol also includes an audit device AD.

Cryptographic Primitives. The extended submission protocol employs the following cryptographic primitives:

1. An IND-CPA-secure public-key encryption scheme $\mathscr{E} = (\mathsf{KeyGen}, \mathsf{Enc}, \mathsf{Dec})$ that allows for re-randomization and special decryption:
   - *Re-randomization* guarantees the existence of a *probabilistic polynomial-time (ppt)* algorithm ReRand which takes as input a public key pk together with a ciphertext $c = \mathsf{Enc}(pk, m; r)$ and returns a ciphertext c^* such that $c^* = \mathsf{Enc}(pk, m; r^*)$ for some (fresh) randomness r^*. We assume that ReRand is *homomorphic* w.r.t. randomness: $\mathsf{Enc}(pk, m; x + r) = \mathsf{ReRand}(pk, \mathsf{Enc}(pk, m; r); x)$.
   - *Special decryption* guarantees the existence of a *polynomial-time (pt)* algorithm Dec' which takes as input a public key pk, a ciphertext c, and a randomness r, and returns the plaintext m, if $c = \mathsf{Enc}(pk, m; r)$, or fails otherwise.[5]
   Note that neither ReRand nor Dec' require knowledge of the secret key sk associated to pk. Example cryptosystem which provide these operations are the standard ElGamal encryption (see Sect. 6) and commitment consistent encryption [9].
2. A proof of correct re-encryption, i.e., an interactive zero-knowledge proof (ZKP) π_{ReRand} for the following relation: $(pk, c, c^*; x) \in \mathscr{R}_{\mathsf{ReRand}} \Leftrightarrow c^* = \mathsf{ReRand}(pk, c; x)$. The joint input of the prover and the verifier is statement (pk, c, c^*) and the secret input of the prover is witness x, i.e., the randomness used to re-randomize ciphertext c into c^*.

Ballot Submission (Extended). The program of the extended ballot submission works as follows (note that the first two steps are the ones of the basic ballot submission protocol):

(BS1) Voter V enters plaintext vote v to voting device VD.

(BS2) Voting device VD chooses randomness $r \xleftarrow{\$} R$, computes ciphertext $c \leftarrow \mathsf{Enc}(pk, v; r)$, and sends c to voting server VS.

(BS3) Voting server VS chooses a blinding factor $x \xleftarrow{\$} R$ and sends x to VD.

(BS4) Voting device VD computes blinded randomness $r^* \leftarrow x + r$ and returns r^* to voter V (in the practical implementations, r^* can be displayed as a QR-code).

From the voter's perspective, the outcome of the submission protocol consists of the blinded randomness r^*, which is used for individual verification purposes, as described next.

---

[5] Special decryption is given for free if the message space is polynomially bounded: one can simply brute-force all the potential plaintext messages and encrypt each with the given randomness until this produces c. It becomes, however, impractical especially for elections with write-ins.

Cast-as-Intended Verification. The program of the voter's individual cast-as-intended verification works as follows. It is executed, if the voter chooses to audit his/her ballot. As for the ballot submission, in what follows, we implicitly assume that the channel from V (via the audit devices) to the voting server VS is authenticated.

(BA1) Voter V enters r^* to the audit device AD (in practical implementations this is done by scanning a QR code produced by VD), which contacts voting server VS.

(BA2) Voting server VS computes ciphertext $c^* \leftarrow \mathsf{ReRand}(pk, c; x)$ (i.e., the original ciphertext c re-randomized with the blinding factor x) and sends the original ciphertext c along with c^* to the audit device AD.

(BA3) Voting server VS and audit device AD run an interactive zero-knowledge proof π_{ReRand}, where VS is the prover and AD the verifier, with joint input (pk, c, c^*) and voting server's secret input x in order to prove/verify that c^* is a re-randomization of c.

(BA4) If the verification algorithm in the step above returned 1, then AD decrypts the re-randomized ciphertext c^* using blinded randomness r^* to obtain $v^* \leftarrow \mathsf{Dec}'(pk, c^*, r^*)$ and returns v^* to voter V. Otherwise, AD returns 0 (indicating failure) to V.

(BA5) Voter V returns 1 (accepts) if AD returned v^* such that $v = v^*$ (where v is the voter's intended choice). Otherwise, V returns 0 (reject).

4   Security

Our cryptographic security analysis of the cast-as-intended protocol (as introduced in Sect. 3.2) consists of two parts. In the first part, we prove that this protocol is an interactive zero-knowledge proof (ZKP) protocol, run between voter V and audit device AD, jointly playing the role of the verifier on the one side, and the voting device VD and voting server VS jointly playing the role of the prover on the other side. This fact establishes the *cryptographic deniability* of our cast-as-intended method: the protocol transcript (the data gathered by the audit device) is useless as a receipt, because an indistinguishable transcript can be generated by any party, using the simulator algorithm (for an arbitrary election choice, independently of the actual voter's choice).

In the second part, we prove that the voting server VS does not learn more information about the voter's secret choice than what VS already learns in the basic ballot submission protocol. Note that this statement is not directly covered by the zero-knowledge (simulation) property of the protocol, because VS is part of the prover.

In Sect. 5, we will explain how to extend the cast-as-intended protocol analyzed in this section so that it provides full individual verifiability.

4.1   Zero-Knowledge Proof

We now show that our cast-as-intended protocol is an interactive ZKP proving that a given ballot contains a vote for a particular candidate. From the soundness of this ZKP, it follows that even if the voter's voting device VD and the voting server VS collude, then they are not able to convince the voter V (who uses an honest audit device AD) that her submitted ballot contains a vote for her favorite choice v when it actually contains a different choice. Moreover, due to the zero-knowledge property, VD and VS prove that the submitted ballot contains a vote for the voter's favorite choice without revealing any information beyond this statement; in particular, the protocol does not leave any information which could undesirably serve as a receipt that could be used for vote buying.

Let Verify be the composition of the programs run by voter V and her audit device AD after the basic ballot submission protocol is completed, i.e., steps (BS3)–(BS4) in the extended ballot submission protocol followed by the cast-as-intended protocol; in short: Verify $= (V\|AD)$. Analogously, let Prove be the unification of the programs run by the voting device VD and the voting server VS after the basic ballot submission protocol is completed; in short Prove $= (VD\|VS)$.

Observe that the resulting interactive protocol with joint input (pk, v, c) and prover's secret input r can be re-written as the following protocol:

1. Prove chooses $x \xleftarrow{\$} R$, computes $r^* \leftarrow x + r$ and $c^* \leftarrow \mathsf{ReRand}(pk, c; x)$, and returns (r^*, c^*).
2. Prove and Verify run the interactive ZKP π_{ReRand} with joint input (pk, c, c^*) and prover's secret input x.
3. Verify returns 1 if and only if the execution of π_{ReRand} returned 1 and $v = \mathsf{Dec}'(pk, c^*, r^*)$ holds true.

We now state that this protocol is an interactive ZKP for proving that ciphertext c encrypts vote v.

Theorem 1. *The interactive protocol $\pi_{\mathsf{Enc}} = (\mathsf{Verify}, \mathsf{Prove})$ is a zero-knowledge proof for relation $\mathscr{R}_{\mathsf{Enc}}$ defined by the equivalence $(pk, v, c; r) \in \mathscr{R}_{\mathsf{Enc}} \Leftrightarrow c = \mathsf{Enc}(pk, v; r)$.*

In order to prove this theorem, we need to show that π_{Enc} satisfies *completeness* (i.e., if Verify and Prove are executed correctly for a true statement, then Verify returns 1 with overwhelming probability), *soundness* (i.e., if Verify returns 1, then the statement is correct, even when interacting with a dishonest prover), and *zero-knowledge* (i.e., the verifier's view can be simulated without knowledge of the witness), each with at least overwhelming probability.

Proof. Completeness: Let x, r^*, c^* be defined as in Prove. Because $(pk, c^*, c; x) \in \mathscr{R}_{\mathsf{ReRand}}$, the verifier returns 1 in an execution of π_{ReRand} with probability p_c, where p_c is the correctness level of π_{ReRand}. Furthermore, the verifier's second check is also positive because

$$c^* = \mathsf{ReRand}(pk, \mathsf{Enc}(pk, v; r), x) = \mathsf{Enc}(pk, v; x + r) = \mathsf{Enc}(pk, v; r^*).$$

Hence, Verify returns 1 in π_{Enc} with probability p_c if both Verify and Prove are executed correctly; in short: $Pr[\langle\mathsf{Verify}, \mathsf{Prove}(r)\rangle(pk, v, c) = 1] = p_c$.

Soundness: Assume that Verify returns 1. Then, due to the soundness of π_{ReRand}, there exists with probability p_s a unique plaintext v^* such that we have $c^* \in \mathsf{Enc}(pk, v^*)$ and

$c \in \mathsf{Enc}(pk, v^*)$, where p_s is the soundness level of π_{ReRand}. Furthermore, since Verify returns 1, by the property of special decryption $\mathsf{Dec'}$, we have $c^* \in \mathsf{Enc}(pk, v)$ and hence $v = v^*$. This means that $c \in \mathsf{Enc}(pk, v)$ with probability p_s.

Zero-knowledge: We can construct a simulator Sim, which does not have access to the witness r and which replaces Prove in the re-written protocol, as follows:

1. Sim chooses $r^* \xleftarrow{\$} R$, computes $c^* \leftarrow \mathsf{Enc}(pk, v; r^*)$, and returns (r^*, c^*).
2. Sim simulates the interactive ZKP π_{ReRand} without knowledge of x.

Due to the ZK property of π_{ReRand}, the verifier is not able to distinguish a real execution and a simulated one with probability p_z, where p_z is the ZK level of π_{ReRand}.

4.2 Simulatability Towards Voting Server

Recall that in the basic ballot submission protocol, the only data that VS obtains from the voter is the voter's encrypted choice $c = \mathsf{Enc}(pk, v; r)$. Due to the semantic security of the public-key encryption scheme $\mathcal{E}$, the probability that VS can derive any information about the voter's vote v is negligible (if VS is computationally bounded).

Now, in what follows, we show that the voting server VS does not learn more information about the voter's vote in the cast-as-intended protocol than what VS learns in the basic ballot submission protocol. To this end, we compare the voting server's view in both protocols and show that all additional interaction between those participants that know/learn the voter's vote (i.e., voter V herself, her voting device VD, and her audit device AD) on the one side and the voting server VS on the other side can be perfectly simulated without any knowledge of the voter's vote v.

From the voting server's perspective, the basic ballot submission protocol can be re-written as follows, where $\hat{V}$ is the unification of the programs of V and VD:

1. $\hat{V}$ chooses randomness $r \xleftarrow{\$} R$, computes ciphertext $c \leftarrow \mathsf{Enc}(pk, v; r)$, and sends c to voting server VS.

From the voting server's perspective, the cast-as-intended protocol (i.e., verifiable ballot submission followed by cast-as-intended verification) can be re-written as follows, where $\hat{V}_{ext}$ is the unification of the programs of V, VD, and AD:

1. $\hat{V}_{ext}$ chooses randomness $r \xleftarrow{\$} R$, computes ciphertext $c \leftarrow \mathsf{Enc}(pk, v; r)$, and sends c to voting server VS.
2. Voting server VS chooses blinding factor $x \xleftarrow{\$} R$, computes ciphertext $c^* \leftarrow \mathsf{ReRand}(pk, c; x)$, and sends (c^*, x) to voting device $\hat{V}_{ext}$.
3. VS and $\hat{V}_{ext}$ run interactive ZKP π_{ReRand} with joint input pk, c, c^* and voting server's secret input x in order to prove/verify that c^* is a re-randomization of c.

Due to the re-written presentations of the two protocols, it is easy to see that from the voting server's perspective, the only task carried out by $\hat{V}_{ext}$ in the cast-as-intended protocol in addition to $\hat{V}$'s tasks in the ballot submission protocol is executing the verification program of the interactive proof π_{ReRand}. Observe that the verification program of π_{ReRand} can be executed by *any* party which knows (pk, c, c^*); in particular no knowledge about the voter's vote v or randomization elements r, r^* is required. We can therefore perfectly simulate $\hat{V}_{ext}$'s additional program in the cast-as-intended protocol. Using the standard (simulation) argument that the voting server VS could run the simulation algorithm (in our case: the verification program of π_{ReRand}) itself, we conclude that the voting server VS does not learn more information about the voter's vote in the cast-as-intended protocol than what VS learns in the basic ballot submission protocol.

Remark 1. In the individually verifiable ballot submission protocol described above, the voting server VS does not learn whether the voter accepted or rejected a protocol run, i.e., whether $\hat{V}_{ext}$ returned 0 or 1. Depending on the overall voting protocol specification, VS may however learn the final output of $\hat{V}_{ext}$, for example, when the voting protocol requires that each voter submits a *confirmation code* to the voting server after she completed her cast-as-intended verification successfully in order to publicly confirm that V accepts the submitted ballot (see, e.g., [11]).

We note that even if VS learns the output of $\hat{V}_{ext}$, ballot privacy towards a possibly corrupted VS is still guaranteed in our cast-as-intended protocol. In order to prove this claim, we show that the probability of the event that the execution of π_{ReRand} returned 1 but $v \neq \text{Dec}(pk, c^*, r + \tilde{x})$ holds true, where $(c^*, \tilde{x})$ is the output of VS, is negligible. Let us consider the set of runs in which this event holds true. Due to the soundness of π_{ReRand}, there exists $x \in \mathcal{R}$ such that $c^* = \text{ReRand}(pk, c; x) = \text{Enc}(pk, v; r + x)$. Now, if $v \neq \text{Dec}'(pk, c^*, r + \tilde{x})$, then there exists $\tilde{v} \neq v$ such that $c^* = \text{Enc}(pk, \tilde{v}; r + \tilde{x})$ holds true. Due to the correctness of the PKE scheme $\mathcal{E}$, it follows that $v = \text{Dec}(sk, c^*) = \tilde{v}$, which is a contradiction to $v \neq \tilde{v}$.

We can therefore conclude that the slightly extended cast-as-intended protocol can be simulated (with overwhelming probability) exactly as in the case above where VS does not learn the output of $\hat{V}_{ext}$ when we additionally specify that the simulator returns 1 to VS if and only if π_{ReRand} returns 1. Note that the simulator does not need to check whether $v = \text{Dec}(pk, c^*, r^*)$ and hence does not need to know v.

5   Full Individual Verifiability

In the previous two sections, we presented the method for cast-as-intended verifiability and analyzed the security properties of this method. Cast-as-intended, which enables the voter to audit his/her ballot and check that it contains the intended choice, does not, however, fully cover the notion of individual verifiability. What is missing is the guarantee that the audited ballot takes part in the tally (sometimes called *recorded-as-cast*).

In this section, we add the standard mechanism to achieve recorded-as-cast verifiability: a public bulletin board and signed receipts. We also state the higher level security properties such a final system provides. The content of this section can be seen as an example for how our cast-as-intended mechanism can be embedded in a more complete protocol to provide full individual verifiability.

As noted, we introduce an additional participant: the public bulletin board. It is used to collect all the cast ballots, where ballots are published together with unique (possibly anonymised) voter identifiers. We assume that the voters (or auditors) have access to this public bulletin board (during and/or after the ballot cast process) and can check that a given ballot is included there.

We also assume that the voting server has a (private) signing key and that the corresponding (public) verification key is publicly known.

The modifications to the protocol presented in Sect. 3 are straightforward. The changes in the ballot submission protocol are as follows.

– The encrypted ballot c submitted in Step (BS2) is published by the voting server on the public bulletin board together with a unique voter's identifier.
– In step (BS3), the voting server VS additionally sends to the voting device VD a *signed ballot cast confirmation s*, that is a signature on the cast ballot c along with the voter identifier. The signature s is then checked by the voting device VD and s is given to the voter in Step (BS4).

We also consider the following changes in the ballot audit process:

– The voting server VS, in Step (BA2), sends additionally to the audit device AD the ballot cast confirmation s, as in the step above. The audit device checks that s contains a valid signature of the voting server on c and the identifier of the voter (who carries out the ballot audit process).
– In the final step of the ballot audit process, the voter is given the signed ballot cast confirmation.

Note that the ballot cast confirmation is provided to the voter twice: once by the voting device and then by the audit device. It is expected that these confirmations are exactly the same (which is the case when both devices are honest).

With such receipt, the voter, having executed the ballot audit process, has the following guarantees which directly follow from the results of Sect. 4.

Theorem 2 (informal). *Assume that at least one of the voter devices (the voting device or the audit device) is honest. If the voter successfully carried out the ballot cast process and the ballot audit process, then the voter is in the possession of ballot confirmation which (1) is correctly signed by the voting server, (2) refers to an encrypted ballot that contains the voter's intended choice (as shown to the voter and confirmed in the ballot audit process) and that is uniquely assigned to this voter.*

At the same time, the second device (even if it behaves dishonestly) is not able to produce a convincing evidence for a third party about the voter's choice.

With this result, given that one of the devices is honest, the voter can check that their ballot, containing their intended choice, is included in the public bulletin board (and if not, given the valid signature, the voter can demonstrate that the voting server misbehaved) and by this also included in the final tally (where the correctness of the tallying process is given due to the universal verifiability). Note that the second part of property (2) of the above theorem protects against clash attacks [23], where different voters audit the same ballot, each believing that the ballot belongs to herself/himself only.

Note that to strengthen this result, the voter can even carry out the ballot audit process using more than one device. With this, even if only one of these devices was honest, it would be enough to guarantee cast-as-intended.

6 Instantiations

Our cast-as-intended protocol can be instantiated with common cryptographic primitives. Our protocol can therefore be used to extend important e-voting protocols for cast-as-intended verification. In this section, we describe the natural instantiation of our method based on the standard ElGamal group; an instantiation for commitment-based e-voting schemes is presented in the full version of this paper.

Let us consider an ElGamal group of order q with a generator g. In this setting, the public key is of the form $h = g^{sk}$, where $sk \in Z_q = \{0, \ldots, q-1\}$. Given a plaintext message message $m \in Z_q$, the encryption of m with randomness r is $c = (g^r, m \cdot h^r)$.

Special Decryption: For a ciphertext of the form $c = (u, w)$ encrypted using randomness r (which means that $u = g^r$ and $w = m \cdot h^r$), the randomness r allows one to easily extract the plaintext message by (checking that u is in fact g^r and) computing $w \cdot h^{-r}$.

Re-randomisation of a ciphertext $c = (u, w)$ is of the form $c' = (u', w')$ where $u' = u \cdot g^x$ and $w' = w \cdot h^x$. In order to prove that c' is a re-randomisation of c, one can use the well-known sigma-protocol for equality of discrete logarithms, that is the proof of knowledge of x such that $X = \frac{u'}{u} = g^x$ and $Y = \frac{w'}{w} = h^x$ [6], and **transform it into an interactive zero-knowledge protocol** using, for instance, the technique from [17,24] (note that the sigma protocol cannot be used directly, because it is only *honest-verifier zero knowledge* and is **not** known to provide the zero-knowledge property in the general case). A detailed instantiation is provided in the full version of this paper.

We note that the *computational cost* of this method is low and the protocol can, therefore be easily handled even by low-end general purpose devices: There is essentially no extra cost on the voting device (no additional modular exponentiations). On the server (prover) side, the ballot audit process requires 6 modular exponentiations (2 for re-randomisation and 4 for the ZKP). The audit device (verifier) needs 8 modular exponentiations: 6 for the ZKP and 2 for special decryption To put this number in a perspective, it is comparable to the cost of ballot preparation in a typical ElGamal-based voting system which, in the simplest case, requires 3 modular exponentiations. For an implementation using elliptic-curve-based ElGamal group, on an Android phone with a relatively modern CPU (Qualcomm® Snapdragon 865 CPU) the ballot audit process takes only roughly 0.08 s, for a simple ballot which can be encoded as one group element, and it scales linearly with ballot length.

References

1. Adida, B.: Helios: web-based open-audit voting. In: van Oorschot, P.C. (ed.) USENIX Security Symposium, pp. 335–348. USENIX Association (2008)
2. Benaloh, J.: Simple verifiable elections. EVT **6**, 5 (2006)
3. Bonneau, J.: Guessing human-chosen secrets. Ph.D. thesis, University of Cambridge, UK (2012)
4. Brelle, A., Truderung, T.: Cast-as-intended mechanism with return codes based on PETs. In: Krimmer, R., Volkamer, M., Braun Binder, N., Kersting, N., Pereira, O., Schürmann, C. (eds.) E-Vote-ID 2017. LNCS, vol. 10615, pp. 264–279. Springer, Cham (2017). https://doi.org/10.1007/978-3-319-68687-5_16

5. BSI. Technische Richtlinie TR-03162 (2021). https://www.bsi.bund.de/DE/Themen/Unternehmen-und-Organisationen/Standards-und-Zertifizierung/Technische-Richtlinien/TR-nach-Thema-sortiert/tr03162/TR-03162_node.html

6. Chaum, D., Pedersen, T.P.: Wallet databases with observers. In: Brickell, E.F. (ed.) CRYPTO 1992. LNCS, vol. 740, pp. 89–105. Springer, Heidelberg (1993). https://doi.org/10.1007/3-540-48071-4_7

7. Cortier, V., Filipiak, A., Lallemand, J.: BeleniosVS: secrecy and verifiability against a corrupted voting device. In: IEEE CSF 2019, pp. 367–381 (2019)

8. Cortier, V., Galindo, D., Küsters, R., Mueller, J., Truderung, T.; SoK: verifiability notions for e-voting protocols. In: IEEE S&P 2016, pp. 779–798 (2016)

9. Cuvelier, É., Pereira, O., Peters, T.: Election verifiability or ballot privacy: do we need to choose? In: Crampton, J., Jajodia, S., Mayes, K. (eds.) ESORICS 2013. LNCS, vol. 8134, pp. 481–498. Springer, Heidelberg (2013). https://doi.org/10.1007/978-3-642-40203-6_27

10. Ehin, P., Solvak, M., Willemson, J., Vinkel, P.: Internet voting in Estonia 2005–2019: evidence from eleven elections. Gov. Inf. Q. **39**(4), 101718 (2022)

11. Galindo, D., Guasch, S., Puiggalí, J.: 2015 Neuchâtel's cast-as-intended verification mechanism. In: Haenni, R., Koenig, R.E., Wikström, D. (eds.) VOTELID 2015. LNCS, vol. 9269, pp. 3–18. Springer, Cham (2015). https://doi.org/10.1007/978-3-319-22270-7_1

12. Grewal, G.S., Ryan, M.D., Chen, L., Clarkson, M.R.: Du-vote: remote electronic voting with untrusted computers. In: IEEE CSF 2015, pp. 155–169 (2015)

13. Guasch, S., Morillo, P.: How to challenge *and* cast your e-vote. In: Grossklags, J., Preneel, B. (eds.) FC 2016. LNCS, vol. 9603, pp. 130–145. Springer, Heidelberg (2017). https://doi.org/10.1007/978-3-662-54970-4_8

14. Haenni, R., Koenig, R.E., Dubuis, E.: Cast-as-intended verification in electronic elections based on oblivious transfer. In: Krimmer, R., et al. (eds.) E-Vote-ID 2016. LNCS, vol. 10141, pp. 73–91. Springer, Cham (2017). https://doi.org/10.1007/978-3-319-52240-1_5

15. Haenni, R., Koenig, R.E., Locher, P., Dubuis, E.: CHVote system specification. IACR Cryptology ePrint Archive, 2017 (2017)

16. Haines, T., Lewis, S.J., Pereira, O., Teague, V.: How not to prove your election outcome. In: IEEE S&P 2020, pp. 644–660 (2020)

17. Hazay, C., Lindell, Y.: Sigma protocols and efficient zero-knowledge. In: Hazay, C., Lindell, Y. (eds.) Efficient Secure Two-Party Protocols. ISC, pp. 147–175. Springer, Heidelberg (2010). https://doi.org/10.1007/978-3-642-14303-8_6

18. Heiberg, S., Willemson, J.: Verifiable internet voting in Estonia. In: Krimmer, R., Volkamer, M. (eds.) 6th International Conference on Electronic Voting, EVOTE 2014, Lochau/Bregenz, Austria, 29–31 October 2014, pp. 1–8. IEEE (2014)

19. Karayumak, F., Kauer, M., Olembo, M.M., Volk, T., Volkamer, M.: User study of the improved Helios voting system interfaces. In: IEEE STAST (2011)

20. Kremer, S., Rønne, P.B.: To du or not to du: a security analysis of du-vote. In: IEEE EuroS&P 2016, pp. 473–486 (2016)

21. Kulyk, O., Volkamer, M., Müller, M., Renaud, K.: Towards improving the efficacy of code-based verification in internet voting. In: Bernhard, M., et al. (eds.) FC 2020. LNCS, vol. 12063, pp. 291–309. Springer, Cham (2020). https://doi.org/10.1007/978-3-030-54455-3_21

22. Küsters, R., Müller, J., Scapin, E., Truderung, T.: sElect: a lightweight verifiable remote voting system. In: IEEE CSF 2016, pp. 341–354 (2016)

23. Küsters, R., Truderung, T., Vogt, A.: Clash Attacks on the Verifiability of E-Voting Systems. In: 33rd IEEE Symposium on Security and Privacy (S&P 2012), pp. 395–409. IEEE Computer Society (2012)

24. Lindell, Y.: Zero-knowledge from sigma protocols-an erratum (2018). https://u.cs.biu.ac.il/~lindell/errata-zk-sigma.pdf. Accessed 18 Aug 2022

25. Müller, J., Truderung, T.: A protocol for cast-as-intended verifiability with a second device. arXiv:2304.09456 (2023)
26. Council of Europe. Council of Europe adopts new Recommendation on Standards for E-Voting (2017). https://www.coe.int/en/web/electoral-assistance/-/council-of-europe-adopts-new-recommendation-on-standards-for-e-voting
27. Ryan, P.Y.A., Rønne, P.B., Iovino, V.: Selene: voting with transparent verifiability and coercion-mitigation. In: Clark, J., Meiklejohn, S., Ryan, P.Y.A., Wallach, D., Brenner, M., Rohloff, K. (eds.) FC 2016. LNCS, vol. 9604, pp. 176–192. Springer, Heidelberg (2016). https://doi.org/10.1007/978-3-662-53357-4_12
28. Weber, J., Hengartner, U.: Usability study of the open audit voting system Helios. Retrieved August 3, 2012 (2009)

Estimating Carbon Footprint of Paper and Internet Voting

Jan Willemson[1]([⊠])[iD] and Kristjan Krips[1,2]

[1] Cybernetica AS, Narva mnt 20, Tartu, Estonia
{jan.willemson,kristjan.krips}@cyber.ee
[2] Institute of Computer Science, University of Tartu, Narva mnt 18, Tartu, Estonia

Abstract. This paper compares the carbon footprint of paper voting in polling stations with the emissions of remote vote casting via the Internet. We identify the process steps with the most significant emissions in terms of CO_2 equivalent, design a methodology to quantify these emissions and give a comparative analysis based on the example of the Estonian parliamentary elections of 2023. Our results show that paper voting has about 180 times higher carbon footprint, owing largely to the need to transport the voters to the polling stations and back.

Keywords: Paper voting · Internet voting · Carbon footprint

1 Introduction

To guarantee generality of the elections, the voters must be provided with convenient and easily accessible voting methods. Voting in a specified location (polling station) on a specified date (election day) is one of the typical options, but there are also a number of other complementary methods. Many countries allow votes to be cast in polling stations during the advance voting period, and it is also common to provide the option to vote via mail. In some cases, it may even be possible to cast votes via phone, fax or Internet [8].

While positively impacting availability, multi-channel elections also pose several challenges. To retain uniformity, care has to be taken that only one vote per voter gets counted even if the voter attempted to use several channels [13]. Even though, in principle, electronic channels provide cheaper ways of voting, full paper-based infrastructure is still typically kept running, increasing the total cost of operations [12].

In this paper, we take a different approach to comparing alternative channels of vote casting, and instead of the direct monetary cost, we consider their environmental impact.

To the best of our knowledge, the environmental impact of voting methods has not been explicitly studied. However, there are a few related studies on general governance issues.

In 2011, Zampou and Pramatari assessed paper-based public services provided in Greece and estimated their carbon footprint. They argued that the

M. Volkamer et al. (Eds.): E-Vote-ID 2023, LNCS 14230, pp. 140–155, 2023.
https://doi.org/10.1007/978-3-031-43756-4_9

footprint could be lowered by digitalising the services but did not give precise estimates on the respective gain [19].

The same year, Larsen and Hertwich estimated the carbon footprint of various public services offered by the Norwegian county of Sogn og Fjordane [14]. Unsurprisingly, the largest CO_2 equivalent emissions were connected to the transportation and energy supply.

In 2015, Tehnunen and Penntinen identified that moving from paper-based invoicing to electronic invoicing decreases the carbon footprint of one invoice lifecycle by 63%. The greatest effect came from the elimination of unnecessary manual work, while material and transportation were significant factors as well [17].

In 2022, Zioło et al. studied the correlation between the E-Government Development Index (EGDI) and several societal development aspects (including environmental) based on data from 26 European countries. The correlation between the EGDI and the environmental parameters was positive and statistically significant but lower than the correlation between EGDI and other social and economic parameters [20].

Even though digital technologies allow to lower the amounts of paper and ink required, they may come with a significant environmental footprint of their own due to increased computational demand. In 2009 it was estimated that, as a result of one Google search query, 0.2 g of CO_2 equivalent is emitted[1]. Depending on the methodology used, watching 1 h of an HD movie over Netflix is estimated to emit $432 \ldots 1681$ g of CO_2 equivalent [3]. In 2015, data centres were estimated to contribute 2% of global greenhouse gas emissions, equal to the emissions from global aviation [11]. Bitcoin mining is estimated to contribute almost the same amount [5].

Thus the question of whether the introduction of digital technologies actually lowers or raises the carbon footprint is a non-trivial one and needs to be addressed in a particular context. In this paper, we will concentrate on voting and attempt to assess how the transition from paper to remote electronic vote casting would affect the environmental impact.

We will be using Estonia as the case study as there the numbers of paper *vs* Internet voters have been roughly equal since 2019 [7], and the share of Internet voters slightly surpassed 50% during the 2023 parliamentary elections[2]. Being a small country with good infrastructure and efficient data management processes, the raw data required to estimate the environmental impact was also relatively easy to obtain.

Our paper makes two main contributions. First, we develop a methodology to assess the carbon footprint of different voting methods (see Sect. 2). Secondly, we apply this methodology to two specific methods – paper voting (Sect. 3) and Internet voting (Sect. 4). A lot of the base data that we were able to obtain for our computations is approximate. Hence the final numbers should also be treated

---

[1] https://googleblog.blogspot.com/2009/01/powering-google-search.html.
[2] https://rk2023.valimised.ee/en/participation/index.html.

as estimates. However, we feel that our general approach to the methodology is valuable in its own right as well.

2 Methodology

The fundamental document for assessment of environmental impact is the Kyoto Protocol, which was first adopted on 11 December 1997 and entered into force on 16 February 2005.[3] The Kyoto Protocol states the approach to assess environmental impact in terms of greenhouse gas emissions but does not specify a concrete methodology for it. Of course, several methodologies have been proposed by international organisations in the following years of implementation.

There are seven gases reported under the Kyoto Protocol framework: carbon dioxide (CO_2), methane (CH_4), nitrous oxide (N_2O), hydrofluorocarbons (HFCs), perfluorocarbons (PFCs), sulfur hexafluoride (SF_6), and nitrogen trifluoride (NF_3). However, these are often re-computed into CO_2 equivalent (also noted as CO_2e) that can be determined by multiplying the share of each gas by its respective factor of Global Warming Potential [2].

US-based World Resources Institute has developed Greenhouse Gas (GHG) Protocol used by the leading industrial players in the US and also some other countries.[4] Their methodology is built around the product life cycle and thus can not be directly used on something like voting, which is a state service rather than a product. However, the GHG Protocol also has guidelines for cities to report their greenhouse gas emissions [2], and several aspects of these guidelines are applicable to our research.

European Environment Agency (EEA) released a report presenting different perspectives on accounting for greenhouse gas emissions [1]. The report focuses principally on emissions of CO_2e as there is the most information available on carbon dioxide. In addition, focusing on one compound also makes it easier to understand the differences between the different emission perspectives. The report lays down three common approaches to comparatively assess these emissions in different countries. These approaches are based on territorial, production and consumption information, respectively.

Our methodology can be viewed as a combination of GHG Protocol's City reporting and EEA's consumption-based approach. Accordingly, we defined the following phases for our methodology.

1. **Boundary definition.** We concentrate on the actions directly related to the preparation and conducting of the elections. The amortised general costs (like building the community houses or schools where voting took place) are not taken into account. Also, in this research, we only look at the activities that relate to only paper or Internet voting, but not both.
2. **Identification of the key activities.** There are several dimensions that help us to identify the key activities. The GHG protocol [2] categorises emission

---

[3] https://unfccc.int/documents/2409.

[4] https://ghgprotocol.org/.

sources into three large scopes: stationery (buildings, manufacturing, etc.), transportation, and waste management (disposal). As the next step of the research, all three scopes were instantiated with the appropriate activities from the voting processes [12].

3. **Assessment of the CO_2e emissions of the identified activities** This phase consisted of two major steps. First, we conducted expert interviews with the Estonian Electoral Management Body (EMB), the Estonian State Information Agency and the vendor of the Estonian Internet voting system. These institutions provided estimates of various parameters concerning the process steps (e.g. what distance needed to be covered to distribute the ballot sheets to the polling stations or the power consumption of the i-voting servers). We also used the results of the regular post-elections survey performed in Estonia. At the last stage, we estimated the carbon footprint of the identified steps, presenting the results in terms of CO_2e emissions per vote.

3 Paper Voting Processes

In our analysis, we will be using the carbon footprint of travel measured in grams of CO_2e per passenger kilometre as estimated by Our World in Data.[5] An excerpt of their dataset relevant to our study is given in Table 1.

Table 1. Estimates of CO_2e emission per passenger kilometer

Mode of transportation	CO_2e emission (g)
Car	192
Bus	105

However, travelling on foot also has an impact on CO_2e emissions as the energy used when walking has to be replaced by food, the production of which has a certain carbon footprint.

Cohen and Heberger assess that assuming an average diet, walking emits about four times less CO_2e than driving a car [4]. Thus, we will use the value $\frac{192}{4} = 48 \frac{g}{km}$ for the average CO_2e emission of walking.

In the following, we will estimate the CO_2e emission per paper vote, of which there were 301620 given in the 2023 Estonian parliamentary elections.[6]

3.1 Printing the Ballots

According to the EMB, the number of printed ballots was somewhat lower than the number of eligible voters (966129), as it was predictable that many people

---

[5] https://ourworldindata.org/grapher/carbon-footprint-travel-mode.
[6] https://rk2023.valimised.ee/en/participation/index.html.

would vote online. So we estimate that about 900000 ballots were printed. Ballot sheets used in Estonia are relatively small, about A5 in size. Thus we estimate that for the parliamentary elections of 2023, approximately 450000 sheets of A4 paper were used for ballots.

Also, about 11000 sheets of A4 paper were used to print out candidate lists at the polling stations. Adding the paper used for information leaflets and advertisement of polling stations, we estimate the amount of paper used to be about 500000 A4.

According to Diaz and Arroja [6], the CO_2e footprint of a sheet of A4 office paper is between 4.26 and 4.74 g depending on the exact type and manufacturing standards of the production. The ballot paper had an FSC-C022692 responsible forestry certificate, so we will use the lower end of the Diaz and Arroja estimate interval, concluding that production of the ballot paper emitted about $500000 \cdot 4.26\,g = 2.13t$ of CO_2e. Dividing by 301620 paper voters, this amounts to approximately 7.1 g per vote.

3.2 Transporting the Ballots to the Polling Stations and Back

The geographical coordinates of the polling stations of the Estonian 2023 parliamentary elections were freely available as a part of the map application designed for the elections.[7] According to the information obtained from the EMB, the ballots were first taken to the county centres and then transported to the polling stations from there.

Thus, we first estimated the distances from Tallinn to the county centres and then from the county centres to the polling stations. To find the shortest routes, we used Openrouteservice[8] together with the routingpy utility.[9] As we needed to get an estimate for the distances, we assumed that the ballots were distributed following a star-like network graph, where the county centres acted as the distribution hubs.

As a result, we found that the total distance needed to the transport the ballots to the polling stations was about 14000 km. Taking into account the need to later also transport the ballots back to the district centres for counting, we estimate that the total distance covered was about 28000 km.[10]

This result is aligned with the estimate by Krimmer et al. [12] that 40743.4 km of transportation was required for about 400000 paper votes given during the Estonian local municipal elections of 2017.

---

[7] https://jsk.valimised.ee/geojson/RK_2023.geojson.

[8] https://openrouteservice.org/.

[9] https://routingpy.readthedocs.io/en/latest/.

[10] The sum of distances from Tallinn to county centres was about 2300 km. Even though the ballots were not taken back to Tallinn, there were still computers and other equipment that needed transportation back, so we decided to account also for this part of the trip both ways.

Assuming that most of the ballots were transported by cars or minivans, we take $192 \frac{g}{km}$ from Table 1 for the CO_2e emission. Thus, we get

$$28000 \, \text{km} \cdot 192 \frac{g}{km} \approx 5.38t$$

for the total emission. Dividing this by 301620 paper voters, we estimate the average CO_2e emission of ballot transportation per vote to be about 17.8 g.

3.3 Transporting the Voters and Polling Station Staff to the Polling Stations and Back

After the 2023 parliamentary elections of Estonia, a population-wide study was conducted, engaging 1001 voters.[11] At our request, the coordinator of the study included questions concerning the mode and time of transportation to the polling station. For 404 polling station voters in the sample, the distribution of answers is given in Table 2. The table shows the number and percentage of voters using a specific form of transport, the average time it took them to get to the polling station and back, and the percentage of persons who only took this trip for voting *vs* people who also did something else (shopping, visiting a friend, etc.).

Table 2. Transportation to and from the polling station

Mode of transport	# of voters	Percentage	Average time	Only voting	Other chores
Car	191	47.3%	25.9 min	41.0%	59.0%
By foot	186	46.0%	18.7 min	57.6%	42.4%
Public transport	21	5.2%	50.0 min	43.0%	57.0%
Bicycle	2	0.5%	20.0 min	–	–
Not specified	4	1%	–	–	–

Only 2 out of the 1001 respondents said they took a bike ride. Also, no one claimed to have taken an electric scooter (even though this option was provided for an answer). The timing can explain such low shares, as the 2023 parliamentary elections of Estonia took place in late February and early March when the weather conditions did not support biking or riding an electric scooter. We expect the respective numbers to be higher for the European Parliament elections taking place in May 2024. As the number of bicycle riders was so small, we do not take them into account in this study.

During the 2023 elections, there were 301620 paper votes cast. According to Table 2, we estimate that $0.473 \cdot 301620 \approx 142700$ voters went to the polling station by car. It took them 25.9 min on average. Assuming an average speed of

---

[11] It was actually an event in a long series of studies, organized regularly after elections by the Tartu University Johan Skytte Institute of Political Studies. The interviews were conducted both via phone and in the form of a web-based questionnaire.

$60\frac{km}{h}$, this translates to a trip of 25.9 km on average. The CO_2e footprint of 1 km of travel by car is about 192 g, resulting in about 4970 g of CO_2e emission per trip.

Out of the 142700 voters who took a car, $0.41 \cdot 142700 \approx 58500$ made the trip only for voting, and $0.59 \cdot 142700 \approx 84200$ also did something else. Accounting for the other chores, we use the weight 0.5 for the latter group, amounting to

$$58500 \cdot 4970\,g + 0.5 \cdot 84200 \cdot 4970\,g \approx 500t$$

of CO_2e emission for all the voters using the car. Dividing by 301620 paper voters, this amounts to approximately 1660 g per vote.

Similarly, we estimate that out of the 301620 paper voters, $0.052 \cdot 301620 \approx$ 15700 took public transport. It took them 50 min on average, which we again translated to 50 km using the average estimated speed of $60\frac{km}{h}$. The CO_2e footprint of 1 km of travel by bus (which is the predominant mode of public transport in Estonia) is about 105 g, resulting in about 5250 g of CO_2e emission per trip.

Out of the 15700 voters who took public transport, $0.43 \cdot 15700 \approx 6750$ made the trip only for voting, and $0.57 \cdot 15700 \approx 8950$ also did something else. Again, using the weight 0.5 for the latter group, we estimate the amount of CO_2e emission for all the public transport users to be

$$6750 \cdot 5250\,g + 0.5 \cdot 8950 \cdot 5250\,g \approx 59t.$$

Dividing by 301620 paper voters, this amounts to approximately 195 g per vote.

For the voters who went to the polling station on foot, we estimate that there were about $0.46 \cdot 301620 \approx 138700$ of them. It took them 18.7 min on average, which we translated to 1.56 km using the average estimated speed of $5\frac{km}{h}$. The CO_2e footprint of 1 km of walking is about 48 g, resulting in about 74.9 g of CO_2e emission per walk.

Out of the 138700 voters who took a walk, $0.576 \cdot 138700 \approx 79900$ only went to vote, and $0.424 \cdot 138700 \approx 58800$ also did something else. Again, using the weight 0.5 for the latter group, we estimate the amount of CO_2e emission for all the walkers to be

$$79900 \cdot 74.9\,g + 0.5 \cdot 58800 \cdot 74.9\,g \approx 8.2t.$$

Dividing by 301620 paper voters, this amounts to approximately 27.1 g per vote.

All in all, transportation of paper voters to the polling station and back gives rise to about $1660 + 195 + 27.1 \approx 1880\,g$ of emission per vote in terms of CO_2e.

There is also a carbon footprint associated with transporting the polling station staff to and from the polling stations. There were 484 polling stations established for the 2023 Estonian parliamentary elections. Assuming 4 persons per polling station, we estimate the total personnel to be about 1940 people. This forms about 0.64% of the total number of paper voters. Hence we estimate the CO_2e emission caused by the transport of the polling station staff to be 0.64% of 1880 or about 12 g per vote.

3.4 Transportation for the Home Voting

Krimmer *et al.* [12] estimated that in the 2017 local municipal elections of Estonia, 24273.4 km of travel was required to support home voting. The Estonian EMB was unable to give a similar estimate for the 2023 parliamentary elections.

Thus we will use an approximation based on the observation that in 2017, the distance required for home voting was $\frac{24273.4}{40743.4} \approx 60\%$ of the distance covered for distributing the ballots. Based on our above estimate that the CO_2e emission coming from ballot transport was 17.8 g per vote, we assess that the corresponding quantity for the home voting would be about 10.7 g.

However, we also have to take into account that the share of Internet voters in Estonia has risen from the 31.7% in 2017 [7] to 50.9% in 2023.[12] This is an increase of about 1.6 times, and we estimate that the need for home voting has decreased accordingly. Thus our final estimate is $\frac{10.7\,\text{g}}{1.6} \approx 6.7$ g of CO_2e emission. Note that we are still considering this footprint per all the paper votes given.

3.5 Running the Polling Stations

According to the information received from the EMB, during the 2023 Estonian parliamentary elections, there were 484 polling stations altogether. Out of these there were

- 76 stations in the premises of local municipalities,
- 102 stations in community centers,
- 100 stations in cultural establishments,
- 35 stations in libraries,
- 121 stations in schools,
- 28 stations in shopping centres, and
- 22 stations in other buildings.

One of the 22 stations in the latter category was a 300 m² tent set up in the centre of Tartu. This is noteworthy because, during the voting period of 27 February – 5 March 2023, it was still winter, with the outside temperatures varying between $-10°$ and $0°$ C. The tent was heated using diesel heaters, and the total fuel consumption was approximately 2500 litres, according to the data we obtained from the Tartu city government. CO_2e emission from diesel combustion is approximately 2500 g per litre, and it is about the same for both mineral and biodiesel.[13] Altogether, heating the tent contributed to about 6.25 tons of CO_2e emission. As there were 301620 paper votes cast, heating this tent alone contributed 20.7 g of CO_2e emission per vote.

In general, it is very difficult to estimate CO_2e emissions related to the energy consumption occurring as a result of running the polling stations. As we saw above, the vast majority of the buildings have some other continuous use and

---

[12] https://rk2023.valimised.ee/en/detailed-voting-result/index.html.

[13] https://www.forestresearch.gov.uk/tools-and-resources/fthr/biomass-energy-resources/reference-biomass/facts-figures/carbon-emissions-of-different-fuels/.

would be heated anyway. We know that there is some extra energy consumption due to elections as e.g. the temperature in schools is typically lowered for the weekends but not for election Sunday. However, identifying the share of extra energy consumption occurring due to voting is very challenging.

In this paper, we propose an indirect methodology based on the general CO_2e emissions from public services. We use the estimates given by Larsen and Hertwich [14]. According to their calculations, the yearly CO_2e emission attributed to transportation is about 26600 tons in the case of the Norwegian county of Sogn og Fjordane, which has a temperature similar to Estonia. On the other hand, the yearly CO_2e emission attributed to electricity and heating is about 4500 tons. Thus, we estimate that in Sognog Fjordane the electricity and heating emissions are about $\frac{4500}{26600} \approx 17\%$ of the emission occurring as a result of transport.[14]

Taking the estimated transportation emission to be 1880 g per vote as computed above, we find that the total emission stemming from running the polling stations is about $0.17 \cdot 1880\,g \approx 320\,g$ per paper vote. Adding the 20.7 g spent on just one tent in Tartu, we get the final estimate of about 340 g of CO_2e emission per vote. Note that given the climatic conditions in Estonia, the carbon footprint of heating in winter is definitely higher compared to other seasons. Parliamentary elections happening in late February and early March are hence a more extreme case compared to the local municipal elections taking place in mid-October and European Parliament elections taking place in late May.

3.6 Disposing of the Ballots

Paper ballots are counted manually at the polling stations, and afterwards, they need to be stored for at least one month. We estimate that neither of these procedures adds a significant amount of CO_2e emission.

Once all the disputes are resolved, the ballots are destroyed. Our enquiry to the EMB revealed that the destruction of the paper ballots is the responsibility of each district, and there are no centrally imposed rules on how the paper ballots

---

[14] Of course, the energy production and consumption profiles of Estonia and Norway are different. In Estonia, the largest share of produced energy in winter is spent on heating the buildings, and this energy is mostly delivered in the form of district heating. In Norway, the predominant form of energy is electricity, which is used for heating as well. Norwegian electricity is produced mainly by hydroelectric power plants with relatively low CO_2e emissions. 58.3% of the district heating energy in Estonia, on the other hand, is produced from wood chips. This method of energy production can be considered carbon neutral or even have a slightly negative emission [15]. Thus, the overall comparison of the CO_2e balance is not necessarily too far off. The exact share of space heating vs general electricity consumption during the 2023 Estonian parliamentary elections would require a detailed analysis of all the polling stations, but the complete data for this analysis was not available to the authors.

have to be disposed of.[15] In Tartu (which is one of the largest districts), for example, the ballots are shredded, and then the remains are sent to recycling.

While we can assume that shredding is the standard practice for destroying ballots, we do not have complete data concerning what is done with the remains everywhere in Estonia. In general, there are two options to what can happen to the shredded paper: it can be sent to recycling, or it can be mixed with regular waste and sent to a landfill[16]. We will analyse these two possibilities in more detail.

Ximenes *et al.* studied the greenhouse gas emissions from landfills and found that, over time, one gram of shredded copy paper emits on average 326 ml of methane [18]. The density of methane is $0.657 \frac{kg}{m^3}$ (given the temperature of 25° C and pressure of 1atm). Therefore, over time, $0.657 \cdot 0.000326 \approx 0.00021$ kg of methane is emitted from one gram of shredded copy paper, which is equivalent to 0.005 kg of CO_2e emission according to the Greenhouse Gas Equivalencies Calculator[17]. As stated in Sect. 3.1, about 500000 A4 paper sheets were used during the 2023 Estonian parliamentary elections, and the approximate weight of one A4 paper sheet is 5 g. Thus, dumping paper sheets into a landfill would generate about $500000 \cdot 0.005 \cdot 5 = 12500$ kg of biogenic CO_2e emission.

According to the Greenhouse Gases Equivalencies Calculator – Calculations and References[18], for every short ton (equivalent to 907.185 kg) of unspecified waste recycled instead of landfilling, CO_2e emission is reduced by 2.89 metric tons. Given the approximate weight of one A4 paper sheet as 5 g, the weight of 500000 paper sheets is 2.5t, which means that recycling instead of landfilling could lower the CO_2e emission by an estimated amount of

$$\frac{2.89 \cdot 2.5}{0.907185} \approx 7.96t.$$

A more detailed methodology was proposed by Merrild *et al.* [16]. They provided estimates of CO_2e emissions for upstream processing of waste paper ($1.3 \ldots 29$ kg of CO_2e per tonne of waste paper), direct waste management ($2.7 \ldots 9.4$ kg of CO_2e per tonne of waste paper), and downstream processing, i.e., reprocessing of sorted waste paper ($-4392 \ldots 1464$ kg of CO_2e per tonne of waste paper). The large range provided for the downstream processing is caused by different assumptions on the effects of recycling.

Three cases were considered in [16]. In the first case, recycling does not affect paper production (resulting in the $488 \ldots 1464$ kg of CO_2e emission per tonne of waste paper). In the second case, recycling reduces paper production, which can reduce CO_2e emissions ($-1269 \ldots 390$ kg of CO_2e per tonne of waste paper). In

---

[15] In our analysis, we assume that other paper materials, like candidate lists and advertising materials, will also receive the same treatment as the ballots.

[16] Part of the waste sent to a landfill may be burned to get energy, thereby reducing the amount of fossil fuel that needs to be burned. We do not cover this aspect due to the lack of data.

[17] https://www.epa.gov/energy/greenhouse-gas-equivalencies-calculator.

[18] https://www.epa.gov/energy/greenhouse-gases-equivalencies-calculator-calculations-and-references.

the third case, it is assumed that due to recycling, less wood is used for producing paper, and instead, the wood is used to replace fossil fuel energy (resulting in $-4392\ldots-1854$ kg of CO_2e emission per tonne of waste paper).

The third case holds quite well for Estonia, where wood is used both for paper production and for generating electricity by mixing it with oil shale. Thus, we took an average of the range presented in the third case, which gives an estimated emission of -3123 kg of CO_2e per tonne of recycled waste paper. The weight of 500000 paper sheets is 2.5t, resulting in approximately -7.8t of emission, which is close to the estimate provided by the Greenhouse Gases Equivalencies Calculator. Dividing by 301620 paper voters, this amounts to approximately -25.8 g of CO_2e emission per vote.

3.7   Summary of CO2e Emissions for Paper Voting

Table 3 gives an overview of CO_2e emissions for paper voting. The table shows that the transportation of voters had the biggest influence on the CO_2e emission per vote. Discussion regarding the results is provided in Sect. 5.

Table 3. Summary of the CO_2e emissions for paper voting

Parameter	CO_2e emission per vote (g)
Paper for the ballots and candidate lists	7.1
Transporting ballots to the polling stations and back	17.8
Transport required for the home voters	6.7
Transporting voters to the polling stations and back	1880
Transporting the polling station staff	12
Running the polling stations (electricity, heating)	340
Disposing of the ballots	-25.8
Total:	≈ 2240

4   Internet Voting Processes

The environmental impact of Internet voting is primarily connected to the power consumption of computers involved in the various stages of the process (development, running the servers and client applications). Thus we will calculate most of the emissions via the energy consumed. For conversion, we will use the estimate that producing one kWh of energy causes 464 g of CO_2e emission in Estonia.[19]

We will estimate the CO_2e emission per Internet vote (i-vote), of which there were 312181 given in the 2023 parliamentary elections.[20]

---

[19] We used Our World in Data estimate from 2022, as the data for 2023 was not yet available. https://ourworldindata.org/grapher/carbon-intensity-electricity?tab=chart&country=~EST.

[20] https://rk2023.valimised.ee/en/participation/index.html.

4.1 Software Development

According to the information obtained from the software vendor, development efforts targeted towards the Internet voting of the Estonian 2023 parliamentary elections spanned over roughly 1000 h hours. Assuming 100 W as average power consumption of a developer machine, approximately 100 kWh of energy was required for development.

This amounts to

$$\frac{100\,\text{kWh} \cdot 464 \frac{\text{g}}{\text{kWh}}}{312181} \approx 0.15\,\text{g}$$

of CO_2e emission per i-vote.

To run the test environment, Amazon t3.small hosting based in Stockholm was used for about 57500 h. Using the AWS carbon footprint estimator[21], this gave rise to about 63000 g of CO_2e emission, which is about 0.2 g per i-vote.

All in all, we estimate the total CO_2e footprint of the software development to be 0.35 g per i-vote.

4.2 Running the Servers

According to the information received from the Estonian State Information Agency, the server side of the Estonian Internet voting system is divided into a number of services running on approximately 160 virtual machines. These machines were deployed for the whole duration of the preparation, testing and running of the elections, with the period spanning across four months. An average monthly cost of a virtual machine was estimated to be 3.2 euros (including VAT). Thus the total electricity cost of running the servers for the 2023 parliamentary elections can be estimated as $160 \cdot 4 \cdot 3.2 \approx 2050$ euros.

The average price of one kWh of electricity from November 2022 to February 2023 on the Nord Pool market was about 17.3 cents before taxes[22]. Adding the transmission cost and renewable energy supplement ($5.7 \frac{\text{cent}}{\text{kWh}}$ altogether) and the VAT (20%), we get approximately $27.6 \frac{\text{cent}}{\text{kWh}}$ as an end-user cost. Thus the estimated energy consumption of running the servers for Internet voting was

$$\frac{2050\text{eur}}{27.6 \frac{\text{cent}}{\text{kWh}}} \approx 7430\,\text{kWh}.$$

Using the above estimate that producing one kWh of energy causes 464 g of CO_2e emission in Estonia, we obtain the total carbon footprint to be about 3.4t of CO_2e. Dividing by the 312181 i-votes, we obtain the final emission to be about 11 g of CO_2e per i-vote.

---

[21] https://engineering.teads.com/sustainability/carbon-footprint-estimator-for-aws-instances/.

[22] https://www.energia.ee/en/era/elekter/elektriturg.

4.3   Running the Client Applications

According to the study by Paršovs *et al.*, the average time it takes an Estonian i-voter to cast a vote has varied between 140.3 and 193 s in different election events [9,10]. Assuming 50 W as a power consumption of an average household PC during voting and 167 s as an average length of a voting session, we obtain $50\,W \cdot 167\,s = 8350\,Ws \approx 2.3\,Wh$ worth of energy spent on casting one vote. As a result, the carbon footprint of casting one i-vote is, on average, $2.3\,Wh \cdot 0.464 \frac{g}{Wh} \approx 1.1\,g$ in CO_2e.

4.4   Disposing of the i-voting Artefacts

The vast majority of the machines and equipment used for Internet voting are general-purpose computing devices that will not be destroyed after the elections but will be used for other applications.

The only things destroyed are one SSD storage device that is used for restoring the decryption key, the 9 chip cards that are used to store the shares of the private key, and about a dozen of DVD-s used to transport various data files between the computers during the processing of the votes.

We estimate the CO_2e emission of these disposals to be marginal, and emission per one of the 312181 i-votes being efficiently 0.

4.5   Summary of CO2e Emissions for Internet Voting

Table 4 gives an overview of CO_2e emissions for Internet voting. A discussion regarding the results is provided in Sect. 5.

Table 4. Summary of the CO_2e emissions for Internet voting

Parameter	CO_2e emission per vote (g)
Software development	0.35
Running the servers	11
Running the client applications	1.1
Disposing of the i-voting artefacts	0
Total:	≈ 12.5

5   Discussion

By comparing the values presented in Tables 3 and 4, we can see that the total CO_2e emission per vote is about 180 times higher in the case of paper voting. The main contributor to this difference is the emission occurring as the result of transporting the voters to the polling stations and back, followed by the emissions from running the polling stations.

However, we have to take into account that many of the parameters used in our assessments are approximate estimations which are inherently impossible to obtain precisely. Several values (carbon footprint of running the polling stations, the amount of transport required by the home voting) we had to estimate indirectly, and their margin of error may accordingly be higher. Also, our information was limited in regard to the ballot disposal methods applied in different districts.

Our study concentrated on the case study of Estonia, and hence several input parameters are specific to this country. For example, Estonia uses relatively small ballot sheets, which limits the amount of paper required. Also, in the 2023 parliamentary elections, vote casting via the Internet was used by more than half of Estonian voters. Accordingly, per-vote estimates similar to the ones in Table 4 would be larger in other jurisdictions where the amount of i-votes is smaller.

A significant role was probably played by the weather, which is still quite cold in Estonia in late February and early March. As a result, many voters may have opted for taking the car, and the need to supply energy to the polling stations had a remarkable footprint, too.

Our study does not cover the emissions caused by the activities necessary for both modes of voting. These activities include candidate registration, developing and running the elections information system, resolving disputes, etc. If we would also consider these emissions (say, adding half of them to both the estimated emissions of paper and Internet voting), the relative advantage of Internet voting in terms of CO_2e emission would be smaller.

6   Conclusions and Further Work

Voting is the core mechanism of implementing democratic decision processes in modern societies. As no significant alternatives to voting currently exist, one can not attach a price tag to it.

However, the existing technical solutions used for elections have evolved over the years and will probably continue to do so in the foreseeable future. Hence it does make sense to ask how to organise voting in a more optimal way, where different measures of optimality may be considered.

In this paper, we took the viewpoint of an ecologist and asked whether the introduction of new voting technologies (more specifically, vote casting via the Internet) has the potential to decrease the carbon footprint of elections. The answer is affirmative.

Even though preparing and running the voting software both on the servers and on the client side does contribute to CO_2e emission, nothing compares to the carbon footprint of the logistics of the voters to and from the polling stations. As parliamentary elections happen in late winter in Estonia, almost half of the paper voters chose to take the trip by car, which is one of the worst options from an environmental point of view. It would be interesting to calculate how much energy could be saved by moving the election date to a warmer period. However, at least in the case of Estonia, the date for parliamentary elections has been set in the constitution, so changing it is not really an option.

The second largest share of the carbon footprint can be attributed to running the polling stations (including heating and electricity supply). This was, however, the most challenging component to estimate, and the margin of error may be significant. Further research is needed to establish a reliable methodology for giving such estimates.

Another interesting future direction is determining the carbon footprint of other voting methods. For example, machine voting potentially has an even higher emission as the need to transport the voters to the polling stations is still there, but instead of (or in addition to) paper, one also needs to produce a large quantity of single-purpose devices, and this process carries a significant environmental footprint of its own. Postal voting from overseas is also a potentially interesting subject as there the environmental impact of ballot transport (e.g. by plane) would be significant.

Acknowledgements. This paper has been supported by the Estonian Research Council under the grant number PRG920. The authors are grateful to the Estonian State Electotal Office, Information System Authority, Tartu city government, Smartmatic-Cybernetica Centre of Excellence for Internet Voting and Tartu University Johan Skytte Institute of Political Studies for their help in data gathering.

References

1. European Union CO_2 emissions: different accounting perspectives. Technical report 20/2013, European Environment Agency (2013). https://www.eea.europa. eu/publications/european-union-co2-emissions-accounting
2. Global Protocol for Community-Scale Greenhouse Gas Inventories. An Accounting and Reporting Standard for Cities Version 1.1 (2021). https://ghgprotocol.org/ ghg-protocol-cities
3. Batmunkh, A.: Carbon footprint of the most popular social media platforms. Sustainability **14**(4) (2022). https://doi.org/10.3390/su14042195, https://www.mdpi. com/2071-1050/14/4/2195
4. Cohen, M., Heberger, M.: Driving vs. walking: cows, climate change, and choice (2008). pacific Institute, https://pacinst.org/wp-content/uploads/sites/21/2013/ 02/driving_vs_walking3.pdf
5. de Vries, A.: Bitcoin boom: what rising prices mean for the network's energy consumption. Joule **5**(3), 509–513 (2021). https://doi.org/10.1016/j.joule.2021.02.006, https://www.sciencedirect.com/science/article/pii/S2542435121000830
6. Dias, A.C., Arroja, L.: Comparison of methodologies for estimating the carbon footprint - case study of office paper. J. Clean. Prod. **24**, 30–35 (2012). https:// doi.org/10.1016/j.jclepro.2011.11.005
7. Ehin, P., Solvak, M., Willemson, J., Vinkel, P.: Internet voting in Estonia 2005–2019: evidence from eleven elections. Gov. Inf. Q. **39**(4), 101718 (2022). https:// doi.org/10.1016/j.giq.2022.101718
8. Gibson, J.P., Krimmer, R., Teague, V., Pomares, J.: A review of E-voting: the past, present and future. Ann. Telecommun. 279–286 (2016). https://doi.org/10. 1007/s12243-016-0525-8
9. Heiberg, S., Parsovs, A., Willemson, J.: Log Analysis of Estonian Internet Voting 2013–2015. Cryptology ePrint Archive, Paper 2015/1211 (2015). https://doi.org/ 10.1007/978-3-319-22270-7_2, https://eprint.iacr.org/2015/1211

10. Heiberg, S., Parsovs, A., Willemson, J.: Log analysis of Estonian internet voting 2013–2014. In: Haenni, R., Koenig, R.E., Wikström, D. (eds.) VOTELID 2015. LNCS, vol. 9269, pp. 19–34. Springer, Cham (2015). https://doi.org/10.1007/978-3-319-22270-7_2

11. Hodgson, C.: Can the digital revolution be environmentally sustainable? The Guardian, November 2015

12. Krimmer, R., Dueñas-Cid, D., Krivonosova, I.: New methodology for calculating cost-efficiency of different ways of voting: is internet voting cheaper? Public Money Manag. **41**(1), 17–26 (2021). https://doi.org/10.1080/09540962.2020.1732027

13. Krimmer, R., Triessnig, S., Volkamer, M.: The development of remote E-Voting around the world: a review of roads and directions. In: Alkassar, A., Volkamer, M. (eds.) Vote-ID 2007. LNCS, vol. 4896, pp. 1–15. Springer, Heidelberg (2007). https://doi.org/10.1007/978-3-540-77493-8_1

14. Larsen, H.N., Hertwich, E.G.: Analyzing the carbon footprint from public services provided by counties. J. Clean. Prod. **19**(17), 1975–1981 (2011). https://doi.org/10.1016/j.jclepro.2011.06.014, https://www.sciencedirect.com/science/article/pii/S0959652611002253

15. Latõsov, E., Umbleja, S., Volkova, A.: CO_2 emission intensity of the Estonian DH sector. Smart Energy **6**, 100070 (2022). https://doi.org/10.1016/j.segy.2022.100070, https://www.sciencedirect.com/science/article/pii/S2666955222000089

16. Merrild, H., Damgaard, A., Christensen, T.H.: Recycling of paper: accounting of greenhouse gases and global warming contributions. Waste Manag. Res. **27**(8), 746–753 (2009). https://doi.org/10.1177/0734242X09348530

17. Tenhunen, M., Penttinen, E.: Assessing the carbon footprint of paper vs. electronic invoicing. In: 21st Australasian Conference on Information Systems (2010)

18. Ximenes, F.A., Kathuria, A., Barlaz, M.A., Cowie, A.L.: Carbon dynamics of paper, engineered wood products and bamboo in landfills: evidence from reactor studies. Carbon Balanc. Manag. **13**(1), 1–13 (2018). https://doi.org/10.1186/s13021-018-0115-3

19. Zampou, E., Pramatari, K.: How green are e-government services? In: Proceedings of MCIS 2011 (2011). https://aisel.aisnet.org/mcis2011/25

20. Zioło, M., et al.: E-Government development in European countries: socio-economic and environmental aspects. Energies **15**(23), 8870 (2022). https://doi.org/10.3390/en15238870, https://www.mdpi.com/1996-1073/15/23/8870

Author Index

© The Editor(s) (if applicable) and The Author(s) 2023
M. Volkamer et al. (Eds.): E-Vote-ID 2023, LNCS 14230, p. 157, 2023.
https://doi.org/10.1007/978-3-031-43756-4

Printed in the United States
by Baker & Taylor Publisher Services